THIS WAY OUT

The Power to Change

Diane Light

THIS WAY OUT

The Power to Change

Order this book online at www.trafford.com
or email orders@trafford.com

This title is also available at major online book retailers as are most Trafford titles.

Printed in the United States of America.

Cover Art and Design, "Healing the Lineage" by Kelly Dietrich.
www.kellydietrich.com

NOTE: The clients referred to as examples in the various scenarios and case examples are composites of the many clients and students I have worked with over the 30+ years of my career as an educator, counselor, and life coach. Any similarities to specific individuals simply reflects general characteristics that can be typical of people who are seeking greater maturity and a better way to live.

ISBN: 978-1-4269-2626-6 (sc)
ISBN: 978-1-4269-2627-3 (hc)
ISBN: 978-1-4269-6829-7 (e)

Library of Congress Control Number: 2010901048

Trafford rev. 09/21/2011

www.trafford.com

North America & international
toll-free: 1 888 232 4444 (USA & Canada)
phone: 250 383 6864 • fax: 812 355 4082

With love to

Lisa and Jason,

Jean and Robert,

Judy and Bob.

Acknowledgements

This book has taken many years to write, and many (too many to name here) have helped along the way. I lovingly appreciate each and all of you and all your efforts.

To Lois Gannon, my dear, encouraging friend, go great thanks. Without your well-timed "encouragements," technical assistance, and other dedicated efforts this volume would still be in the works.

Special thanks go to Lorin Buck for astute editorial comments, general encouragement, and assistance with Chapter 2.

Thank you to Sara Callanan for insightful comments and for proof reading the entire manuscript, and to Celeste Goodwin for edits of the Introduction and of Chapter 1.

Thank you to Kelly Dietrich for the rendering of Diagram 2, for the beautiful Cover Art, "Healing the Lineage," and for the Cover Design.

I extend profound gratitude to Lisa Light, Jason Light, Lucia May, Ann Hagan, Donna Gingerich, Dr. Bob Rose, Judith Pugsley, Daniele O'Brien, Dr. Bob Smith, Dr. A. Ramos, and Renee Rutkowski for all the support, encouragement, and assistance each of you provided to me and to this project.

To my amazing and creative clients and students, you have been great and beloved teachers each and all.

Read Me.

Escaping Never Land

"Can't be done!" the grown man said. "I've tried… at least twice before. There's no way to get out of your own damn head with all its tricks and traps."

"Well," said the woman seated across the small divide, "let's try again. Perhaps this time you'll want to use your magic powers… and *all* of them… and in the right ways."

"Naw. Paul Simon said it best. In *The Boxer* he said it…

'After changes upon changes, we are more or less the same. After changes we are more or less the same.'"

"Real Life," she said, "is never superficial. Thoughts like that don't take you to the depths. Real Life is not any kind of tragedy. But it can at times feel like one… especially if you don't believe in the magic that lies deeper than bones."

Where doubt sees the obstacles,
Faith sees the way.

Table of Contents

A Fable

Once upon a time…
…In a land far away lived a beautiful, perfectly loveable child, the child of a king, who through a certain mysterious event became lost and all alone in a very dark forest. How this came to be is a story for another day. But here we find the little one caught in great difficulty. The thick and tangled woods are filled with many strange creatures and a cacophony of hideous sounds. Some are harmless, but all are terrifying to the weary wanderer. There are witches and goblins and trolls. There are lions and tigers and bears. Stumbling through the thick brambles, sharp briars and thorns grab and scratch at every limb, leaving once beautiful garments tattered and torn. All seems dark and hopeless, indeed. But suddenly, as will happen in dark and troubling times, just as all hope seems truly lost, something amazing and wonderful occurs. It changes everything. Our tiny struggling traveler stumbles upon a lighted path. It has been there all along. Now, even though the dear child is every bit as deep in the dark forest as ever, and even though the briars still scratch and pull at every step, it does not matter any longer. *The darkness has lost all its power* over our precious one because the way home is now certain. This royal child has found…

The Way Out.

The Beginning…

Overview

"To the dull mind all of nature is leaden. To the illumined mind the whole world sparkles with light." --Emerson

A New Spirit

People have too long accepted their lot in life. People have too long accepted the idea that some have it and some don't. People are waking up to the idea that some are not more entitled to the good life than others. People are tired of playing in and paying in to corporate greed. People are becoming savvier and are calling for a more equitable system.

A New Model

Along the same lines, people have too long accepted the concept of mental illness, of being sick and seeking a cure. *This Way Out* is a groundbreaking book that catapults mental health and prosperity into the arena of growth and maturity by placing the power in people's own hands. It presents a humanistic, transpersonal, and cognitive approach to self mastery and beyond even to self liberation. It rejects the traditional view of people with complaints, symptoms, struggles, and problems as passive, powerless, and sick. *This Way Out* describes a new way of looking at mental health that is in alignment with what many have called the fourth wave of psychology, which follows the first three waves: psychodynamic, behavioral, and humanistic psychology. This book not only identifies and presents the newly emerging model, but names it as well. What this author has dubbed the "Maturity Model" is the model that mental health professionals are increasingly adopting in place of the outdated pathology oriented "Mental Illness Model." Under this broad new umbrella, transpersonal psychology, existential psychology, and many of the more modern theories and therapies can be found.

A New Theory

This Way Out introduces Personality Integration Theory and Personality Integration Therapy, a breakthrough and empowering new system of concepts and techniques in sync with this newly emerging Maturity Model and psychology's fourth wave. People are frustrated and looking for answers, for a better way to achieve a happier life, for a "way out" of whatever makes them feel stuck, for a "way in" to the life they really desire. This book gives them a down-to-earth system and effective methods and directions for getting control of their lives in all aspects, including family, relationships, career, finance, and spirituality.

A New Tool

Further, it identifies and incorporates what has been a significant *missing piece* in our understanding of how we tick. With this missing piece Personality Integration Theory and Therapy provide an important key for use with its practitioners and for use with other therapies under the modern umbrella of the Maturity Model as well. This missing piece, in other words, can greatly assist practitioners in the application process of this and various other therapies and systems.

A New Way

The theory, system, and methods presented in this book as Personality Integration Theory and its Therapy provide an intensive, original model for growth and self mastery that works synergistically with other theories arising in the new paradigm. It builds on the work of William James—the father of American psychology, Gordon W. Allport—the founder of individual personality as a field of study, Rollo May, Abraham Maslow, Roberto Assagioli, and Carl Rogers. The works of contemporaries like William Glasser, Eric Berne, Alice Miller, and John Bradshaw are reflected in its development as well, as they have helped shape the new paradigm. Further, it is firmly rooted in the work of the masters in psychology, such as Freud, Adler and Jung, but transcends their approaches and offers readers a unique and useable method for self mastery and self liberation.

There are no other sources that deal with this original breakthrough material. The author is the sole developer and owner of Personality Integration Theory, Personality Integration Therapy ("IT"), and all associated methods and techniques.

Introduction

Breaking Freud's Spell

Want to live a more abundant life?
Want loving relationships that last?
Want peace in your soul?
Contentment?
How about a real sense of happy accomplishment?

Do any of these sound familiar?

You're sick and tired of being sick and tired.

Or, perhaps you never thought of yourself as sick in any way mentally or emotionally; but still your life doesn't seem to work and you feel powerless to make the necessary lasting changes.

Or, maybe your life looks pretty good from the outside, but inside you feel like a phony, or at the least, not quite real.

Then again, perhaps you're very happy with yourself but can't seem to get anyone else to agree with you. In other words, your relationships don't seem to work—at least not the important ones.

Maybe you tried personal growth plans, or workshops, or programs. Maybe you tried certain therapies, various therapists. Maybe you tried various spiritual paths or religious movements. Maybe these trials have worked for a while but never brought about the lasting change you sought in you, in your life, never really changed you from the inside out. Maybe they never worked at all despite any guarantees or promises and you felt disillusioned with the system, or even worse, felt more of a personal failure than ever, set apart from your fellows by your flaws and inadequacies, or just more hopeless than ever. It may have seemed that there was nowhere else for you to turn.

What if the changes never took because you, like vast numbers of other adults, were held back by hidden immaturity? Wouldn't you want to uncover it? Root it out? Deal with it? Just consider this...

What if:
Depression ≠ sick, but = immaturity?
Anxiety ≠ sick, but = immaturity?
Mood swings ≠ sick, but = immaturity?
Panic attacks ≠ sick, but = immaturity?
Migraines ≠ sick, but = immaturity?
Perfectionism ≠ real, but = immaturity?
Feeling driven ≠ trapped, but = immaturity?
Financial struggle ≠ your "lot in life," but = immaturity?

Just to name a few.

What if there were some truth to these possibilities? Wouldn't you then surmise there might be a way to get control? Wouldn't you want to find it and put it to work? Wouldn't you want to find a map to help you grow; to help you achieve your goals and heart's desires?

William James brilliantly hinted at it and laid the groundwork for where we are going by applying his mind to returning to what he called revitalization, or returning (from depression) to life.

Freud's insight created an incredible foundation for understanding ourselves with the hope of getting control of ourselves—our lives. Yet, Freud may just have gone too far. Unlike his forerunner, William James, he imagined the power in the wrong hands, those of the therapist, the doctor, the authority. The result has been the great mental illness hoax—the spell under which most of us in western civilization have suffered whether we have been personally diagnosed or not. Freud was not, of course, the originator of the Mental Illness Model. He merely fell into step with that belief system, much as science throughout the ages has worked within the confines of the paradigm of its time. The new Maturity Model represents what can be called a paradigm shift. A paradigm is a framework or a model that is unquestionably or widely accepted—until it is outgrown. Some examples are concepts such as "The earth is flat," and "The earth is the center of the solar system." Firmly held but outmoded ideas have clouded and confused life on earth throughout the ages even as developments and new discoveries were being made.

Developments continue under the restrictions of the prevailing paradigm until finally a realization begins to dawn on those on the cutting edge of change that there is a better way to look, another place to look from, and that the new paradigm is more in line with how things really are and what we are coming to know than is the old belief system. The tight skin of the old paradigm is thus slowly shed and the new paradigm is born. Freud mapped the inner psyche of humans, discovering and describing the inner psychic structures—the parts in all of us. Working out of the illness paradigm, he developed theories of behavior from the pathology oriented vantage point, a reflection of the limitations of his illness filter.

On the issue of human agency in personality theories, in the seventh edition of *Beneath the Mask*, Monte and Sollod (p. 654) reference A.R. Buss and state:

Active human agency means that the person is portrayed as masterful, planful, resourceful, resilient, and capable of overcoming obstacles. Passive human agency means that the theory portrays people as shaped by factors over which they have little control. Feelings of powerlessness and incompetence are the result.

Monte and Sollod (pp. 654-655) further go on to state:

Classical psychoanalysis and radical behaviorism are generally viewed as portraying human control as weak in the face of reality. Freud's dictum that "reality made much of us" and his use of the concept of Anake (destiny) reflect a fundamental theme in classical psycho-analysis: Human reason should take charge of inner and outer reality, but it is rarely as strong as our instinctual makeup or the influence of early experience. Similarly, radical behaviorism depicts humans as largely determined by the sum total of their biology and environment, with very little room left for individual choice or the decisions of reason. Psychoanalysis and radical behaviorism picture humans as having less self-control, less self-efficiency, and less self-competence....

...Many of the more recent trends in personality theory have shifted toward an active human agency view.

Like Dorothy of *The Wizard of Oz,* with her ruby slippers, the power has been with us all along. The slippers were just a device to help her believe in herself; a way for her to find her power. Was it worth the journey and the struggle? The new Maturity Model with all its emerging methods is like the ruby slippers. Just as the concept of the earth as a globe came to be more real in our minds and helpful in many more ways than the flat earth paradigm, so too is the new paradigm in mental health. We are at the very dawning place; that point in history when we begin to see ourselves in an almost entirely new way. This shift has been formulating for many years. Some would say William James (who was the first to use the term "transpersonal psychology" in his Harvard lecture notes) opened the door and encouraged the quest. Some would say Roberto Assagioli's psychosynthesis provided a foundation for broader ways of looking at the psyche. Some would say that the first hints appeared in the 1930s as the recovery movement. Alcoholics Anonymous (A.A.) and its Twelve Steps is certainly a forerunner. There are many systems that have appeared simultaneously in the relatively recent history that do not fit comfortably into the old paradigm. They are of the new structure and are creating the shift to new and more functional ways of conceptualizing humankind.

Freud's theories, methods, and models, and those derived thereof have always fallen short of the mark in certain ways. For example, when helping people diagnosed with character disorders (personality disorders such as borderline personality disorder [BPD], or narcissistic personality disorder, etc.), Freud's techniques for the most part would result in very little progress for the "patient." Yet a substantial proportion of the population suffers in varying degrees from just such disorders. This seems to be a phenomenon of our somewhat self-disordered society. The new paradigm resolves this and other such issues and conditions and calls them by a more realistic and more workable name—immaturity.

Another example of the limitations of Freud's work can be seen in the following quote:

The cigar was solace. The cigar was something when you suck, you've got something you love. You've got the original source of nurturing when you suck. Now, Freud's analysis, which was a breakthrough, was limited. I think Freud's addiction was never analyzed, and it killed him.

-- Leo Rangel, MD
Psychoanalyst

Freud smoked ten to twenty cigars per day even after he developed mouth cancer. And as to Freud and women, he called women "the dark continent."

The essential critique of Freud is that Freud thought that you were a superior human being if you had a penis, and if not, you weren't.

-- Gloria Steinem

And:

For women, the bedrock is their penis envy, "Won't they always feel inferior because they lack this magnificent organ?" There's a statement [by Freud] to the effect that a woman about the age of thirty is so rigid she can't change. Then, of course, there's the statement that a woman has a defective super-ego.

--Judith M. Hughes

Such beliefs easily demonstrate the limits of the old paradigm thinking. And to go even further, they illuminate the fact that immaturity existed in significant and powerful ways not only in Freud's "patients," but also can be readily discerned within the great doctor himself! Freud's analysis was limited by such assessments of women, and his limiting view of people in general. When he named the psyche (the Greek word for the soul), Freud originally believed that the soul played a part in the mental life of a person. Later he came to reject spirituality as an ingredient in the psyche—another important example of the limitations of his work. Thankfully, as Bob Dylan sang, "The times, they are a'changing!"

Maybe you've heard the old Arabian story of the camel's nose under the tent. Before too very long if the nose got in, the entire camel was sure to follow! A.A., with its significant healing impact, and its central dimension of practical spirituality, has been said to be the camel's nose under the tent of western psychology and western thought. As we move into the new millennium the camel pushes. The Jamesian "Vital Self," Roberto Assagioli's scientific contributions, A.A. and the Twelve-Step programs that followed, Carl Jung's "collective unconscious," the human potential movement, *A Course In Miracles,* William Glasser's *Reality Therapy*, Eric Berne's Transactional Analysis, Eckhart Tolle's *The Power of Now*, the New Thought Movement, the work of Tony Robbins, The Beatles, The Stones, and even the rebellious energy and "out of the box" new ideas that emerged with a vengeance in the sixties are all parts of the camel, as are other systems of belief and action (such as Zen and meditation) which have been present in the world for eons, but have only recently been embraced by the west.

We are moving into a new era on the planet—one that more realistically views science and spirituality as compatible and connected in the study of the human psyche. Approaches that work for the betterment of the mental health of the individual and for society-at-large are already in play. This book attempts to name the camel, to clarify and add to the synergy and to begin to see its parts come together and to see it as a whole, and to add a vital missing piece. The theory and methods presented here for mental health and self mastery are from the new paradigm. They have been formulated and discovered and developed by me over a 30-plus-year period in clinical work as a psychotherapist, an educator, counselor, and coach. I owe much, of course, to the strength and creativity and curiosity of my students and clients themselves. They have never failed to demonstrate the fact that they have within themselves the keys to self control and self liberation. Together we have come upon the treasure map for the new millennium.

The new paradigm shakes off the spell Freud cast so artfully in the early days of the last century. William James, Roberto Assagioli, Carl Jung, and William Glasser, all pioneers in the new paradigm, were among the first to challenge the old spell. With the breaking of the spell we must take responsibility for ourselves. As we drop the labels of mental illness that define us as victims without power, we must be willing to become self honest. We must bravely consider our immaturities—many of them deeply hidden under layer upon layer of fear, self-deceit, and shame. We must become self responsible. We have had the power to do just that within us all along, but like Dorothy, we just didn't know it.

As we begin the journey and the quest, we must be willing to take the leap-of-faith—often difficult, sometimes frightening—that will take us to new levels of functioning and real self mastery. In that state of true self mastery (real maturity/actual adulthood), perhaps we will discover that we are that elusive Holy Grail of legend, that we have within us and newly emerging the "second coming" so long foretold by so many.

We need new maps. With them and our determination for a better life we can begin to reshape and really integrate the inner psychic terrain. This book offers a blueprint, a new map. It also introduces an important missing piece. It outlines the camel, names and orders its current parts, and presents a new personality theory that can easily be superimposed over other systems of the new paradigm already effectively in use, thereby breaking the old spell and creating a new synergy of change.

The new paradigm for mental health has created the Maturity Model, which is replacing the antiquated Pathology Model of yesterday's psychology. With it we have already begun to break the bonds of the spell that bound Freud and all of western psychology for ages. Already we have grown and changed in ways that the outmoded psychiatry of the old "passive human agency" paradigm could never have predicted or allowed. We are not sick, nor are we passive victims of fate, but we are significantly underdeveloped and immature. With this viewpoint, with proper methods, guides, and maps, with determination, courage, and support, we can grow up. *This Way Out* puts a name to the new paradigm, giving it the dignity it deserves, and puts the outdated and currently dysfunctional old system into proper perspective, thus helping to loosen its hold on our psyches. With the introduction of Personality Integration Theory and Personality Integration Therapy and its methods, it provides a new and functional set of directions and new tools to grapple more directly, more effectively, and more actively with the real problem—our mistaken notions about ourselves and our immaturities.

The good news is we are not sick.
The bad news is we have to take responsibility to change ourselves.

It takes hard work.
There are guides available.
May you find your way now.
May you discover your Great Treasure.
Self Mastery and Self Liberation can be yours.
Click your heels three times...

Chapter 1

The Family: The Flawed Mirror and the Impact of Focus

"We are all victims of victims, and they could not possibly have taught us anything they didn't know." --Louise Hay

There Are Three Phases
In the Developmental Evolution of Our Species:

Phase I: Survival
Phase II: Self Development
Phase III: Creativity

Phase I: Survival

We were hunter-gatherers. We were cave dwellers. We were surrounded by danger at all times. In our ancient past we were survivors. That was the goal—survival. All instinct and behavior was geared to it and survival meant the group. To survive we needed the safety of the group. The group was our safe space in the wild and our collective group focus had to be tuned to the jungle out there.

Think about the life of a wild bird. Think about the life of an antelope on the African plain. Think about the life of a fish in the ocean. Think about daily life moment-by-moment in the wild for any creature. Everything is geared to three basic needs: avoid being eaten, eat, and multiply. When we were in the wild as a species the same was true for us. Not that there weren't sparks of fun and creativity—there probably were. But the main gist of life was centered around be safe, eat, and multiply.

If the goal of Phase I in the evolution of our species was to survive, the focus had to be on any possible danger or possible food source in the outer environment. Let's say one day a saber-toothed tiger wandered by the old family cave. There was only one job in the world at the time—spot and kill (and cook up) the tiger! It could be said therefore that basically the ideal function of a Phase I family was to kill the outsider. Many skills were required for success in that venture, and every family member went to work. A Phase I family then was by necessity focused on the world out there—on danger and dinner. In Phase I the focus was on the saber-toothed tiger. In that phase of our evolution a dysfunctional family was one that probably got eaten. A functional Phase I family would look something like the diagram that follows:

Diagram A

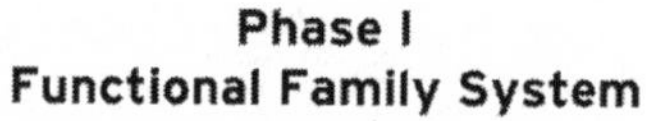

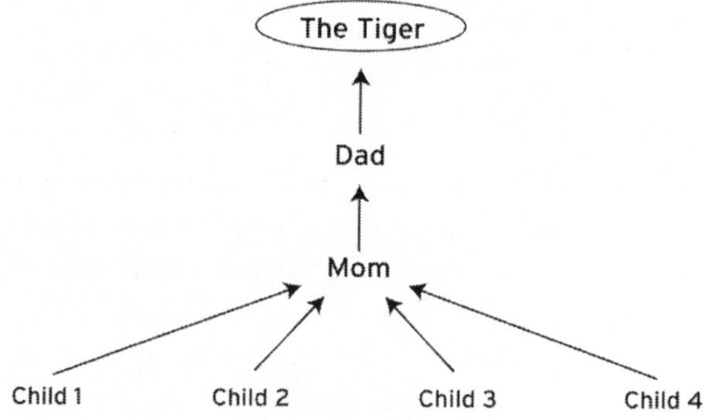

The impact of Phase I focus for your personal stone-aged family (if you are here to read this) was survival. It worked. We did it! Yea! But now we have come indoors.

Phase II: Self Development

In Phase I the focus was on the tiger and life was brutal. Now we have advanced as a civilization; i.e., we are in the process of becoming civilized. Indoors now, we find ourselves moving into Phase II, the self development phase, and our focus must necessarily shift. In this second phase of our evolution, having created our manufactured safe space to live in, we find the opportunity to delve into greater aspects of who we really are and what our true potential as a species and as individuals really is. These are exciting times, but as with all times of transition, they can be confusing and difficult as well. Some of the old brutality of the survival phase remains and can adversely affect our lives and our family life. Out of habit we sometimes create our own tigers. As Qui-Gon Jinn, the JEDI Master who trained Obi-wan Kenobi, said to young Anakin Skywalker in *Star Wars*, Episode I, *The Phantom Menace,* "Always remember…your focus determines your reality."

I once heard a story about the color blue. It goes something like this: At one time in our ancient past the color blue could not be discerned from the color gray by the human eye, and that in the days of Plato the ability to see blue began to evolve. If the story is true you can imagine that at first only a few lucky people were on the cutting edge of seeing blue. One could also imagine that many generations came and went before the average fellow had the new vision. Evolution is like that. Trends first appear on the horizon, on the cutting edge, sporadically at first then more consistently make their way into the entire group.

In Phase II we finally begin to discover the meaning behind certain mysteries hinted at through the ages. For example, we've been told that we are "the salt of the earth," "more than we know," "the light of the world," and that we only use 3-13% of our brain. We've been instructed, "Man, know thyself." Phase II in the evolutionary process is to self develop, i.e. to know thyself. The focus must therefore necessarily shift from the tiger "out there" to the individual—to answer the question that the caterpillar put to Alice in *Alice in Wonderland*, "Who Are YOU?"

Phase II will give way to, or unfold into, yet a third stage in the not too distant future. Phase III can be called the Creative Phase. Safety combined with unity and wholeness achieved for each individual opens the way for creativity. Some attention will be given to this exciting "outcome" phase in later chapters, but it is not the focus of this book. For now we will concern ourselves largely with Phase II work and issues and adjustments.

In society in general, and in the family in particular, the current state of affairs reflects the remnants of our ancient history (the survival phase—the group), even as it begins to show signs of the new (the self development phase—the individual), and hints at the future (the creative phase—integration, or wholeness). Our future looks bright when viewed from this vantage point, but things can sometimes seem to be quite dark and even frightening in certain ways for those of us caught up in the process. We are evolving. In fact, we seem to be evolving out of the dark ages of man but we are not out yet. There is much work to be done. There is much light to be shed.

In this chapter we are going to look at the impact of evolution on the family. In Chapter 2 we will look at the impact on the individual. The rest of the book will look at what kinds of things we can do about it.

The Phase II Family Focus

In Phase II the focus can and must now shift. The function of a Phase II family is to focus on, to nurture, and to raise the children. The focus is on first seeing and then drawing out the true nature of the individual child. This includes assisting the child that is becoming an adult in discovering (uncovering) their life purpose. We are safe enough now to make this shift, but old habits die hard. Our ancient training and its "look for the flaw" brain has a tight hold. When we were in the wild our focus was not only "out there," but also was constantly scanning the landscape for danger—not for what was good, but more for what was bad. Again, survival of our species was dependent on finding the tiger on the hill, the flaw in the picture—on finding the fly in the ointment. Even though we've been coming more and more inside for 10,000+ years, we are now beginning the real transition out of the dark and dangerous past to Phase II—Self Development. The function of a family today is to focus on, to nurture, and to raise the children. The family is to raise the children to become fully developed adults. A fully developed adult is an individual who among other qualifications is fully aware of their interests, their curiosities, and their individual life purpose.

The term "dysfunctional family" is widely known and used in our current popular culture. But the definition of functional family seems to have been understandably missed. Hence, many confusions and misunderstandings have naturally arisen. It will be useful to all further considerations on this subject to get clear about this one fact. The only function of a modern-day family is to focus on, nurture, and raise the children. A dysfunctional family therefore is any family that fails to do just that, in any way, to any extent, for any reason.

It is common in our families today, as it has been for generations as far back as can be determined, for the dynamics to be turned around (i.e. for the children to be focused on the parents). That is survival mode. The children warily observed the adults and imitated all behaviors in order to survive. Mom and dad were busy watching for the tiger. We are ready now as a species to move out of the survival mode and into the self-development phase. In this next phase of our evolution a functional family, according to many family therapists and theorists, might look something like the following diagram:

Diagram B

Phase II: A Functional Family System

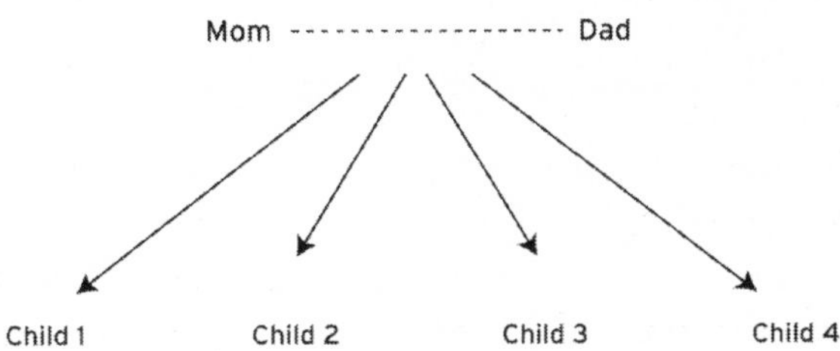

*Arrows denote direction of focus.

In the diagram above of a functional Phase II family, mom and dad meet, fall in love, and marry and give each other genuine adult love and attention. As the children arrive, mom and dad have the personal maturity and the strength of their love for each other to turn their attention together to the needs of the children. Virginia Satir makes these points clear in her book *Conjoint Family Therapy*. With their needs met, the children in this family system are free to bond with each other and to experiment with self-discovery and self-development. With proper exposure to various choices and experiences their talents and true interests will naturally become apparent. And because mom and dad are focused on them, the children will be seen, supported and encouraged to pursue and develop their emerging interests and natural abilities. The children are really seen by mom and dad. They become more and more visible and distinct and their true uniqueness is allowed to develop. Competition within the family (between family members) remains at a minimum.

In a dysfunctional family there is always a condition or event that creates dysfunction by taking the focus of mom or dad off the children. It can be any stress maker: alcoholism, serious or chronic illness in any member, financial worries, etc. Any serious long term stress maker will become the dysfunctional piece. The dysfunctional piece affects the focus of every individual in the family. The dysfunctional piece throws the family into survival mode (Phase I). A dysfunctional Phase II family might look something like diagram C below:

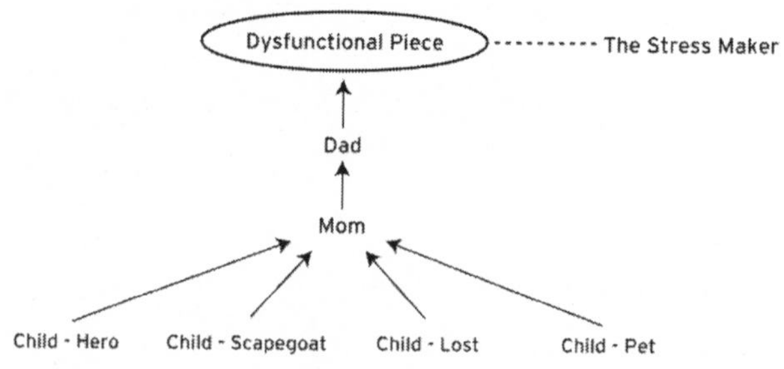

Does this model look familiar? It seems to pattern a Phase I family system. For the sake of example let's say the dysfunctional piece in the family in the diagram above is not the old saber-toothed tiger, but alcoholism. But it could just as easily be a severely and/or chronically ill child, a grandparent moving in, or poverty. Let's say that dad is the alcoholic. He is focused on alcohol—where to drink, when he will next drink, what might interfere with the next desired drink, etc. Not to mention actually being drunk. What is mom focused on? She becomes more and more focused on dad. The children are not really seen by mom or dad. According to Sharon Wegscheider-Cruse, noted addictions author and founding board chairperson of the National Association for Children of Alcoholics (NACoA), "They are just kind of left floating out there." They stay connected to mom and dad by focusing on them and even attempting to meet their needs instead of focusing on each other and on their own interests and on their true current day childhood tasks. They don't really get to grow up. They don't become self-developed. They don't become their true selves. "Who" they really could become remains stifled.

If mom and dad had each grown up in a Phase II functional family they would have the maturity and the inner fortitude to bounce back from stress and make the necessary adjustments to return the system to normal proper Phase II functioning fairly quickly. If, however, one or both parents were raised in a basically dysfunctional family, there will always be a stress maker taking the focus. This occurs because one and more likely both parents didn't really grow up. That is they grew to chronological adulthood carrying hidden unmet crucial needs from childhood. In effect, they came into adulthood stuck in survival mode. Adults stuck in survival mode function as children in the world-at-large and they tend to create chaos.

In the dysfunctional family diagram one parent is focused on the stress maker of the moment and the other parent is focused on the unavailable spouse. The children are left on their own. They turn their focus to mom and dad in order to survive. The whole system runs backward. Mom and dad are not aware of this consciously. In most cases they may even be doing all the "right things" a parent should do for basic care taking. But they may not be doing much more for the children. In this backward family system the children do not connect with each other. They are thrown into Phase I survival mode and are often like the birds that fight for bread crumbs in your back yard in winter. They must fight each other, sometimes as bitter rivals, for any crumbs of love or true focus that may fall their way from the basically unavailable parent(s).

In this system the parents have the "problem" of dealing with the children, i.e. they see the children as a burden, and the children must be gotten out of the way. That's where family roles come into play.

Family Roles

It is human nature to evolve toward efficiency in all matters. We see this phenomenon at work in our living languages. For example, over time habit of use causes words that once were crisp and distinct to contract; i.e., can not becomes can't, is not becomes isn't. In families establishing roles through habit, stereotyping, and categorizing, is a way of developing efficiency for interactions. Role assignments are not in and of themselves a problem. It is the extremity of the roles assigned and the rigidity with which they are adhered to that matters.

Much has been written and said about the roles that emerge among the children in a dysfunctional family, and birth order seems to play an important part in the assignment of these roles. The oldest child is often assigned the role of the Hero. This is done unconsciously, of course, by mom and dad. It is done because mom and dad are gnawingly aware that something is amiss and they need the world to view them as good parents with a good marriage. The Hero child proves this. Generally speaking she is good at school, good at sports, good at something significant and visible to the school and the community, good at something public, and brings praise or even glory to the family. This child performs the function of proof.

The second born is often what is called the Scapegoat. Renowned family therapist, Virginia Satir, was first to recognize the acting out child as part of a system. She labeled this child the Identified Patient (IP) and pointed out that the child was performing a function that helped to keep the whole system going. At first it was thought that the IP was the only child forced into a role. Later, during the recovery movement of the seventies and eighties it was discovered that each child in the dysfunctional family was assigned a distinct role. This discovery came out of the family work done in treatment centers and inpatient alcoholism treatment hospitals. Eventually it became clear that this was not only true for families dealing with alcoholism, but for families dealing with any major stress maker when the parents are immature or otherwise unstable. This second child in the dysfunctional family system would be the "sick one," the deviant, the bad child, the black sheep. This child performs the function of the distracter. She takes mom's and dad's attention off the fact of the miserable marriage and gives them a project they can agree, or disagree about.

The third child comes when energies are spent and there is little at all left over for him. This child often becomes the Lost Child. This is the child who seems to have no needs, who seems quietly content and self contained. This child is generally very little bother and rarely makes waves. This child is almost invisible. He gets attention by performing the function of validating all others. This child is the listener.

The fourth child is often what is called the Mascot or the family Pet. This child is viewed by the family as cute and performs the function of discharging the family energy and entertaining the troops. She is energized by the unnamed tensions in the stressed-out family. In fact, her main job in the family is to discharge the constant build up of tensions. She is not taken seriously as a person.

We will be looking in more detail at these roles and how they develop, and their impact on the child later on in this chapter, but at this point it is important to understand that they are roles. It is important to become aware that they have nothing to do with the true latent talents or interests, or the potential true personality of the child. These roles are thrust upon him for the sole benefit of the dysfunctional parents. In the family, and then in the world-at-large, and worst of all to the child, they define the child. This is a fundamental false beginning for the child. The child stretches into the role and squelches most if not all true self development that is out of character with her family role and quickly comes to believe (though forever with unease) in a fundamentally false identity.

The Shapers

The child is shaped by the family to fit the unconsciously desired role. He is shaped first by mom and dad. The cues are quickly picked up by all other family members and everyone takes part in the shaping. The role shaping is done in subtle ways and with no conscious awareness by the shapers. It is done unconsciously by behavioral techniques that reinforce the unconsciously desired behaviors. It is also accomplished

by interpreting generic behaviors as behaviors that support the family role assigned to the particular child.
For example:
Behavior: cleaning your plate (eating everything on it) at dinner.
Interpretation:

1. Hero child: "Good job!"
2. Scapegoat: "You eat too fast!"
3. Lost Child: completely ignore the behavior and the child. Say nothing.
4. Pet: "How cute you are! You ate it all up!"

Shaping by the parents profoundly shapes not only the child's view of himself, but also the view of the child by onlookers. A modern public example of shaping can be observed in politics. Shaping is a common, conscious, knowingly deceitful practice among politicians. In politics this purposeful tactic is called "framing the opponent." In a given political race Candidate A may try to "define" candidate B before he gets to make himself known, i.e. to define himself for the voters. Framing is done by words, gestures, and tone. To diminish an opponent in the eyes of the voters, a candidate might begin laughing about him. With the goal to diminish his opponent's stature, or even to destroy his character, he may begin acting as if his opponent is just a silly youngster or a villain. The point is once the "framing" of the politician takes, it is very difficult for candidate B to change his false public image.

For the child in the family, the shaping is done in similar fashion (even though it lacks the conscious awareness of political framing). For example, the designated Hero will only be noticed for high achievement. In some families this child is raised to the level of an emotional partner or pseudo-spouse for the neglected parent. (But this can happen to a child in any role.)

For even minor accomplishments high praise as well as pressure for more success is generously doled out to the Hero. Any and all negative behavior by the Hero is ignored, not reinforced, and thereby quickly extinguished. The Scapegoat gets attention mainly for bad behavior and is referred to as a problem child in conversation with others. The

Lost Child is shaped into passivity by parents who do not respond to or even look at him when he asks for attention or expresses needs. This child is ignored, not heard or seen, and he therefore gives up on trying to have any impact on anyone and just kind of fades into the background. The Pet is given focus generally only when acting funny or cute, and is kept sheltered from knowing the true nature of the family problems. However, this child feels and carries all the stress of the family; the Pet is the family drain. This can only result in the child being perpetually frightened of the vast unknown. This child is not taken seriously, even as an adult.

There are complexities and variations, of course, but that is the gist of role shaping. Further, once mom and dad begin their shaping behaviors (generally at the time of birth of each child) all other family members follow suit. Everyone in the family comes to believe the Hero is exceptional, to believe the Scapegoat is intrinsically bad, to believe the Lost Child has no needs and large shoulders to cry on, to believe the Pet is just cute, silly, and fun. The Hero performs to higher and higher standards. The Scapegoat deviates, rebels, and exasperates. The Lost Child disappears. The Pet performs—consistently. These behaviors have nothing to do with the undeveloped talents and interests of the child. But even the child has bought the bridge to Brooklyn. The child has been defined by the family. The child has not been seen. The child has been defined incorrectly. Everything else that unfolds for the growing child in terms of identity and behaviors and even career and other future life decisions is built on this fundamental error. The child feels a strange sense of unease, but has little power to question. The child has been defined from the outside in. This is a problem.

Outside/Inside the Child in the Role

Role	Outside	Inside	Family Function
The Hero	Achievements	Tremendous pressure	Proof of parents' skills
The Scapegoat	Troublemaker Rebel Defiance	Shame Despair Desperation	Take focus off of bad marriage
The Lost Child	Content Easygoing Invisible	Unimportant Not Real	Ease burdening parents and validate all others
The Pet	Adorable Silly Frivolous	Anxious Unnamed worries Fear/ Terror	Drain off family stress

It is important to realize that the parents "see" only the good behaviors of the Hero child. That child has a secret inner sense of inadequacy in light of such lavish praise and strives harder to achieve more. The parents see only the bad behaviors of the Scapegoat and give him messages of discouragement, anger, disapproval and disgust, messages of negative expectations. "You'll never amount to anything." They hardly see (or hear) the Lost Child, and in fact, they barely look at him at all. They see the Pet as very cute and minimize her accomplishment. The family's perception is often in marked contrast to the observations of outsiders. For example, an outsider may not see the Pet as cute at all, and may, in fact, feel annoyed at the parents' doting admiration toward that child. They may even describe that child as obnoxious. All behaviors from the children that do not meet the role expectations are simply not "seen" by the shapers.

When a child's entire family acts towards him as if he is not there (Lost Child), as if he is not saying anything of significance (Pet), as if he is set apart from his siblings by glory or special authority (Hero), or as if he is evil (Scapegoat), his picture of himself is profoundly affected. The family has acted like a powerful mirror--distorted and powerful. The child can only see himself as reflected back by the family mirror. This powerful family mirror is in effect, the child's only feedback system. In large part the child can therefore only "know" himself through the eyes of the family. The real substance of the child is denied, a consequence of the natural reluctance to make the shift from survival to self development.

Level of Rigidity

All families do some shaping. In a family with basically mature parents there is more real or true focus on the children which permits more of the child's true potential to emerge and form. The roles will therefore be less discernible and less damaging to the child. The more dysfunctional the family system, the more rigid the roles and the less a child accurately knows himself. When there is severe immaturity in the parents the roles will be very rigid and extreme. The Hero will have to become a great hero (president?), or will breakdown altogether, suffering severe physical or mental symptoms, or she may just drop out (in which case one of the other children will step up to the Hero role). The Scapegoat will act out so severely that addiction and or criminality might occur. The Lost Child will withdraw into depression and or prescription drug addiction. The Pet will demand to be the center of attention to an extreme (class clown, extreme sports, rock star, movie star, or maybe even president).

In the extreme all four roles are highly susceptible to suicide. Of course, the roles are never exact and can be handed from one child to another depending on the circumstances and the needs of the family at any given moment. For example, should the Hero fall from grace, the Scapegoat will suddenly find himself assuming the Hero role. The Scapegoat will suddenly become responsible and "good." There can also be overlapping of roles and the roles can occur in different birth order. Further, if the family consists of only two children the four roles will be divided between the two. A Hero may also pick up some characteristics of the rebel at times or may entertain the troops. If there is only one child that child becomes all things to serve the hidden needs of the dysfunctional parents. (An only child can be burdened indeed!) But generally speaking, the roles tend to follow the outlined pattern. And the sad irony is that the parents who have unconsciously assigned these roles are often pitied for "the child who went bad" and lauded for the "successful one." The bottom line: the "family mirror," the family feedback system, is not a true mirror for the child.

Cracks in the Mirror: The Impact of Abuse and Neglect

Roles in the dysfunctional family are just the first layer of impact in the development of the false identity of the child. There is a second and even more sinister and horrifying set of phenomena that creates a second layer in the development of the false identity. The second layer comes about as a result of degrees and types of abuse and neglect perpetrated on the child.

Abuse and neglect are significant factors in the developing psyche of the growing child. Whereas roles suppress "true self" emergence and create a false identity, abuse and neglect leave wounds and scars and contribute to the coping strategies and survival tactics developed by the child. Many of these tactics and strategies will harden into symptoms once the person has outgrown or moved beyond their true situational usefulness. They do not tend to fade or go away, nor do the scars. Rather, they can begin to turn on the person as the years go by.

Roles are shaped by the parents and imposed on the child from without like a mold. The child develops wounds and survival tactics from within in reaction to trauma such as abuse. In other words, roles shape the outside layer, but the trauma of abuse and neglect creates wounds that affect the internal mechanisms of the child's developing psyche. Such wounds create triggers and serve as filters on the world out there and can greatly distort the view. This will be covered in greater depth in future chapters in this book. At this point in our study of the family and its impact on child development, it is important to note that the level of immaturity in the parents coupled with the stress level of the moment as well as family history of abuse and neglect all intertwine and overlap to affect the incidence and frequency and severity of these factors in the family-at-large and within each individual. In other words, if mom or dad was abused or neglected the pattern is likely to be repeated. Author and noted psychotherapist, Alice Miller (1983, p.97) writes:

Among the adult's true motives we find:

1. *The unconscious need to pass on to others the humiliation one has undergone oneself.*
2. *The need to find an outlet for repressed affect.*

3. *The need to possess and have at one's disposal an object to manipulate.*
4. *Self-defense: i.e., the need to idealize one's own childhood and one's parents by dogmatically applying the parent's pedagogical principles to one's own children.*
5. *Fear of freedom.*

The Impact of Phase II Focus

The impact of Phase II focus, when the ideal becomes a reality, will be full self development for all adult members of the family and accordingly, the child's true nature is drawn out. In the interim the impact of the outdated focus is significant and problematic. Chapter 2 will look at the dilemma many of us find ourselves facing in this period of transition when the danger of the wild has largely passed and we have nothing solid and constructive firmly in place to replace it with.

"*Always remember*...your focus determines your reality."

--George Lucas
Character: Qui-Gon Jinn
Star Wars
Episode I, *The Phantom Menace*..

Q & A

Ask Yourself

In your family of origin:

1. Q: What was your role?
   A:

2. Q: Where was your focus? Where was your mother's focus? Where was your father's focus?
   A:

3. Q: Was there a major stress maker? What was it?
   A:

4. Q: On a scale of 1 to 10, 1 being least severe, how would you rate your family level of rigidity in terms of roles?
   A:

5. Q: Was abuse, neglect, or trauma present?
   A:

6. Q: Can you identify what happened?
   A:

And:

7. Q: Who Are You?
   A:

Summary

1. There are three phases in our evolution:
   Phase I: Survival (Creating a Safe Space)
   Phase II: Self Development (Discovering Our Full Potential)
   Phase III: Creativity (Expressing That Potential)
2. We are currently moving from Survival to Self Development, with glimpses of what is to come.
3. The function of a Phase II family is to focus on, to nurture, and to raise the children.
4. Family focus plays a primary part in the development of the individual.

5. The four basic roles in a dysfunctional family system are: Hero, Scapegoat, Lost Child, and Pet. They are assigned to the children usually by birth order.
6. Roles tend to meet the unconscious needs of the parents and can profoundly stunt the development of the child.
7. Abuse and neglect trigger–set the growing child for future "issues."

Chapter 2

The Individual: Seeking the True Mirror

"A sad soul can kill you quicker, far quicker than a germ."
--John Steinbeck

Life in the Reflection of the Fun House Mirror

What happens to the children from dysfunctional families when they reach the age of adulthood in our culture? What happens to them as adults in a Phase II world? Anyone born into and growing to adult age in a family system that is dysfunctional as is described in Chapter 1, and remember that today this includes most of us, can sense that something might be amiss. It may be just a faint (and ignored) little sensation somewhere very deep inside, it may be a tendency to cry unexpectedly and without understanding at certain movies, or it may be fully bloomed in conscious awareness. But it is there. We know when we are not quite genuine, when something inside just seems a little "off." We can sense when there is a certain unexplainable (no matter how slight) feeling of emptiness. It may be just a tiny itch or a little gnawing feeling. It may rage in our consciousness or, unfortunately, for many, it can lay dormant forever in this life. But either way, we know.

Growing up in such a dysfunctional family system sets us up to spend our adult years hiding this unhappy condition from ourselves and our fellows, or to search endlessly for a way to heal, to become whole, to become real i.e., to become genuine and functional in a Phase II sense. To become "who we really are." This is often not a conscious quest, though for some it is. But it is (as psychologists have discovered) often the unconscious driving force in much that we do and throughout our entire lives. We are driven to root it out, fill it up, or to cover it up.

The point is that it does drive us. When the urge to maintain the status quo, to "not rock the boat" is a driving force, this "opposing energy" sets up tensions and inner conflict and turmoil, because as we shall see in Chapter 3, there are other forces also driving us. Either way we are unhappy and stressed.

Those of us who are avoiding the search for the truth do so because the pain of knowing the truth about the emptiness of childhood is too great to face. Or, we are driven to maintain the connection (in our psyche and in real life) with our parents. We are driven to protect them and ourselves from our own awareness of the truth. To look back at our caregivers and to see them as the neglectful, unavailable, immature people that they were is just too hard, too scary and too lonely. It can feel as if there was nothing holding us up and nothing substantial to stand on. We fight down the truth inside and we don't want to know.

Seekers are those of us for whom the pain of not knowing has surpassed the risk of discovering the truth.

Whether there is a cover-up or not, we remain driven to fill the awful emptiness. Whether we are consciously aware of the emptiness or not we are driven to fill it. Either way it is part of what drives us at this stage of our development. We strive constructively or destructively, but we strive. Because we have had false identities (roles) imposed upon us from without to one degree or another by our family of origin, we do not feel genuine and we feel a great sense of loss. What we are empty of and what we have lost touch with is the self.

There are three elements to happiness:

1. Belonging: We need to feel we belong, to our families, to our communities, to some human group.
2. Accomplishment: We need to feel we are accomplishing something of value to us.
3. Authenticity: We need to be living an authentic life. Authenticity is a Phase II addition to the other two requirements which have their roots in the survival phase.

Numbers 1 and 2 were with us in the Survival Phase. They remain with us in the Self Development Phase which adds No. 3, "Authenticity." All three will play a part in Phase III.

Many of us are stuck in our roles assigned in childhood and do not even know that they are roles. By living as the role we lose out on discovering who we really are. We are empty—empty of the genuine self. This phenomenon is rampant in our current stage of evolution. It can explain, in part, why today we find ourselves dealing with so many addictions and obsessive compulsions in our personal lives and in our self-disordered culture.

Addictions can be said to be our quest for "God" in a bottle. They are born, in part at least, of an absence of the True Self. Something is missing.

We fill it with:

a. work
b. shopping
c. alcohol
d. a doughnut
e. drugs
f. gambling
g. new love
h. something!

Or, we try to regain the pack. We either try to fill the new sense of emptiness, or we try to go back to the security of the pack.

In Phase I, the survival stage, we simply held our collective breath and fought against physical danger and hardship. Our thinking was largely limited to strategies, tasks, and tactics. We were busy. We were focused. We were accomplished. We belonged—we were a group. We each quickly found our place in the pack (or we were eaten) and we worked together for the common cause.

Suddenly, some of us find ourselves with spears and clubs still in hand but with no saber-toothed tiger to fight! No group! No real fight to fight. Yet, fight we do. Our targets are in our homes, our jobs, our friendships, and our communities. Our relationships are suffering.

It seems we are either trying to fill the "hole in the belly with the wind blowing through it" feeling—the inner emptiness that we feel as we arrive in Phase II unprepared, or we are striving to regain the pack—to go backward to Phase I where we knew our place and what to do.

To go forward in Phase II we need to develop boundaries. Since we no longer have a pack or a place in it we now have to find our own place in the world. Boundaries set the border for defining the True Self. They protect me from you and you from me. They tell us both where I stop and where you begin. Boundaries are sacred. To get them we need a true mirror.

Since mom and dad were stuck in survival mode, they did not know to, or know how to focus on, nurture and raise the children. They did not establish for us the boundaries we now need in a Phase II world. We grew to adult age in a system running backwards, focused on the needs of the parent and there was no true mirror reflecting back a true image to the child. A true mirror accurately reflects back the picture before it and offers validation, definition, and proof that you exist. Our boundaries were not formed.

Boundaries are sacred. Imagine a lake without a shoreline. The lake disappears. It thins out and evaporates. Imagine a country without borders. It is soon overrun by its neighbors and soon does not exist. A child without boundaries has no safe inner space to develop. Boundaries are required to become whole and distinct. It is the job of Phase II mom and dad to give you your boundaries. They do this by seeing you, by reflecting you back to you. They do this by respecting you and what should be your growing domain. They do this by giving you proper feedback and discipline—not to be confused with punishment (more on this in future chapters). In other words, they do this by being true, firm and loving mirrors. Mom and dad are responsible for teaching you what your domain is. When they are needy people, taking from you and not making decisions in your best interest, they are teaching you that you are an extension of their domain and that is where we find ourselves. To put it in stronger language, according to Phase II standards, they have trained us as slaves or they have trained us as tyrants.

As children in such circumstance we experienced very little sense of personal rights, meaningful personal choice, or personal preference, and basically lived in open territory unprotected. We did not learn how to protect ourselves because without borders there is nothing to protect. With no sense of the border between self and parent/ruler the slave mentality is automatic. The over-controlled unprotected child can't discover who he is. He takes this sense of slavery out into the world with him, putting the needs and demands of most, if not all, others before his own best interest at his own expense. Or he identifies with the rulers and he dominates. He becomes the doormat or the tyrant but he does not become his real self. An underdeveloped, unboundaried adult is like a borderless energy center. The world will take unfair advantage or he will. The world will wipe its feet on him or resent and resist and reject his unwelcome intrusions. Either way relationships suffer. A child "owned" by mother and father can't say no. That child grows into an adult who cannot say no, or who tries to own others. Either way, doormat or tyrant, that adult can never say a true yes.

Boundaries set the border for defining the true self. Adults raised in the dysfunctional families of Phase II, lacking good boundary formation, tend to become blended into their relationships with others. They have a vague (or pronounced) sense of losing the self or of not having one at all. They build thick walls to compensate or they become tyrants. Personal power vs. power over others is very confused in these relationships. Without proper boundary formation adults cannot successfully come together and form loving, satisfying, life-enhancing, give-and-take relationships.

But come together they do. In fact, many rush together at the outset of a new relationship unconsciously striving to get their "true loving mirror experience" from their new "love." In truth, they can't really come together as two separate loving beings, capable of both giving and receiving mature love. They will either become enmeshed, or estranged. They will either blend to the point of suffocation or build impenetrable walls between them, or they will fight for control. More likely a fourth scenario will occur. One of them will strive for closeness and the other will build an impenetrable fortress to live in. They cannot really see each other and therefore cannot be seen. They are each alone.

Relationships today often reflect the unmet needs from childhood of the participants. The sometimes abused, largely neglected, incorrectly defined (defined by assigned roles) adult arriving fresh from a dysfunctional childhood is set up to have problems and dissatisfactions in all relationships—at home, at work, and in the bowling league. It is a set up for power struggles, ego wars. Each spouse marries expecting on an unconscious level to be seen and nurtured at long last. Each wounded partner brings a tendency to over-sensitivity and misunderstanding to the relationship. Each expects that finally their time has come; each expects finally to be the "star" in their own movie. During the dating and courtship phases that probably was the case as both partners tend to put a "best foot forward" during the acquisition phase. Once the dust settles on the honeymoon they begin to naturally clash. This can occur as quiet or even silent simmerings or loud explosions, and anything in between. They inevitably begin to clash.

Growing to adulthood without an accurate definition of self is, first and foremost, not growing to adulthood. That being said, the pseudo-adult feels alone. Never having been really seen, s/he is alone. Every aspect of life and all relationships are affected. If the trauma of childhood abuse and/or neglect was added to the deadening experience of role shaping, everything is intensified and made more complex. To deal with the abuse trauma the child has added complex coping strategies needed for survival at that time. In adult life with adult responsibilities and expectations, they begin to really backfire. Some examples of such coping strategies for abuse survivors include:

1. Rigid adherence to a principle or principles.
2. Split off parts of the child stuck in time.
3. Oppositional behaviors that can harden to anti-social and even criminal behavior.
4. Obsessive compulsions.

Adult survivors of dysfunctional family systems are survivors. They often project onto the world their own distorted mirror and see circumstances and events and people not as they actually are. They are literally not themselves and they see others through the distorted vision of their projections.

Example: Let's say "Connie" was the family scapegoat and therefore used to being accused and blamed and chastised. Let's say she took a job with a kind and reasonable boss. Before very long our subject would most likely be expecting criticism and would begin to see the authority figure as blaming. To go a step further, before long, the kind boss would begin to see Connie as a problem because she begins to behave as if guilty of something. We teach others how to define us and how to treat us. Poor Connie would have effectively and unwittingly re-created her former family environment at the workplace through her expectations of chastisement and the behavior she displayed as a result of that.

Adult survivors of such family systems are stuck in their roles and stuck with their coping strategies. They are not themselves, and somewhere deep inside, we now know, the thwarted kernel of true self somehow knows it. This is our hope for the future. And there is *a way out,* but for now, it sets the trigger for relationship wars.

In relationships today many of us seem to be doing things backwards. Just like mom and dad in the dysfunctional family in Chapter One we are functioning with unmet needs and we are striving to get them met. We are in hot pursuit of the true mirror. Whether we realize it consciously or not is another matter. Be assured, if the need went unmet we are trigger-set to strive to meet it. Sadly then, we seem to be "looking for love in all the wrong places" just like in that old country song. We're looking for definition and proof of our existence, and for that unconditional love mom was supposed to give us—but we're now looking for it from our mates. When that fails we seek it out in our captive audience—our children. This does not heal us, but it salves the wound. We look to our spouses, we look to our children and we are unavailable to them.

And we now know what it is doing to our children. They are growing older with the focus going in the wrong direction once more. As they reach adult age they will take their unmet needs into all their relationships. But we're beginning to figure it out. Like Harry Truman, we too can draw the line where we stand and decide "The buck stops here!" There is *a way out* of the mess that we find ourselves and our children in. There are proven methods for change available. Our excuses are beginning to evaporate.

If you have children ask yourself this question: *Am I getting a sense of support from one or more of my children in any arena of my life?*

Flawed mirroring, faulty focus, and brutality leading to abuse and neglect in our families are among the most unwanted inherited remnants from Phase I. These three issues have created the phenomenon of the adult child syndrome and our self-disordered society. This is a temporary condition. Starting on the cutting edge we are beginning to find *the way out.*

We now realize that vast numbers of us are, as Thoreau eloquently penned, "living lives of quiet desperation." Our lives are not based upon who we really are. And the forces within us will not be wholly quieted. Our lives are not authentic. You may be asking yourself what's the point of living if it's not really "me" doing it?

Don't despair. In the context of evolution the current state of affairs becomes less frightening, not less painful or urgent, but less frightening. This current angst we are experiencing seems to be a necessary step in the evolution of our species. Some comfort! But we now know why, and that there is a better way. It can be a difficult step with some struggle and pain, but it can shift in the wink of an eye! As you gain realistic understanding and effective tools, you can, in a flash, make the leap-in-consciousness to authenticity and gain self mastery and freedom. Remember the story of the color blue? Some among us have already begun to make the leap. Some have already made it. Let's not linger here long.

Q & A

Ask Yourself

1. Q: Have I ever really been seen?
   A:

2. Q: Am I looking for a true mirror?
   A:

3. Q: Where am I looking?
   A:

4. Q: Who Am I *really*?
   A:

Summary

1. We need to be seen.
2. Boundaries are sacred.
3. We are "looking for love in all the wrong places."

4. We can learn the way to achieve true self mastery.
5. At this stage of our development there are 3 elements to happiness:

   a. Belonging
   b. Accomplishment
   c. Authenticity

   The first two are from the Survival Phase. The third, Authenticity, is newly introduced in the Self Development Phase. Without this one today we feel UNHAPPY! We feel that something is missing. It drives us to grow.
6. You now can find out HOW to find your SELF.

Curious?

Commentary

Choice

What choice have you? Only, it seems, as much as you are free to give yourself.

There are five basic freedoms:

1. Physical
2. Political
3. Religious
4. Financial
5. Psychological

By far the purest and most fundamental, the most precious, is psychological freedom. Psychological freedom *is* the freedom of True Choice. And yet, it seems very few of us truly have it. Very few of us truly operate out of it much of the time.

Every freedom listed that we enjoy had to be fought for and earned. It is only now that we seem ready to work for our psychological freedom.

What is psychological freedom? What is true choice? Let's take a look at what it is not: How much of what seems like choice in life is actually just bowing to inner or outer forces? Reacting rather than acting? Reacting based on fears or foes? Present or long past?

If we are truly children of the Most High and have been endowed with free will, then why is it that most of what most of us "choose" seems to make us unhappy, less than wealthy, frustrated, and stuck?

Could it be that finding our free will (which is different from our stubbornness or our self-sacrificing) is a necessary, but not easy, first step to fulfillment and joy?

What does all this mean? If you have uncovered your true power to freely choose in life, you will understand. If you have not, you can. There are, remember, maps and guides available. And it is never too late.

The choice is yours.

Chapter 3

The Theory: Introducing Personality Integration Theory "IT"

"In the depth of winter, I finally learned that within me there lay an invincible summer." --Albert Camus

The Power to Change

A Question

Here we find ourselves at the turn of a new millennium, at the dawn of the 21st century with the technology to travel to the moon, Mars, and beyond, and corruption abounds, wars rage, people starve, tent cities pop up, and the divorce rate rises. We know how to build a robot, clone a dog, save the earth from ourselves, but we don't know how to get along with each other, or even what really makes us tick. Our whole human culture is based on a paradigm that tells us we are creatures with limited intellect, abilities, resources, and power. We live as if some of us were endowed with greater potential than others of our fellows, and we are determined to figure out which is which. Fierce rivalry and competition abound. They are reflections of our lack mentality of "only so much to go around," and the idea that, "There's only one number one!" We're survivalists; victims of our environment, genetics and social conditioning. We tend to live within the limited vision we hold for our species, accepting our "lot" in life. We accept ourselves at face value and look to the hereafter for some purpose to our existence and for our reward.

What if we were really more than all of that? What if there was an amazing sleeping part in each of us just waiting for some event, or condition, or force, or decision to trigger its great awakening? Some evolutionary push? Some gathering momentum of energy? What if the time has come and the great sleeping giant within, like the butterfly in its dark cocoon, is now stirring in the souls of humankind? What if deep within each one of us we have the power to change?

In Search of an Answer

Some Foundational IT Concepts

Old Belief:

There is something wrong with me. There is something wrong with you.

IT Belief:

The only thing wrong with either one of us is the mistaken belief that there is something intrinsically wrong. From the flawed foundational thought that there is something intrinsically wrong with you comes all manner of difficulties; layer upon layer of cover ups, including roles, defense mechanisms, self-protective self-deceit, and various other blocks to true self understanding and acceptance. Self understanding and acceptance are requirements for real maturation and freedom.

One village in Africa seems to understand this very well. Dr. Wayne Dyer appeared some time ago on PBS and spoke about his book, *The Power of Intention.* He told the story of a woman who had traveled around the world. While visiting a particular village in Africa, she learned how they handle deviants in their community. As I remember from Dr. Dyer's account, the traveler's story is that when someone breaks the village law or rules and is caught he is brought to the middle of the village and seated as the villagers gather around him. For however many days and hours it takes (usually about three days) all other business in the village stops. Over the course of the event each of the villagers takes their turn at sitting directly in front of the "offender" to confront him with everything they know and can remember throughout their lifetime of knowing him about what is wonderful and functional about him. They go back through the years and recount everything good that they remember about the person. They include behavior and attitudes, kind acts, talents, and evidence of intelligence. Only the good is fed back to the person. Every person in the village takes their turn with the entire village as witness, for as long as it takes. The village becomes a true mirror.

The result of this treatment is that the bad behavior stops from that individual and they go on to take their rightful, responsible place among their fellows. This sure seems to be powerful evidence of the basic truth that we are intrinsically good and that the only thing wrong with us is the mistaken "belief" that there is something wrong with us. As well as saving human lives and reducing human misery, the village method seems pretty cost effective, too!

The only thing holding you back from dream fulfillment and joy is a false self-concept!!! That seems simple enough. Most *truth* is. But fixing it, since most of us do not live in such a wise and wonderful community as that village yet, isn't necessarily an easy process.

Old Belief:

We are limited beings.

IT Belief:

We are more powerful than we realize and are limited only by our own individual limiting beliefs (i.e. If you don't know you can walk, you won't.) and our false fears.

Old Belief:

If I do what is truly best for me, it might harm you.

IT Belief:

That which is for my highest good will never, can never, clash with your highest good.

Old Belief:

People don't fundamentally change. "You can't teach an old dog new tricks."

IT Belief:

Change is coming.

****

On Children…

On children…
We all are.
In some ways
We all are children…

Some would say we are Children of the Divine, Children of the Universe, Children of the Earth. Some would say that inside each of us there is a part of our psyche that is the little child of our own past that stores the hurts and joys of our seemingly long-lost childhood. Some would say that inside each of us is the Divine Child, the Playful Child, and the Magical Child. Some would say that our inner child of the past holds the key to our spontaneity, our individuality, to our creative genius.

People spend hours of effort and pockets of dollars on books and tapes and lectures and workshops to find that childlike part, only to lose sight of it again for not knowing what to do with this great discovery, for not knowing how to deal with the Child once found. Anyone who has been through an inner-child discovery experience can tell you there is a child within. Yet, there does not seem to be a lot of practical guidance out there about how to integrate that precious, fractioned off part into the whole of you.

On Children and Goblins and Ghouls...
Then, there are the *tapes.* We must look carefully at the tapes that can rule so many of us—those shoulds from the dusty past. Many are like outmoded traditions that have lost their underpinning of purpose, or

worse yet, never had any. Those tapes when left to rule will mishandle the precious inner child and force a retreat to some inner sanctum. Those critical tapes—those recorded messages from our past—do not nurture, encourage growth, experimentation, or creativity. For the most part they squelch, and at worst, they injure.

And Here's The Rub...

Many of us, without being aware of it, can be ruled by the immature child part. As you examine your life, do you find you ever display impulsivity? Compulsivity? Addictions, for example, are a signal that the out of control child within is in charge. If you are operating out of your inner child, you are often operating out of fear, or anger (which is pretty much based on fear) and are likely showing signs of lacking discipline in some ways. You may be rebellious or stubborn. These are all signs of a child in charge.

Others may largely be operating out of the critical tapes. Perhaps you hound yourself to "get your work done!" You may chastise harshly for any perceived mistakes. Or overachieve. All this sends the frightened inner child to the far corner of the psyche, sentenced to hide out sometimes for a lifetime!

Many of us flip back and forth from the child in charge to the critical tapes ruling the roost:

"Gimme!"

"No!"

"I want!"

"Shame on you!" etc., etc. and the intra-psychic battle rages. Child creates chaos; tapes shame and frighten.

Neither of these modi operandi is adult!

How does an adult really deal with the inner child in all its aspects—the frightened child, the playful child, the tyrant child, the traumatized child, the magical child, the angry child? First by recognizing that it is the child that is trying to express and *not* the true self. Then by discerning—considering—i.e., "Is this the right time to take a walk in the surf, or do I need to protect my welfare by being on time for work?

I'll take that walk later." Or, "Should I really go ahead and yell at my boss?" Or "Will s/he really hurt me?" Or is it just a child's way of looking at whatever the situation is? Often we do not realize that we are in our child and judging the situation as a child, through a child's eyes, or making the demands of a child. As we become more aware of this we can begin to access the adult part inside (which includes the observer aspect) to gently but firmly reign in the child with *love.* The adult is that quiet little voice that is so rarely listened to (if even heard at all). The more we center on that small quiet voice, the more we strengthen this part that is the key to our True Self.

Sometimes we let the critical tapes do the reigning in—shaming the child, punishing the child. *This is never helpful, constructive, or necessary!* We need just access that always loving, wise, discerning, adult part inside to let the child know that s/he is far too loved to let our life be jeopardized in any way. With adult security, peace, and wisdom we silence the critical tapes and hush, guide, and comfort the inner child.

There is all the difference in the world between being childish and being childlike. The first is a child run amok in an adult body. The second is a grown up with the freedom to access the spontaneity, creativity, and joy of the inner child and integrate that into a balanced whole. Between inner tapes and inner child must emerge a discerning adult to do the integrating. Let's learn how to pull ourselves together and enjoy!

****

Definition: Theory (n.):

1. *Systematically organized knowledge, esp. a set of assumptions or statements devised to explain a phenomenon or class of phenomena.*
2. *Abstract reasoning: speculation.*
3. *A set of rules or principles for the study or practice of an art or discipline.*
4. *An assumption; conjecture.*

(<GK.theeoria.)
The American Heritage Dictionary, third edition.

Personality Integration Theory can be said to fit the criteria for each of the above 4 stated definitions of a theory. Theories are not absolute, nor are they complete. Rather, they are ways of looking at, studying, and or organizing for practice and for practical purposes. Perfection will not be found in theory; not in this one or in any other. Greater functionality for the student of the theory is the goal.

Personality Integration Theory

The Goal: Personality Integration / Self Mastery
Once consistently achieved, the sky is the limit!

The Structure of the Psyche

The Parts

The KID, the DTL, and the IS

The psyche is made up of three basic parts.

1. **The Key Individual Dynamic (KID)**
   The first part to consider here, the "KID," is very roughly comparable to Sigmund Freud's "Id" in Analytic Theory (AT), and to Eric Berne's "Child" in Transactional Analysis, (TA).

2. **The Dead Tape Library (DTL)**
   The second part in Personality Integration Theory (IT) is the "Dead Tape Library" referred to in IT as the "DTL." This part is roughly comparable to Freud's "Super Ego" and also to Berne's "Parent."

3. **The Inspired Self (IS)**
   The third and central part in IT is the "Inspired Self"—the (IS) (also referred to as the "True Adult.") It is very roughly comparable to Freud's "Ego" and Berne's "Adult." It has access to the unconscious. See diagram 1.

Diagram 1

Freud—AT	Berne—TA	**Light—IT**
↓	↓	↓
Super Ego	Parent	Dead Tape Library (DTL)
Ego	Adult	Inspired Self (IS)
Id	Child	Key Individual Dynamic (KID)

In IT the parts can be conceptualized like a shamrock. We are, it seems, something of a trinity. Maybe St. Patrick got it more right than even he realized! Picture a shamrock in full bloom with the top center leaf representing the Inspired Self, the left lower leaf representing the KID, and the right lower leaf representing the DTL. Each part is interdependent, yet seems to function independently. Each is present at birth, much like a bud, and each is connected to the others and is part of the whole. There is also a stem that has access to the dimension of the All There Is. Like any stem, it serves as a conduit for nourishment. The

KID and the Inspired Self are living creative parts. The DTL, however, is just that—a library of videos and audio recordings. Nothing in the "library" is creative. It contains *only* stored information units. All are dead. They make up the non-living part in us. The DTL is a computer-like resource to be drawn on or dismissed. This part functions like a robot. The KID functions like a child. The Inspired Self is actually the Adult Self, and will function as the master of the control panel for the entity, according to Personality Integration Theory, but only when properly activated. In IT the goal of the individual is for the Inspired Self to emerge and expand and to stand between the KID and the DTL, to integrate them into the whole, to filter and make use of their elements as is helpful, reasonable, and life enhancing for the entity, and to be the only part that interacts in the world-at-large. The goal, in other words, is Self Mastery. Only when the Inspired Self is directing our lives can we live from true inspiration. *Only then can we live in the present.* Only then can we really choose. Only then can we live creatively. This requires proper integration of parts. See Diagram 2.

Diagram 2

The Three Faces of Adam

Life for humankind up to now has been largely a reflection of the kind of life that is limited to, and can be delivered by, the KID and the DTL, interspersed occasionally with brief appearances by the Inspired Self. Each of the three parts when on the "Throne" of the psyche feels and functions like the entire consciousness of the person. But it is not. Each is a distinctly different face of Adam, the individual.

At the broader developmental and evolutionary level the three faces of Adam (as humanity) are Survival Mode, Self Development, and Creative Mode.

The Key Individual Dynamic

The Key Individual Dynamic (KID) contains all our feeling life. It functions like a KID, thinks like a KID, sees the world and all events, inhabitants, and relationships from the eyes of a child, and is never meant to grow up. It has many aspects, such as, the creative child, the angry child, the playful child, the fearful child, the magical child, the sickly child, etc. The KID contains all our symptoms, and is the main beneficiary of any and all medicines and treatments.

The Dead Tape Library

The Dead Tape Library (DTL) contains all the tapes from our formative years. This seems to be a temporary resource of information on how to be civilized, how to get along with our fellows, and hopefully how to succeed in our contemporary society. The Library can have its scary sections too. Some of its contents can be distorted. It also contains a fair share of misinformation and some outright lies. The only "emotions" expressed by the Tapes (almost always overblown) include anger to rage, harsh judgment, approval and disapproval (almost always with a strong sense of urgency and/or emergency). And they can contain dire warnings that could be categorized as fear mongering. These are not primary (or even genuine) emotions. But they can stir up all kinds of strong emotions in the KID. They are recordings. They are dead. They are not a living or creative part, but in our heads they can howl like the banshee! The DTL may well be a holdover from the Survival Phase and may ultimately be replaced by the full emergence of an "inspired" and flexible living part. The DTL cannot create accurate assessments for the entity and as we are evolving beyond mere survival they therefore need to be carefully screened. Who or what can do the screening? It has to be another part.

The Inspired Self

The Inspired Self (IS) is where wisdom, discernment, intuition, peace, and joy reside. This is the seat of our power. Wisdom and discernment are necessary ingredients for the ability to make choices. Free will lives here. The Inspired Self contains the big picture—the blueprint for our lives. It has the ability to constantly observe the other two parts. It is the observer self. The Inspired Self is actually the True Adult. It is the "missing," or rather, underdeveloped and dormant part in many of us today. It is also the only part that has access to a wormhole into another dimension, the spiritual dimension, which Bill Wilson, an original founder of A.A., once referred to as the fourth dimension of living. The IS is our spirit and is meant to direct our lives. Often we have to work to bring that about.

The Structure of Consciousness

To quote one of the masters in the field of psychology:

It is a mistake to believe that science consists in nothing but conclusively proved propositions, and it is unjust to demand that it should. It is a demand only made by those who feel a craving for authority in some form and need to replace the religious catechism by something else, even if it be a scientific one. Science in its catechism has but a few apodictic precepts; it consists mainly of statements which it has developed to varying degrees of probability. The capacity to be content with these approximations to certainty and the ability to carry on constructive work despite the lack of final confirmation are actually a mark of scientific habit of mind.

--Freud

The Three Levels of Conscious Awareness

In the IT Model the structure of the conscious mind includes three levels of conscious awareness. The first level of consciousness is the functioning level on which one of the three parts of the psyche is operating in any given moment of wakefulness. Whether actually *operating* on level one or not, the Inspired Self part is *always aware* of both level one and level two simultaneously. Further, the third level of consciousness is continually accessible to the IS.

Level One

Level one consciousness is located on what IT has labeled the Throne of Your Being. Generally, most of the more established theories of personality limit their definition and description of human consciousness to this one level only (with the notable exceptions of transpersonal psychology, integral psychology, and psychosynthesis). It is this *functioning* level, i.e., the control panel of personality, that most theories exclusively recognize and deal with as consciousness. In IT theory level one is considered to be the most obvious level of consciousness. According to IT theory, the part that is in control of the psyche at any given moment is functioning on the *Throne* of level one consciousness. Only one part sits on the Throne at any given moment and it could be occupied by any one of the three—the KID, the DTL, or the IS. When the DTL is in control of level one it functions like a pre-programmed robot that then pushes the buttons of the KID and/or attacks others in the outer environment. When the KID is in control of level one it functions like a child. The Throne belongs to the IS.

Level Two

Level two consciousness, the Superconscious Mind, includes what is roughly comparable to what is sometimes referred to in the literature of psychology as the subconscious. Level two consciousness is located *in* the always aware IS. The IS is the observer-self and is continuously aware of the other parts in the psyche and of all that is happening to and within the individual even during periods of sleep. The Superconscious is not ever unconscious. It is always aware. This observer-self is perfectly connected through the wormhole to the All There Is.

Level Three

The Superconscious IS can draw from the third level of conscious awareness—the Cosmic Consciousness of the All There Is. With the Superconscious IS traversing the wormhole, there are within it levels of Cosmic Conscious Awareness at any given moment. All consciousness is always available to the awareness of the fully developed IS—always.

Integration of Consciousness

It is optimal for the individual that the Inspired Self is operating on all three levels of consciousness simultaneously, and generally so at all times. Under such circumstance the IS smoothly handles the mundane, and the unique personality—the emancipated, integrated, True Self of the individual—can flourish. For the individual, life flows along its unique, creative, and joy-filled path. "Things" just seem to work out. Synchronicities abound—as all is connected—and life is filled with accomplishment, magic, and love.

It is with proper integration of consciousness that we can also experience what Abraham Maslow and others have called Peak Experiences, i.e., what IT would describe as intersections of the IS and level three—Cosmic Consciousness. And though various methods referred to and discussed herein can lead the practitioner to such experiences, it is beyond the scope of this present volume to focus on or study such phenomena to any great degree or in any depth. Many eminent professionals from various scientific fields have for a number of years considered such areas of study worthy, including William James, Maslow, and Carl Jung. Many others are currently conducting such research and work, both scientifically and experientially. Psychologists, physiologists, and anthropologists, among others, have experimented with, researched, and studied the known heights of the intersections of Superconsciousness and Cosmic Consciousness in great detail. Much has been discovered regarding such human states of consciousness and potentials. Some noted names in the field of higher consciousness studies include contemporaries Stanislav Grof and Ken Wilbur, as well as the late Willis Harman (past president of IONS).

Occasional, or even quite regular, profound peak experiences enhance our faith in the cosmos and our place in it. They can be a seeker's joy. Such phenomena serve a mighty purpose. Yet, as important as such peak experiences are, it is important to achieve the quiet serenity of living and moving competently, lovingly, among our fellows, in our families, our work, our communities, in the capacity of our fully integrated higher selves. The main focus of IT is on the magic of the mundane. For practitioners to master the ability to operate relatively consistently out of the integrated Superconscious (the Inspired Life) in everyday living is the major thrust and goal of Personality Integration Theory and Therapy. To function as a fully integrated adult is the very definition of functional living. Being able to tap into and draw from the Cosmic Consciousness when needed and desired in order to improve the quality of living, for higher creativity, for the wisdom called for in everyday life, and to experience the welcome sense of connectedness, are all equally important potential benefits and outcomes of IT work.

The focus herein is to lay the groundwork for identifying and dealing with the Lower Life structures in the psyche (the KID and the DTL) for the attainment of self mastery and self liberation, and to present useable methods that lead to operating from the Inspired Self, i.e., the Superconsciousness, and maintaining access to Cosmic Consciousness to the benefit of ordinary everyday living.

Just how to achieve such self mastery and beyond toward self liberation is for most one of the great mysteries of life. There are roadmaps available. Personality Integration Therapy can be one of them. To learn how to achieve such psychic harmony and then to increase the ability to apply such learning *consistently* in daily living is the goal of IT work. Personality integration, self mastery, and full emancipation from enslavement to the Lower Life is our destiny. Evolution is taking us there. Let's consciously use any and all reasonable available methods and work to help move things along.

The Unconscious

The unconscious is *in* the KID. Only the KID part contains the unconscious in the traditionally accepted meaning of the term. In IT the unconscious exists in relation to level one consciousness only. The unconscious includes various *aspects* of, or *all* of the KID at any given moment. The DTL is not conscious or unconscious. It is a system that includes a movie camera, tape player/movie projector, tapes/movies, an on/off button, a volume control dial, and lots of storage space for recordings. The IS is always and only conscious.

How It Works

When the KID is on the Throne, and making decisions, and having impact on the person and the world-out-there (running the show), it is *only the particular aspect of the KID part that has been triggered* that comes to conscious awareness to inappropriately claim the Throne. All other aspects of the KID, the IS, and the vast stores of the Dead Tape Library are all closed off from the conscious awareness of the KID. The IS, however, remains aware of all. The KID is experiencing level one consciousness, and *experiencing it as a child.* The KID may be aware of the triggering message(s) from the DTL (including any intensity stored or encoded within), but the actual DTL is not conscious in the KID. The KID thinks that the messages from the DTL are its own thoughts. They seem very real and commanding. DTL messages are very compelling to the KID. As to the IS, only the "still small voice" may gently whisper through to the conscious awareness of the KID at any given moment. The IS will not ever impose its will. The KID can choose to pay attention to such a nudge from the voice of reason within, or (more likely) choose to ignore it. The KID is not really aware of the IS, but the IS is aware of all. When either the DTL or the IS is on the Throne of consciousness, the KID is generally unconscious. All aspects of the KID remain beneath consciousness with the exception of those feeling aspects of the KID that are provoked at times by the DTL (such as fear and shame), or those aspects of the KID that are summoned by the IS for participation when the IS is on the Throne. Those particular aspects of the KID that the IS might summon could include, for example: creative impulse, curiosity, laughter/sense-of-humor, playful expression, etc.

By its very label, it is clear that the Dead Tape Library is not actually conscious. It is dead—a library of dead tapes. When it is on the Throne of level one consciousness, when it is seemingly in control of the person, it can be said to be functioning like a movie, just "mindlessly" and robotically running its course. Or it can function like a movie projector that has captured the attention and the focus of the KID. In other words, it seems to have triggered, overwhelmed, and taken over the conscious awareness of some aspect of the KID. Much like reading a vivid story, or watching a compelling movie, it can seem completely real and alive and fill level one consciousness. When the outer environment provides the stimulus to select a particular pre-recorded thought (tape), the light of level one consciousness shines upon it and the movie comes blaring on. The KID defaults and cowers as the movie runs its course. The DTL takes center stage and attacks the KID and/or acts its part out on the world-at-large.

The IS is the observer-self. It is the watcher. The Inspired Self is entirely conscious at all times; this includes awareness of all activity taking place in level one consciousness. The IS comes to level one consciousness, comes onto the control panel of the Throne, only when *invited* by the KID. The IS does not impose itself on the KID. The IS does not perform any coup—does not impose itself on the KID or take over the Throne. The IS respects the free will of the KID to ask for help or not. When the IS is invited by the Key Individual Dynamic (KID) onto the Throne of level one consciousness, the first two levels of consciousness are merged. The *first two levels of consciousness are merged*, the individual is fully and properly integrated, the KID slips freely off the burdensome and scary Throne into the unconscious to play, and/or to be dealt with internally by the IS for any healing called for. And the IS is in the decision-making position. This may be the case for only a moment, or for a more extended period of time. Further, when the IS is on the Throne, the integrated personality (which is the True Self) also has access to level three resources—Cosmic Consciousness—as needed and desired.

How So?

How can it be that most, if not all, of these concepts are possible? Some may seem quite strange to the person whose head is filled with the collective system of beliefs that are commonly held today. Yet, lets look at some of the current research. According to recent research findings from many different scientific fields, it is becoming evident that various super skills and abilities can be developed in the human mind. The field of noetic science is currently providing evidence that extra-sensory perception, natural healing abilities, remote viewing (ask the CIA about this one!), precognition, increased creativity, access to "genius" level ideas and inspiration, are just a few of the amazing powers humankind is beginning to understand, develop, and harness. These powers, according to IT theory, can be developed as a matter of course by all of us by developing the Superconscious activity of the IS—some in conjunction with Cosmic Consciousness.

Still Wondering?

Raised as I was in the traditions of Western science, I had been taught that mind is a creation of neural structure and function, and of neurochemistry, that mind plays a small role in human behavior, and that when the brain dies, the mind disappears. Case closed.

This is the "brain first, mind second" hypothesis. It is the prevailing model in contemporary science. It is presumed to be true and, for all practical purposes, it is taken on faith by modern Western science. Until a few years ago, I took it on faith, too.

However, there is an alternative model, as current as today's visionary science yet as old as recorded history, looked on as truth by scholars like Plato and Pythagoras more than two thousand years ago. And it was held by scholars like Sir John Eccles, the Nobel prize-winning neurophysiologist, and Dr. Wilder Penfield, the distinguished neurosurgeon, in the last century. It was also held by Dr. William James; David Bohn, Ph.D., the distinguished quantum physicist student of Einstein's; and Tom Slick, who established the Mind Science Foundation.

This model says that mind is first. Consciousness exists independently of the brain. It does not depend upon the brain for its survival. Mind is first, the brain is second. The brain is not the creator of mind, it is a powerful tool of the mind.

--Schwartz (p. 267)

For Much More of What We Are Discovering From Current, Rigorous, Cutting-Edge Scientific Research About the True Nature of Our Astounding Universe Read:

The Afterlife Experiments by Professor Gary E. Schwartz, Ph.D., and William L. Simon,

Esteemed physicist, Michio Kaku's, *Physics of the Impossible,*
Michael Talbot's, *The Holographic Universe,*
The Hidden Reality, by Columbia U. theoretical physicist, Brian Greene,
And *Feeling the Future* by Cornell Emeritus Professor, Daryl J. Bem.

New findings and current research in psychology and in quantum physics and its string field theory suggest that the universe and our human potentials might just be even more magical than ever dreamed of.

"Miracles happen not in opposition to Nature, but in opposition to what we know of Nature." --St. Augustine

How the Psyche Functions;

How the Parts Function Together

The First Relationship

The first relationship is the relationship inside you. The first relationship is your relationship to yourself. This is where so many of us get it wrong in our lives. We don't get this worked out first. As a result, we inevitably screw up our "outer relationships" (our relationships with others) because we don't have the first relationship figured out and worked out.

Inside the psyche the three parts are functioning in relation to one another and interacting at all times. This is true whether we like it or not, or even whether we know it or not. It's just the way it is. It is all-important that this inner interaction be in the originally intended balance. If a person has been properly raised and is mature, the Inspired Self is well developed, substantial, and in control. Then the "Self," the inspired true adult part, is genuine. It includes the other two parts properly integrated. The Self is "on the Throne" and *always* stands between the KID and the Dead Tape Library, and *always* stands between those parts and the outer world. Always means always. If the Inspired Self is underdeveloped or even seeming to be missing altogether (experienced as a feeling of vast emptiness) then the IS is dormant and the internal activity (thinking/feeling) occurs between the KID and The Dead Tape Library. Then the world gets in and they get out. Under those conditions life in the head, the heart, and the world out there is tough indeed! This unfortunately is a very common state of affairs in our world today. And remember this—when the KID gets out it acts like a child. When the DTL gets out it acts like an automaton—very rigid and robotic, and often like a tyrant. And believe me it lacks a sense of humor! Do you know any one who ever acts like a KID, or like a robot? Intimately?

A Bottom Line

You are parts. You are three in one (like the shamrock). You will be successful or not in your life depending on which part dominates and actually runs your life.

The KID will screw it up, and you will feel occasional short-lived elation, but mostly you will feel shame, guilt, anger, and fear. You will avoid all things distasteful to any undisciplined child, and it will matter.

The DTL will be colorless and dull and full of distain. Even if it creates some appearance of success, you will feel less than satisfied, empty, probably quite burdened, and often angry. People will avoid you and consider you unapproachable. Or they will overburden you with tasks and responsibilities. You will judge.

The Inspired Self will be powerful, creative and fair, responsible, stable, and joyful. You will feel whole, productive, adventuresome, and vibrantly alive. You will create. You will love. You will be loved.

In Phase II the task is to develop the True Adult (IS) and to begin to more consistently and to more fully operate out of it. How to make that happen and how to sustain it, for those among us who don't come to it naturally out of a fully functional childhood, is the point and purpose of IT Theory and Therapy and the focus of this book.

The Shift

The Missing Piece

Maturity

"We shall be changed in a moment, in the twinkling of an eye."

--1 Corinthians, 15: 51-52

Maturity is *in* the True Adult. A person is mature to the extent that the Inspired True Adult Self is running the show. Maturity is not a function of helping the KID part grow up; though the KID, with the help of the Dead Tape Library, can become a pseudo-adult. Nor is it a function of "shrinking" the KID. What is the deal?

The answer, it seems, is that maturity is a matter of a Shift. In fact, it is a matter of mastering the ability to recognize which part is currently operating on the Throne, and then mastering the desired Shift. In other words, it is not so much about "growing up" the organism as a whole, as it is a matter of "Shifting into" the grown up part to operate out of, and then properly integrating the other two, i.e. dealing with each of them—the KID and the Tapes—*from* the Inspired Self part. It is a matter of growing the True Adult "muscle" (the IS) if it has been under-developed or under used. Like a muscle, the more you use it the more it develops. The more you use it, the more it grows by drawing in nourishment from the "All There Is" through the wormhole. Looking for evidence? The proof is in the practice. How to do so can be found in Chapter 4.

Maturity is a matter of making a SHIFT into the grown-up part in you. A mature adult is one who operates out of the Inspired Self part.

This IT concept differs from Freud's theory that "The goal of psychoanalysis is to claim a little more ego from the vast sea of Id." (Kornfield.) The goal of IT is to *Shift* out of the KID into the fully intact IS.

The Shift Process

Step One is to recognize which part is on the Throne of your being. The "Throne of your being" is the seat of your acute (level one) conscious awareness.

Step Two is to determine if it is the appropriate part for the situation.

Step Three is to Shift into the appropriate part if needed.

Step Four is to *deal with* the part just removed from the Throne in specific appropriate ways.

IT Therapy can teach you how to make the assessments, how to make the Shift, and then how to deal with the "other" part with methods and techniques for Self Mastery. At this point it is important to begin looking at mental health and maturity in this very different way. It is important to begin thinking about it from the new paradigm.

Application of Self Help Methods

Have you ever left a workshop or seminar with high hopes for applying some wonderful new method to live a better life, only to be crushed by the inability to keep up the good work? The IT concept of the Shift explains why so many seekers of health, truth, and growth can't seem to be able to apply what they have learned in all the books, workshops, therapy sessions, etc. they have tried over the years. Without the missing piece of the "Shift" they have been trying to apply perfectly good self help concepts, methods and techniques *from the KID part in them!* The KID *can't* apply the needed changes. For so many people, the KID part in them has valiantly tried to apply whatever was last learned. People are told to "make better choices." The KID in us has no power to make choices! So, people attend the workshop, study under the "Master," read the next "answer," only to feel more like a failure than ever. All was doomed from the start because the KID can't do it.

With IT we can begin to make real changes from the inside out because the first task is always to get the KID off the Throne. The KID is finally relieved of the burden of impossible tasks. The KID is off the hook.

If you have an addiction and are not aware of it or not dealing with it, the KID in you is on the Throne and you won't be able to apply the new idea or method for self-improvement until you get the abandoned, dug-in KID in you the necessary addiction treatment. I didn't make the rules; that's just the way it is.

The Problem

Immaturity

According to IT, in a chronological adult (anyone over age 21), immaturity (often mislabeled as pathology by other systems of psychology) is always and only the function of the wrong part being on the Throne. In other theories of personality this would be the section labeled "Pathology" or "Mental Illness" and there would be an emphasis on analyzing and healing the wounded psyche as a whole. In IT all "illness" occurs in the KID and is a manifestation of the absence of internal parenting of the KID by the Inspired Self/True Adult part. Or, "illness" can also be unsupervised runaway Tapes. In the absence of the True Adult, the KID may run rampant or the Tapes may go on autopilot and take control of the organism. The "problem" is the lack of an adult in charge. The problem is immaturity. See diagrams 3-6 below.

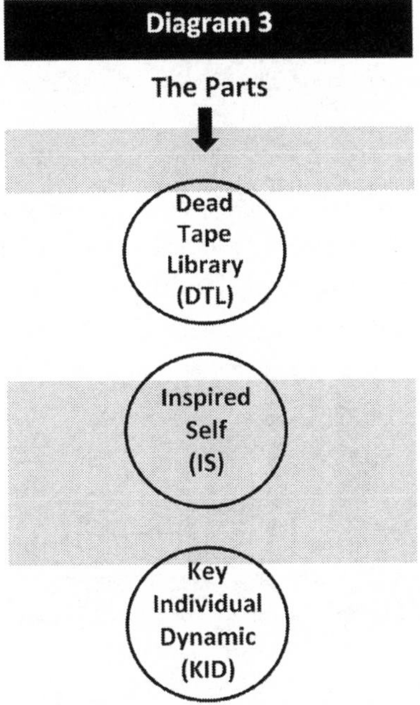

The Dead Tape Library has no ability to discern. It contains every rule ever "learned" (seen, heard, experienced). It simply records every warning, every threat ever observed or received. Every parent, teacher, and authority figure ever experienced, along with his or her opinions and boogymen are simply recorded. The Dead Tape Library selects a particular tape based on triggers from the current environment. The volume level of the selected tape, as experienced in the head, is determined by the noise level or the amount and severity of abuse, trauma, or neglect at the time the recording was made. Or it can be influenced by the volume level of the trigger.

The Inspired Self is the seat of the soul. It is the point of personal power. It is the center of all consciousness and the creative spark in the individual and is connected to the All There Is. We are physical and metaphysical beings. Spirituality is a part of us—the adult part. This is true even for the atheist. The IS contains our Life Purpose—the Blueprint. It holds the broader view, "the big picture." Only from this part can free will be exercised and choice be made. The Inspired Self takes input from the KID and from the Tapes and determines whether and how such input might be put to use. It is meant to be the governing body. It can never be destroyed but it can remain largely dormant for an entire lifetime.

The KID is our individuality—our personality. It is the spice in life. Preference, creative impulse and activity, curiosity, and all our fears and all emotions, reside and spring forth from here. The KID brings much to the table in the expression of our lives, but it is not meant to have a *governing* role. Further, all symptoms reside in the KID and the KID can become stuck at various ages and stages especially when abuse, neglect, or trauma occur in childhood. There can be many aspects to the KID, but like a hologram, each aspect contains the whole.

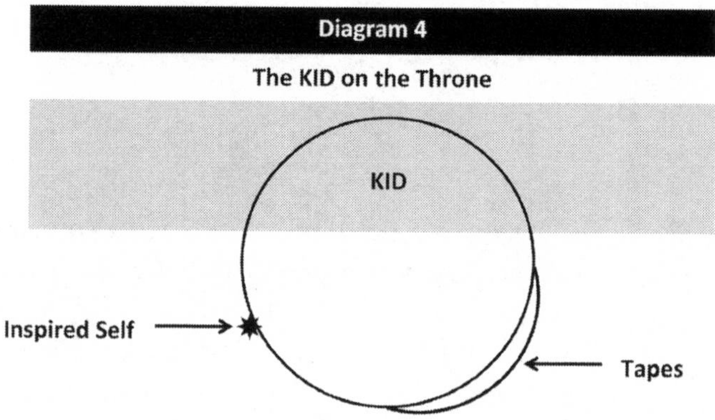

In this scenario in diagram 4 the KID is in charge of the individual. The Inspired Self remains dormant and may faintly express as a "still small voice." For the most part that voice will fall on the deaf ears of the KID. The KID will also drown out the sounds of the Tapes. This person will behave like a child and will actually see the world through the eyes of a child. Impulsivity and instability will be the modus operandi. This is the psychic map of an addict, a criminal, a ski bum, or any other functionally irresponsible person. These individuals may actually have very full, harsh and well-developed Dead Tape Libraries, but they shut them off as completely as they can. This person will feel like this is "who they are." But they will also have at least a dim sense of emptiness.

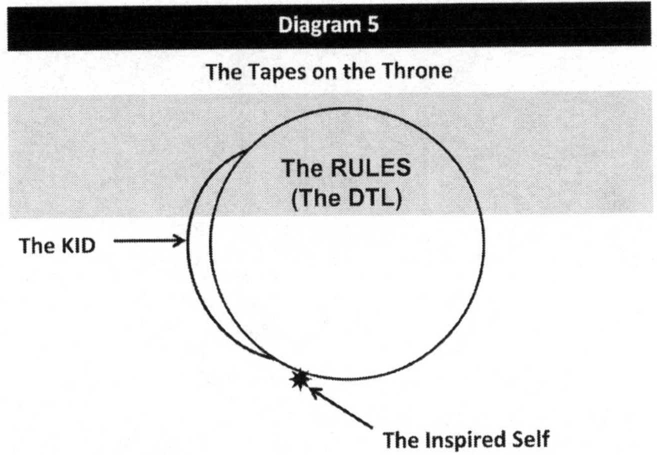

This person, portrayed in diagram 5, is an example of the pseudo-adult. This person comes across in the world as very rigid. This person has gotten the sense of "no adult at home" and the KID part has looked around to try to figure out how to be the grown-up he or she needs to be in the world in order to survive. In this person the "Rules" rule and the KID part is suppressed. They *are* no fun and tend to *have* no fun. Everything is important, urgent, serious, an emergency, hard, and difficult but necessary. This person may be hailed as a great and wise reformer, as tough but just. Or they may just be experienced as unbending, set in their ways, lacking genuine emotion or empathy, and quite like a robot. This person is highly judgmental.

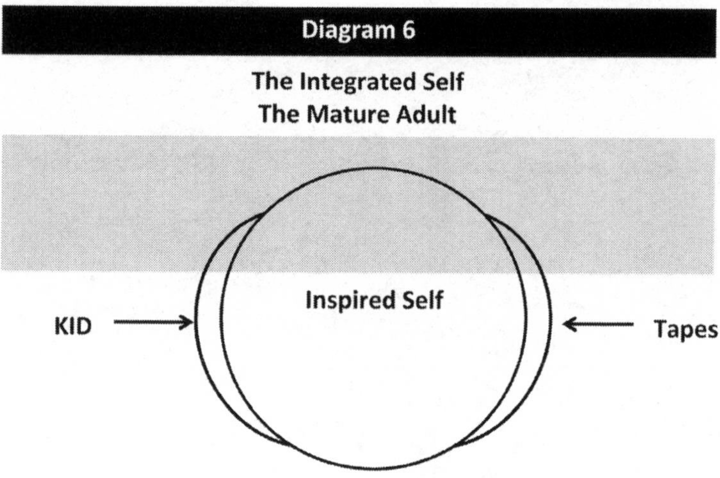

In Diagram 6 the Inspired Self is in control of the personality and draws material and/or takes input from each of the other two parts as needed or wanted. There is true choice. The Inspired Self keeps the KID and the DTL separate at all times and ***never*** lets the Tapes attack the KID with opinions, directives, or judgments period! Any and all material emanating from the DTL is processed through the higher, wiser part—the true adult part—the IS. If and when an impulse from the KID calls for correction by the DTL, the IS will assess the situation and lovingly deliver the correction. Further, the Inspired Self stands between the KID and the outer world, and the Dead Tapes and the outer world. The KID and the Tapes never interact with one another and *they never interact with any other person or event out there*. This is a key aspect of maturity. Everything is filtered through the Inspired Self part, period. Only when operating out of the IS can a person access at will what it chooses to access from the other parts. Only the mature part, the Inspired Self, has the free will to make a real choice. Free will resides in the IS. In relationships the KID and the DTL always and only just react. This explains why people seem unable to change even when they desire to. If they are operating out of the KID, the KID can't change other than to decide to let go of the Throne. If the KID is afraid, letting go is not likely. The KID can't make any mature life changes for the person. It can only behave like a child, or choose to let go. In this way IT explains why it can be so difficult to make a good choice. When operating out of the KID, choice is *impossible!* It is important to note that a choice made by the Inspired Self will never clash with the highest good of the individual, nor will it clash with the highest good of any other person "out there." This is an important fundamental concept of IT. The fully and properly *integrated* Inspired Self is the True Self.

Only when fully integrated does the True Self emerge. The True Self then is the synergy of the sum total of the fully integrated parts.

The Lower Life

What was Henry David Thoreau saying when he spoke of men living "lives of quiet desperation"? Could it be that he was referring to the state of existence that a vast majority find themselves living in today; a state that in IT is called the "Lower Life"? Living the Lower Life is living a life bereft of the Inspired Self—empty of the security, joy and creativity that comes with proper integration of the parts.

For the average person in our current culture it is not unusual to live with the KID being largely in charge or with the DTL running things, or to flip from the KID in charge to the Dead Tapes in charge. Many of us, if not most, live out our lives at this level of development, never developing the Inspired Self, never getting to live life inspired. When operating out of The DTL a person has to force himself to work to accomplish unless he is a workaholic. If that is the case, there is an actual compulsion to work, which tends to serve only Lower Life functions such as distraction and over compensation for seeming lack. Barring the presence of workaholism, life feels like a major effort or just dull drudgery. This can be relieved by periods of letting loose by partying, drinking, over-sleeping, and generally avoiding. The KID has popped onto the Throne for a time and will play like a child until the DTL takes control once again and it's back to the grind. Or the person is living a generally irresponsible existence and the DTL gets to critique it—usually very harshly—and then efforts might be made to straighten up. Those efforts generally inevitably fail and it's back to the old patterns again.

Another phenomenon of the Lower Life is the sparks that fly when the DTL directly attacks the KID. When this occurs, the KID feels incredible shame and terror and is powerless to deal with it. The same is true when the world gets in and the KID is unprotected. Whenever you feel yourself cringe it is because the DTL in you or someone in the outer environment is shaming the abandoned (by you) KID in you.

The Lower Life holds you prisoner to a life of shame, doubt, worry, discouragement (lack of courage), and fear, and sometimes leads to terrible consequences. Or, as Thoreau so poetically put it, it condemns you to a "life of quiet desperation." It buries your dreams. People living the Lower Life of existence may desperately strive for false dreams such as fame and fortune, but never uncover their true dreams. True dreams may include the freedom that wealth can bring, but are always about accomplishing, creating something, and growing. People living the Lower Life throw in the towel and default to the crumbs they can grab to brighten the sad drabness of existence.

Most people allow their thoughts to dwell on selfish purposes, the inevitable result of an infantile mind. When a mind becomes mature, it understands that the germ of defeat is in every selfish thought.

--Charles F. Haanel (p. 39)

The Law of Cause and Effect, sometimes referred to as Karma, can be said to be a function of the Lower Life. The Law of Cause and Effect is triggered by immature behaviors. Our acts have consequences. When immature parts are on the Throne and running things negative Karma is being created and experienced. When operating from the Inspired Self, Karma can be transcended. This is true because the integrated KID and DTL are not interacting directly with anyone in the world "out there" and are therefore insulated from cause and effect. The Inspired Self is not creating a trail of disasters, missteps, or tears. Therefore, negative consequences are not being racked up to come back and haunt. Further, according to the great Indian-American Yogi, as written in his classic, *Autobiography of a Yogi*:

"Seeds of past Karma cannot germinate if they are roasted in the divine fires of wisdom." --Paramhansa Yogananda

A person living the Lower Life may experience depression and anxiety and wonder "Is this all there is?" Life can seem boring (DTL) or out of control (KID), or just horribly sad, and may go on like that until the other lower part is triggered and the flip occurs, or until the person is diagnosed as "sick." But some (maybe most) just take it to the grave, never knowing that there is a better way, and in fact, *a way out* of the misery.

People living the Lower Life are all around us. Do you see them? (Sometimes in the mirror?)

****

Definition: Diagnosis (n.): Identification, esp. of a disease, by examination and analysis. (GK. diagnosis, discernment.)
The American Heritage Dictionary, third edition.

Symptoms, Symptom Clusters, and Diagnosis

In 1865 Freud traveled to Paris to study under the celebrated, world-renowned French doctor of neurology, Jean-Martin Charcot. There, he was to experience a paradigm shift of his own. At the time, the primary accepted belief in the scientific community, which Freud ascribed to, was that either lesions on the brain, or nerve damage were the cause of hysteria and all its symptoms. Mental illness, in other words, was viewed as being caused by physical illness or conditions in the body. Charcot, however, was experimenting with a brand new concept—that mental illness originated in the mind. When Freud arrived to study under him, Charcot was experimenting with hypnosis, and he had discovered what he called the "second mind." Charcot demonstrated through hypnosis that *ideas* can cause physical symptoms, and that those ideas that do so reside in the second mind. From that experience Freud got the concept that ideas cause disease, and that such ideas are hidden in what he came to call the unconscious. That was a brilliant breakthrough. The next major breakthrough, the idea that the "patient" had an ally within that could provide actual *self*-healing, had to wait for yet another century and yet another paradigm shift. That time has now come. It has been brewing for decades. It is now ripe.

According to IT, all psychiatric diagnoses from our traditional "Illness Model" are diagnoses of the KID part only. That is to say that all disease (dis-ease), all symptoms, are *in* the KID, and *only* in the KID. In fact, all dis-ease (what IT calls symptom clusters), whether mental or physical, meets the needs of the Lower Life. IT suggests that dis-ease exists in order to clue the person to deal with the KID in some way, or is created by negative emotions from the KID that impact chemical production in the brain and body and result in symptoms. Therefore, dis-ease performs a Lower Life function. For more information and a brilliant in-depth treatment of this phenomenon read the classic, *You Can Heal Your Life*, by Louise Hay.

The KID can be extremely complex, vexed, troubled, stormy, and strong in certain ways. Childhood shapes, fuels, and determines many aspects in the KID part. This is not the case for the Inspired Self part. Every diagnosis in the mental health books, every assignment of a mental illness label is actually diagnosing just one part of the person in question—the KID. This is a major shift in perception and thinking about illness and the human being. This is a paradigm shift. In the new paradigm it is the KID part that is the schizophrenic, that has obsessive-compulsive disorder (OCD), that suffers from depression, anxiety, bipolar disorder (manic-depression), multiple personality/dissociative identity disorder (MPD/DID), narcissistic disorder, borderline personality disorder (BPD), alcoholism, addictions, eating disorders, and so on. The point, according to IT, is that it is not the whole of you that is symptomatic. The symptoms reside in one part only. It is not the entire person that is dis-eased. The problem resides in just one of three parts. The Dead Tapes can play a role in the development, triggering, and maintenance of the symptoms, but the symptoms reside in the child part—the KID. The DTL, remember, is not a living part. It runs on automatic until the true adult, the IS, emerges and takes control. The child is the victim, container, and expresser of the symptoms.

The truth about our childhood is stored up in our body, and although we can repress it, we can never alter it. Our intellect can be deceived,

our feelings manipulated, our perceptions confused, and our body tricked with medication. But someday the body will present its bill, for it is as incorruptible as a child who, still whole in spirit, will accept no compromises or excuses, and it will not stop tormenting us until we stop evading the truth.
--Miller (1984, p. 316)

And the solution is not so much to "heal" the KID, as it is to "Shift out of" the KID and to "be with" the KID. When symptoms appear, the treatment is to Shift out of the KID and to be with the KID. The treatment is to be *with* the KID instead of *being* the KID. The solution to dis-ease is to grow the true adult muscle, the Inspired Self, to be with and to properly deal with the KID, which is the *only* thing that does calm and restore the KID! It is important to realize that there is a part in every person that is untouched by illness, untouched by the past, untouched by trauma, and untouched by medication. That part, the IS, can be called upon to be the lead player in a person's functioning. The IT Shift is the piece that breaks Freud's spell.

It is also important to realize that the KID is *smart enough* to *create* symptoms. This accomplishes at least two important ends. The first is illustrated by the following passage concerning the impact of abuse and neglect from Pia Melody, on p. 87 in her book, *Facing Codependence,* under the heading: *Mental Illness*:

The reality of what happened in childhood can be extremely traumatizing and horrible. To survive, some people have to keep themselves from fully knowing about and experiencing feelings about that reality. At some level these people are so afraid this painful reality will come up into their conscious life that they unconsciously "restructure" their mental world in very skewed ways to avoid the pain of dealing with what is or was. And this "restructuring" manifests itself as mental illness or psychotic behavior.

Or, as the late, gifted psychiatrist, Ronald David Laing, so succinctly stated:

"Insanity—a perfectly rational adjustment to an insane world."

Symptoms have function. One, they protect us from the unbearable until we are ready to face it and two, they give us the clues we need to figure out what happened to us and what the KID needs from us today in order to heal and calm down. Symptoms are nature's way of giving us the opportunity to figure it all out and fix it for ourselves, to overcome it, once we reach adult age.

Triggers and the Impact of Abuse, Neglect, and Trauma

Abuse, neglect, and trauma affect the child, change the child, infuse the child with shame and fear, and cause intensity of reaction for the purpose of self-protection. The more a child was abused, the stronger the KID will cling to the Throne for fear there is no adult at home to protect them, i.e. the stronger the symptoms will be. If a child was raised in less than perfect circumstances (as most of us were) chances are very high that as an adult-aged person s/he will be trigger-set in some ways. Triggers are caused by trauma, abuse, and/or neglect. When we are little some emotions can be too big to be experienced fully. A child can handle just so much psychic pain consciously. When events go over a certain threshold the child self-protectively simply does not feel those feelings. But the feelings do not go away. They are stored for future processing. The child *seems* fine and appears to be fine and feels fine. But the child is not fine. Fast-forward to adult age and nature has a way of healing us—offering opportunities for our healing. When the trigger is pressed later in life it offers us the opportunity to deal with the earlier trauma.

For example: If in childhood a parent died, the child may have appeared to handle the tragedy better than the adults around him. Now fast forward twenty years and let's say this same young person was in a relationship with someone they felt close to, maybe they were even in love with. Let's say it did not work out and the beloved broke it off. That could serve as a trigger to the earlier loss and all the stored pain from that childhood experience would be unleashed. This person thinks they are reacting to the current loss, when, in fact, it is heavily saturated with very old tears. In this confusion, this person laments the current lost love and unknowingly misses the opportunity to process the deeper grief—the long buried and far more painful grief over the long lost parent.

When a person seems to over-react to current slights, losses, or events it may signal that a trigger has been pushed and an old unhealed wound has been opened. Some people seem to go through life over-reacting to everything. On closer analysis, it probably would be discovered that there were many childhood traumas, or one very big one. The problem is that unless the person begins to realize the truth about the pain being experienced—the true origins of it—it never gets processed and it never gets properly integrated (resolved). The cycle may repeat itself for a lifetime.

Triggered Regression (Trance)

"We are all in a post-hypnotic trance induced in early infancy."

-- R. D. Laing

You might ask what is actually happening in a trigger event? Let's look at the young person in the example again. Let's say he was operating out of the Inspired Self and thereby functioning as an adult. When the relationship ended and the ancient loss was triggered he was thrown into a regression. In that state of regression he began suddenly to see life through the eyes of the child within him. In other words, the tragic child of his past was suddenly on the Throne of his being and running things. And in this matter he began therefore to function as a child. In other words, he went into trance wherein he actually was the child who lost his parent. But he now becomes not just the memory of that past child of his history; he is a living, breathing, current and creative KID. The KID in him that has been stuck for all these years in that unresolved tragedy of his past now comes to the fore in his psyche. That aspect of the KID in him jumps onto the Throne. And it feels to him as if it *is* him and *all* of him. If this goes unrecognized and the person really believes that all the feelings are coming only from the current event, the opportunity for real resolution is missed and he goes through the entire experience operating like a child.

Think of someone you might have observed in just such a situation. Did they behave as if the world had ended? Wouldn't it seem that the world had ended to a small child who has lost a parent? Think about the symptoms you observed. Did they seem excessive? Could it be that what they were really reacting to was an earlier and more fundamental wound?

The young man in our example above will eventually come out of the trance of regression but the tragic KID in him will not have been dealt with and will be triggered anew with each new loss experience. The more a person was abused or neglected, the stronger the hold on the Throne once triggered. This is the case because that KID part fears that no one will protect him.

A brief or lengthy bout of triggered regression is far more common an experience than previously thought. Think about the times when you were fine one minute only to find yourself suddenly thrown into a sea of strong emotion or numbness by some event or incident. If you examine the situation closely, you may find that something triggered you from adult behavior to acting like a child—maybe even to the point of being out of control or completely shut down. What may have actually happened is that the KID part in you got on the Throne of your psyche. Suddenly it is as if you are that KID. You see everything as a child, you think like a child, you feel like a child, you act like a child. You have psychically gone back in time and psychologically you are again that 8-year-old or 6-year-old and reacting today to the past as if it were here now. That is living in a trance. Even in that trance state you are aware of current surroundings and experience. You know your current age and situation, but you are viewing and assessing everything related to the loss with the mind and skill set of a child. Some people live most of their adult years in various states of triggered regression. *They live out their lives in trance!* And remember, the more a child was abused, the more severe the trauma, the stronger the KID's hold on the Throne once triggered.

I repeat: *Many people are living out their lives largely in some level of a state of trance. They are not living in the now. They are not really living a spontaneous, creative life. They are trapped in the past and living in trance.*

Operating Out of the Different Parts

The KID will create a rollercoaster life of extreme negative and positive emotions along with a sense of emptiness. Relationships will be stormy or flat. True love is not possible from this part. Avoidance and control are driving forces.

The Dead Tape Library will bring boring stability, peppered with harsh emotions, and rigid adherence to rules and principles at the expense of spontaneity in relationships. Or the person behaves like a tyrant or a mouse. Much of life feels like pressure. True love is not possible from this part. Dominance and control are demanded.

The Inspired Self will be like a magnet for good in the world, and will live a productive empowered life of love and adventure.

Causation

The central cause of immaturity in adults today is abandonment (by abuse, by neglect or by both) during childhood by the caretaker(s). The result of this is that we arrive in adulthood dragging the baggage of shame, fear, and all the unmet needs from childhood. The abandonment may have been intentional or not intentional. That is secondary to the fact of abandonment. The problem is then severely compounded by the fact that we are set up to continue the syndrome by consistently *abandoning ourselves* and seeking to get our ancient needs met through others out there throughout the remainder of our lives. Unless we become aware of the phenomenon and work to change we will live the unsatisfying Lower Life all the way to the grave. To live the life intended for us, the Inspired Life, there is hope and there are maps to follow.

IT Drive Theory

Drive theory is the theory of what drives us as human beings. It identifies our true needs. We are driven:

1. To be safe (Protection).
   This includes food, shelter, clothing, and safety from all harm (physical and emotional), and to be rescued from the past.

2. To be seen (Boundaries). (I Exist).

3. To be valued (Love, Nurture and Belongingness).

4. To be disciplined/to develop (Develop Self and Self Mastery).

5. To know (Curiosity).

6. To be filled up with the Inspired Self (Integrated).

7. To express/create (Autonomy/Freedom).

Q & A

Ask Yourself

1. Q: What part in you is most often on the Throne of your psyche?
   A:

2. Q: Are you seeking to fill the void with an addiction? Any addiction?
   A:

3. Q: Do you know your Life Purpose?
   A:

4. Q: If so, what is it, and are you on track? If not, why not?
   A:

5. Q: What percentage of your life is lived in peace and joy? Explain.
   A:

6. Q: Are you creating? Write about your answer.
   A:

7. Q: WHO ARE YOU?
   A:

Summary

Key Concepts in Personality Integration Theory

1. The New Paradigm: The Maturation Model of Mental Health
The Maturation Model is replacing the outdated Pathology Model. Under the new model we are not sick. We are immature, which is to say that we are largely operating out of our immature parts.

2. The Shift: The Missing Piece
The Shift is "the missing piece"—the piece that is completely missing in other mental health theories, systems, and models. It has been hinted at in many ancient wisdom teachings and various spiritual systems. *Becoming aware of the Shift* ***as a psychological concept*** *and applying it makes choice more possible,* makes change more possible, and therefore makes life as a real adult more possible. We begin to operate as mature adults only by learning how to Shift into our Inspired Adult Self. If we were properly raised by real adult parents, we learned this naturally. If our family of origin was dysfunctional to a significant degree, we can

still learn it. Once we learn it and practice consistently, it can become more automatic, requiring less focused attention, like learning to swim, ride a bike, or shift a manual transmission. In IT the goal is to Shift the KID part or the DTL off the Throne by Shifting into our Inspired Self. When we Shift and are *with* the KID rather than *being* the KID, when the Inspired Self is present and in charge and we are operating as an adult, the KID calms down and the volume button and the shut off valve on the DTL can be controlled. The focus in most other systems of psychotherapy is for the "KID" to grow up. In IT this is not only unnecessary, it is not possible. The KID is never supposed to grow up. It is meant to remain our childlike enthusiastic and curious part. Rather, it is supposed to be protected, nurtured, properly disciplined, and rescued from the past (emancipated), and thereby properly integrated. Only when properly integrated in our psyche can the KID take its intended place in our functioning and enrich our lives.

3. Integration/First Relationship/The Inspired Life/True Self

In an integrated psyche the Inspired Self stands between the Key Individual Dynamic and The Dead Tape Library at all times, and stands between those two lower parts and the world out there at all times and under all circumstances. When all parts are in their proper places in the psyche, the Inspired Self deals with and draws from the others as appropriate. When the internal relationship (the first relationship) is functioning in harmony and proper balance, when you are living the Inspired Life, you are functioning as your emancipated, well-developed True Self. Life then improves markedly both inside and out.

4. Symptoms and Symptom Clusters

All symptoms reside only in the KID part. All psychiatric diagnoses, as recorded in the medical books, apply only to the KID part. The DTL is not alive, and the Inspired Self is symptom free. In other words, there is a living part in each of us that is not sick and has never been sick. Further, this part can never be destroyed. Any and all medicines used in any treatment process medicate the KID part only. The symptoms serve as clues that we can follow backward to determine what happened to us so that we can determine what the KID needs from the IS in order to heal. In other words, symptoms are functional—they have a function—to clue us in! They are cries for help with directions included!

Symptom clusters found in the KID can be analyzed and categorized to serve as predictors for dealing with the real needs of the KID once s/he is properly De-Throned and the "regime change" is complete in the psyche. Awareness of specific symptom clusters can also be helpful as a part of the process when working with a particular method for creating the Shift.

5. Triggered Regression and the Lower Life

Many people in our culture live much of the time either in triggered regression as the KID, or operate rigidly as the DTL. They live out their days largely in trance, functioning in the Lower Life, and rarely or never experience life as their True Inspired Self. Therefore, they never really experience life.

6. The Parts: the KID, the DTL, and the IS

There are three parts in the psyche: The Key Individual Dynamic, The Dead Tape Library, and The Inspired Self. The Dead Tape Library is not a creative, living part. It is just a computer-like storage unit filled with the recordings of our life experiences. The KID is our *unique* creative expresser. The IS is our wise spirit and is meant to run our show.

7. The Wormhole

The wormhole is our connection to the fourth dimension which includes what Carl Jung called the collective unconscious. It is our pathway and/or organ for perception of our sixth sense. The Inspired Self, otherwise known as the True Adult, is connected to The All There Is through the wormhole. Inspired Self includes our Spirit and is meant to incorporate and properly integrate our lower parts. It holds the blueprint for our lives. Only the Inspired Self part can traverse the wormhole and draw power, information, support, intuition and inspiration from the All There Is. It is our Divine Connection.

8. The Function of the KID

"A little child shall lead them." ~~ Isaiah, 11:6

In our psyche, the function of the KID is to bring fun, interests, curiosity, unique creative activity, and adventure into our lives in proper balance. It is deeply connected to our life purpose and plays a major role in it. When operating properly in the psyche the KID, often through our curiosity, will give us clues that will lead us to discover it. The KID is our individuality. When the KID knows the inner parent (IS) is present and taking care of business (food, belonging, clothing, shelter, and safety stuff), the KID not only calms down, but is free to express its individuality. Here then is the spark, or seed, of a person's individual "personality."

9. Consciousness and the Unconscious

The three levels of consciousness are:

One: the Throne of Your Being/the control panel,
Two: Superconscious Awareness of the IS,
Three: the Cosmic Consciousness of the All There IS.

Only one part at a time can operate on the Throne. The Superconscious IS has access to all three levels, and is meant to be the only part that actually operates on the Throne.

The Unconscious is located in the KID part only. Only the KID is entirely unconscious at times, and always at least partially unconscious. The DTL is recordings; the IS is always aware.

Chapter 4

The Therapy: How IT Works

"The best way out is always through." --Robert Frost

Of Wizards and Kings In the Current Evolutionary Scheme of Things

Our once accepted beliefs about what makes us tick emerged out of the old pack mentality of our ancestors. The authoritative therapists that soon followed to "heal us" (Freud's Spell) emerged out of the overlap between the Survival Phase mind set and the onset of Phase II. At the present stage of evolution in our thinking we are beginning to outgrow both the old definitions of who we are and how to heal. Today as we move deeper into the Self Development Phase, we are realizing that the power lies within and that the old belief system with all its trappings for the ivory tower therapist is antiquated, corrupt, dysfunctional and incorrect by our shiny new standards. The time for the power in the hands of the healer has now passed. We want no kings and we are discovering that we are the wizards.

Just as mere water can destroy the very rocks it glides, so does the passage of time and new knowledge in the general human consciousness erode all before it that blocks the current evolutionary flow. The past is past and has served its purpose. It cannot be revived. But it sure can die a very slow death! There are certain seemingly stubborn remnants of Phase I thinking even in this new era of budding enlightenment.

(One quick example is "punishment.") What matters to us most is to see them for what they are and to begin to label them old school and to realize that they are on the way out. They *will* give way.

Let's look in on what Alice Miller, one of Freud's one time disciples now turned critic, has to say about it... She describes the impact in therapy on the client when the therapist applies even the most therapeutic techniques without an awareness of his own (the therapist's) issues. The psychotherapist with a set apart or superior attitude, such as the attitude fostered in the pedagogical (pack or top dog mentality) systems of training and treatment (the attitude fostered for example in Freudian Analysis), she writes:

> *...can even have such detrimental effects that the patient remains locked in a depression or in the chaos of awakened feelings. Results of this kind are not rare...*
>
> --Miller (1984, p. 313)

In IT language, this is an example of the KID getting stuck on the Throne *in therapy* by being triggered by the therapist's authoritarian stance—i.e. by the DTL of the therapist acting out on the patient!

Miller goes on to make predictions about the modern way of understanding the healing process:

> *...But this expanding knowledge will scarcely emanate from authoritative institutions such as universities and institutes. Once survivors of abuse (sexual and non-sexual) feel truly supported by society and by their therapists so they can find their own voice, therapists will learn more from them than from any teacher. As a result, therapists will find it easier to relinquish many of those misguided beliefs that are based on the pedagogical principles of earlier centuries.* --Miller (1984, p. 314)

In the decades since Miller wrote those words, that is, in fact, what has been occurring. It is out of this climate that the new paradigm with its new therapies and treatments has emerged. As it turns out, we are the wizards in our own lives. What we are looking for is the magic of a darn good map!

Personality Integration Therapy

IT

"Your mind is a tool for you to use any way you wish." --Louise Hay

Some Basic Tenets of IT in Our Perfect Universe

1. You have within you the power to heal (make whole) yourself. (Perfection #2.)

2. In every situation, circumstance, event, and relationship you have power. You have ethical power, personal power, real power, *YOUR* power. We live in a perfect universe and you have power in *every* situation. This is Perfection #3. You can count on it.

3. Only power that you are aware of can be used purposefully by you. Awareness + use of personal power = Empowerment.

4. Abuse is *always* abuse of power. Abuse = any unnecessary and/or uninvited use of power over others.

5. Exercising your true personal power can never do harm to another's highest good. This is Perfection #4. It speaks to our connectedness, to the Jungian concept of the collective unconscious, and to the concept of oneness in the uni (one) verse (word).

6. No one can take your power. (Perfection #5.) Barring childhood, infirmity, or physical force, only you can give your power to another. This is *never* a good idea.

7. You can *always* take your power back. It is *never* too late. (Perfection #6.)

8. Abuse can only come from the DTL or The KID parts.

9. All ethical power (which is the power of choice, i.e. free will) resides only in the true adult part (IS). You can use your ethical personal power only when operating from the Inspired Self.

10. The KID only has free will to let go of the Throne or not. The Inspired Self will never force the KID to relinquish the Throne.

11. Ethical power trumps abuse.

More About Power in This Perfect Universe

In every given situation (unless under some physical threat) we have power. We may have to look for it. It may not be easy to find. And we may not like what it is when we find it. But in every situation we have power. If we are living the Lower Life we may well miss out on this fact completely. Or we may just ignore it. But it is there. We have power. Maybe it's the power to hold one's tongue when the KID really wants to wag it. Or maybe it is the power to leave a broken or otherwise unhealthy relationship when we would prefer to change the other person or somehow change the situation. We have the power to let the person who is wrong for us go and to find a person who better fits the life we want. It is always our job to find the power we have (never power over others; our personal power) and to exercise it for the highest good of all concerned even if the KID in us would rather change someone else.

****

Definition: Integrate (v.):

1.to make into a whole; unify;
2.to join with something else, unite.

(<Lat. Integer, whole.)
(See Integration [n.])
The American Heritage Dictionary, third edition.

How IT Works

The First Relationship and the Inspired Life From Survive, Through Awareness, to Thrive

The first relationship, the inner relationship, is the relationship of the parts within you to each other. When that is properly aligned and consistently maintained, your life will go smoothly. You will handle difficulties that arise *as they arise*, and with wisdom and ease. You will experience mixtures in balance of peace and joy *as your usual state of mind.* You will live the Inspired Life as you were created to live. If in childhood you were abused, neglected, or exposed to trauma, you will most probably arrive to chronological adulthood with a need to work on the inner relationship. This may or may not seem simple, but it is not easy for most of us to achieve. It is very possible with some hard work. Here's what is required: an open mind to new ways of thinking about yourself, a willingness to suspend skepticism, and lots of determination to have a better life. Feeling confused? Good. All major new learning requires a period of confusion to shake up the old and make room for the new.

For many of us the inner relationship does not seem like a relationship at all. Most of us are unaware that different parts are doing our thinking at different times. It can just seem like "I" am thinking. Actually the conscious "thinking" going through the head is being done by one part at a time. Whatever part is on the Throne at the moment is the part that does the conscious thinking. Only one part at a time controls the power of the Throne. The "thinking" part thinks with the characteristics of that given part—i.e., the KID part thinks like a child, the DTL "thinks" like a judge and jury, and the Inspired Self thinks with inspiration, reasoned judgment, wisdom, and compassion. The two parts that are not on the Throne at the given moment remain on the scene, but we are at all times, we are at any given moment, operating out of only one part. Discovering the parts and then discerning which part is doing the conscious thinking at that exact moment is a learning process. It is the Inspired Self in us that has the capacity to function as an observer in the psyche. We can strengthen this function and become better at picking up on this important awareness as it occurs. Realizing which part is meant to be on the Throne at a given time in a given situation and then making the Shift is the way to freedom and self mastery. It calls for the development of mental discipline.

How it is supposed to work is simple. The well-developed Inspired Self (IS) is meant to be the main "control" of our lives. The IS is meant to be the one in charge of all inner and outer activity, i.e. all thinking, feeling, and behaving. As the captain of the vessel, the IS has many functions. One such function is to stand between the KID and the DTL. If you think of the KID and the DTL as being kind of like siblings who squabble, you begin to realize they must be kept apart. These two must be kept apart because if they are allowed to interact it can only mean that one of them is on the Throne and the other is not, and this means trouble. If the DTL is on the Throne, it goes after the KID in one way or another. (It may also go after people "out there" in thought, word, or deed.) Only in a situation of physical emergency can any of this be helpful. Usually the DTL upsets the KID without justification. It's like when in a family the parents leave an older child to baby-sit the younger child. The DTL can attack, scold, shame, frighten, boss, and otherwise control, or completely ignore the KID part. The KID then responds as any child might by screaming, hiding, cowering in fear, cringing in shame, or by attacking back. The result is inner turmoil. The DTL is never meant to "have at" the defenseless inner child, or to be actually responsible for the child's welfare. It is just a library. When the DTL is left in charge, the KID feels like he is home alone. The KID feels abandoned. The abandoned KID might then get on the Throne and begin to run the show. And the KID will do any manner of things (drink to excess, over eat, gamble, etcetera) to quash the nasty Tapes. Or the KID will invite the DTL to become the pseudo-adult (or the DTL will just step in and take over and squash the KID), and then it will rigidly run the show. The two are supposed to be kept separate. There is great need for a real adult to be in charge.

Abandonment

Enough cannot be said, written, or read about abandonment. Abandonment may have its roots in our past, when we were in one way or another abandoned to some degree by our caregiver(s), but the crucial fact is this: *we regularly abandon ourselves* (the KID in us) *today.* Abandonment is for most of us a current and very frequent event. Most of us have no awareness of this sad fact. The KID is not meant to be unprotected in our psyche from the DTL, or from the critics, adult relationships, and any abusers out there. The KID is not supposed to be on the Throne and running our current relationships and activities. There is supposed to be adult supervision at all times. But when the Inspired Self part is undeveloped or under-developed, the KID has to handle things all alone with only the resources of a child. Not a pretty sight as it plays out in our lives. The three things that the KID needs today and that the Inspired Self must provide are:

1. Protection (including rescue from the past).
2. Nurture.
3. Discipline.

These three things are what every child requires in order to be and feel safe, loved and guided. If it wasn't the status quo during the time of actual childhood, it can still be provided. It is never too late to get the parenting we need. We may just have to provide it for ourselves. How do we do this for ourselves as adult-aged people today? There are, for the eager and open minded, many ways. This is where mental discipline comes in.

Internal Parenting: Dealing with the KID

In IT the IS needs to stand between the KID and the DTL, and between those two parts and the world "out there." The IS also needs to deal with the feeling life of the KID. This should be an internal process in the psyche. The KID must not be allowed to act out feelings in outer relationships. But that is, in fact, what happens in so many of our relationships today. Except when appropriate to the activity at hand, i.e. having fun at the beach, enjoying a movie, dancing, etc., the KID should not show up in our interactions with anyone out there. Other than contributing emotion to entertainment, or enjoying creative artistic activities, or adding some other pleasant spice, the KID is not meant to be in direct relationship to anyone out there. But the KID has feelings about many things. Those feelings need to be resolved internally.

The KID's feelings are the feelings of a child. They can be very strong and intense, but they are based on the mind-set of a child. They reflect a child's view of things. They are not right or wrong; they are the feelings that the KID *has*. People get into all manner of difficulties in relationships today in two major ways. They either allow the KID to express feelings "out there" in various relationships, or they cut the KID off entirely and the DTL attacks the KID and represses the feelings deemed inappropriate. There is a third option. It is the only functional option. Option #3 is to first recognize that the KID has a particular feeling, to recognize that it is only the KID part that is having the feeling, and to block the KID'S access to the outer relationship while at the same time validating the KID.

Let's say, for example, you get furious with your son because for the fourth time this week he did not do his homework. It is common for a parent of today to yell at the boy. In IT, it would be best to recognize that it is the KID in you that wants to yell. There is a better, more adult way, a more effective way, to deal with your son. I am willing to bet that you can even figure one out as you read this. That is your IS mind at work. It has the ability to access multiple solutions.

One idea we might consider is to let the boy experience the consequence of going to class unprepared. Another idea might be to impose a logical consequence. Maybe the TV comes out of his room until he improves his behavior. The point is that when a parent has awareness of the parts and access to the IS there is no yelling. At the same time the KID in your head needs to be honored and validated and disciplined (kept from yelling). The KID is taken off the case. The KID in you is allowed to be a child, rather than feeling like he has to parent your son. That is too hard a job for the KID in you, and yelling is probably his only option. Disciplining your son "out there" is an adult task. The KID in you is attempting the task because he thinks he is home alone and there is no adult to rely on. You have effectively abandoned the KID in you to be the parent of your son out there. And you will feel pressure. Also, it should be noted, another reason for the KID in you to yell at your misbehaving son is to do what was done to you. "Now," the KID in you thinks, "it's my turn to do the yelling." In other words, it's payback time. But instead of paying back your offenders (your parents) you are taking it out on an innocent and passing the flaming terrible torch to another generation! Payback is a child's activity. Adults do not seek revenge. This is a way to release old pent up feelings long stored in the KID. It is not, however, a good way. It does not heal the KID in you, and it does harm to your actual child out there.

When we parent our own children from the DTL or from the KID in us it is generally not a good thing. Yet, it is very common in our culture. It can feel very much like good parenting. But it is not. The Dead Tapes can be loud and authoritarian. We are, however, *only* meant to parent from the Inspired Self—the true adult part. We are meant to parent from strength, wisdom, compassion, and the kindness of the Inspired Self. Good parenting never includes harshness—firmness, yes, but never harshness. There is all the difference in the world between being stern and being cruel. To be able to parent from our love and wisdom we must be set free from the Lower Life where our emotions dominate.

To begin to get a grasp of this concept you can ask yourself what your true agenda is. Are you yelling at your son to meet your internal needs or the needs of your external son? Here's a clue: do you want to punish or discipline him? Punishment meets the needs of the punisher. Punishment is about hurting, whereas discipline is about teaching. Punishment exacts some toll or price and is meant to relieve anger in the punisher, or to get revenge. These are Lower Life emotions in the punisher. Discipline meets the need of the object of the discipline. Yelling and spanking, teach yelling and spanking. They may bring about a modicum of cooperation, but the recipient learns to submit rather than to grow up. As a graduate student at The University of West Virginia, one of my favorite professors made a powerful impression on me in this area of applied psychology. Dr. Robert Smith, a behaviorist and noted expert in the area of prisoner psychology, would regularly stress the known impact of punishment on its victims. He pointed out in each class he was teaching that, "Experiments with rats have taught us that punishment really teaches only one thing: *escape from (as possible) and avoidance of the punisher!"* Punishment teaches the punished and the threatened to avoid the punisher! After hearing this over and over, I found myself wondering that if rats can figure that out, could it be that God just might have it figured out, too? Or, as one of our local D.C. suburban preachers, Rev. Lon Solomon, is known to say in his brief radio spots, "Not a sermon, just a thought."

Standing between the KID and the DTL and then keeping them from directly interacting with anyone out there is what a True Adult does. In this scenario, the next steps would then be to deal with the needs of both the internal KID and the kid out there by:

1) Getting the KID off the Throne.
2) Disciplining your child out there.
3) Dealing with the needs of the KID in you.

Dealing with the Parents of Your Childhood

It is important to say something here about dealing with how each of us was parented. There is, as you might have guessed, much work to be done on this. In fact, this is where much of the IT processing work for the KID can be centered. For some people there is a strong desire and tendency to let bygones be bygones, or to avoid looking too closely altogether. One reason for this is what Pia Melody, author of *Facing Codependence,* and founder of the Meadows treatment center for codependency in Wickenburg, AZ., calls the taproot effect. According to Pia, we don't want to become aware that our parents were not really grown up because it means there was no real adult raising us. This is a horrifying thought when you consider the stakes. We have to face that we were virtually on our own, alone, that nobody stood behind us, supported us, had our back, when we were mere children! The trouble with just letting it go with no real examination is this: the KID inside knows full well what wrongs were done by mom and dad, and until they are validated, the KID does not heal and does not trust the IS or anyone out "there." Other reasons why we may want to avoid a clear look at our past might include: that we have a good relationship today with our parents, or we feel sorry for them in current circumstances, or our old role from childhood includes caretaking their feelings. It can be helpful to learn that we do not ever have to confront them. What is necessary is to clear it up in our own heads. We may choose to confront them, but it is never necessary to our own healing to do so. And yet another reason is that we confuse impact with intent, and we may realize that our parents did not intend to neglect or harm us. We don't want to blame them. However, we are left with the impact of their mistakes. Think of it this way: say you were standing at the end of your driveway on the grass and waiting for your mom to back out and let you in the car. Let's say she mistakenly drove over your foot. She certainly did not intend to break your foot. But she did break your foot. Would you ignore it because she didn't mean it, or would you deal with it and get it treated? It is not about blaming. It is about becoming honest with yourself (inside yourself). Impact is what you are living with. No matter the intent, if the impact did harm, treatment is called for. Certainly if there was intent *and* harmful impact it can be more difficult to face and deal with, but intent is not necessary to cause a wound.

One of the most difficult feelings for people to process can be anger. Using logic, they may think that it is not reasonable to be angry about "whatever," or to be angry with "whomever," in a given circumstance. The mistake is this: that is *never* the issue. It is not about *getting angry* or about *not getting angry.* It is about *admitting that you are angry.* It is the KID part that is angry. Therefore, it is about allowing the KID to have its feelings; it is about giving the KID permission to be a KID. It is about being honest.

Yet another reason we may want to avoid knowing the real truth is that we may have a sense of intense unconscious anger. The KID can be very fearful of the power of smoldering rage. With assurance from the IS in you, the KID can come to understand and trust that you will not allow acting out. The KID will not be allowed to attack mom and dad, and over time your anger will come up to be dealt with internally and released.

It can be a lengthy but enlightening process to become realistic about our parents and siblings and their impact on our self-image and development. It can be a worthy struggle to discover and to hold them responsible (inside our own heads) for their stuff if only because without doing so, we don't really know who we are. We need to be seen. The KID needs us to stop making excuses for our parents' mistakes, for our siblings' mistakes. And we need to stop believing their views and definitions of us. When the IS really sees the KID and what happened in childhood, the triggers dissolve and the KID calms down. It then releases its grip on the Throne and can begin to get on with its true role in a person's life.

****

What to Do

Once you begin to recognize that the KID or the DTL in you is indeed inappropriately active in your relationships, and probably screwing them up, the question becomes how to get them off the Throne and properly integrated in your psyche. There are many methods for doing just that! Where to begin…

The IT Process

ONE: Learn the New IT Concepts

a. The Parts and their Intended Functions:
   The KID
   The DTL
   The IS
b. Wormhole Theory

c. The First Relationship
d. Integration
e. Current Abandonment
f. Triggered Regression, Triggers and Trance
g. IT Drive Theory
h. Internal Parenting
i. The Shift
j. Mental Discipline
k. Maturity/Self Mastery
l. The Throne of Your Being
m. The Lower Life (LL) (Operating From the KID and the DTL)
n. The Inspired Life (IL) (Operating From the IS)
o. The Maturity Model For Mental Health
p. Truthink (see Method #5)
q. Superconsciousness
r. Cosmic Consciousness
s. The True Self
t. Symptoms and Symptom Clusters in the KID

****

TWO: Practice Discernment: Self Diagnosis
Are You Living the Lower Life?

a. Grow the Observer Self

If you are primarily or even frequently operating out of the KID or the DTL, how do you know it? How do you catch it going on? Whenever you experience strong or intense feelings it is not the IS. Begin to recognize with your observer self (the IS) that since it is not the Inspired Self in you that is experiencing those feelings, that it must mean that another part is on the Throne. This is probably the case for many of us off and on all day long. Also, look for signs of boredom, or a tendency to judge others silently, with gossip, or to their face. Look for other negative thinking going on in your consciousness and any negative acting-out. Even as you pay attention in this way to what is going on in your psyche and in your actions, you are growing and strengthening the presence of your observer self, which is the Inspired Self.

b. **Analyze This**

Look around you at the people you see. Are they emotional? Are they stiff and robotic? Either an excess of or absence of feelings suggest they are living the Lower Life. You will begin to recognize in others what part of them they are operating out of. The more you practice this the more you will realize that most people are quite immature. People in high places can be living the Lower Life convinced that they are justified in their negativity, justified in their anger, justified to act out. They are living the Lower Life and they think they are adult. Look around you at the politicians. Look at your fellow workers, your bosses, your church elders and congregants. Just look around you and you will begin to see people operating out of the KID or out of their Dead Tape Library. The more you look for it in others, the more you will be able to begin spotting it in yourself. This takes time. And there will be great resistance. Who wants to give up the luxury of a good tantrum now and then or the luxury of some good gossip? Who wants to take up the task of mentally disciplining your own thinking instead of just letting the thoughts roll and rule? It takes time and a burning desire to have a better life.

A cautionary note: Remember that you are observing and assessing others in order to break the cultural spell that binds you so that you can gain Self Mastery and not to become the teacher or the judge. Though for some of us it can become a great temptation, respecting their boundaries is important for our own integrity. Becoming aware of this phenomenon can be helpful to our process of self diagnosis, and it can also help us be better able to set needed limits on others who are operating from the Lower Life.

c. A Fairy Tale Can Be a "Tell All"

What is your favorite fairy tale? Whatever your answer, it is probably telling you clues about the myth you are living with. It can tell you a great deal about what you are afraid of, what you are avoiding, what is holding you back, what you may be afraid to hope for, and even what happened to you that may lie just beyond realization, or even memory. It can tell you, in other words, if you are living the Lower Life and what keeps there.

Sometimes when I am trying to make a particular point with a resistant client, I may ask for their favorite fairy story. From there we can look at the characters and see what they are trying to do. I worked with a young woman I'll call Sally, who was stuck and unable to take a risk that was clearly indicated and one that she really wanted to make. Her favorite story was Rapunzel. In that story, Rapunzel is stuck and needs to be rescued from a very scary witch. She is trapped way up high in a tower and unable to help herself. Once Sally realized that she was operating like a KID and being terrorized by a witch that existed today only in her own head (DTL), she realized that she was *actually trapping herself.* Once she realized she was living the Lower Life, she was then able to appropriately take the task away from the KID in her and handle it from the IS. More about how to make the Shift later, but the first step was to recognize that she was living the Lower Life.

Sally was soon able to move forward toward her goal. In real life there was no tower and no witch. She wasn't really trapped at all, but the KID in her was responding to life as if they were real and that *made her* powerless. In her childhood, Sally had spent much of her time in her room avoiding a very scary mother. It was time for her to be her own prince (the IS) and help herself down from the prison she was unconsciously creating for herself today. Not only did she begin to take more risks, she came to a session not long after that with her long hair cut short!

d. **Check for Boundaries**

As a functioning adult you will set and keep proper boundaries. Well-set and well-honored boundaries make life a breeze! Only the IS can set boundaries. The DTL builds walls (even prisons). The KID withdraws, becomes an outcast, becomes enmeshed and smothers, takes hostages, or runs screaming and kicking into isolation. When we were children, our parents were supposed to set our boundaries for us. If that wasn't done, and done well, then we must do this for ourselves. In adulthood this must be done from inspiration—from the Inspired Self. If you want to change someone else and feel entitled to do so because you are "right," you are not honoring their boundaries. If you are trying avoid conflict or to please someone else you are lacking proper boundaries (whether you are failing or succeeding).

Boundaries are sacred. They set us apart and allow us to join and to connect in life-enhancing ways. Boundaries make community. Boundaries make companionship possible.

Consider if you have proper boundaries in all your relationships and situations. If the answer is no, you may well be living the Lower Life. Boundaries, or the lack thereof, are a powerful diagnostic tool.

e. **The Acid Test**

If you are still confused and unsure, and wonder if one of your Lower Life parts might be on the Throne in a given situation or relationship, ask yourself what your real agenda is. This is the acid test. What is your real agenda for whatever actions you plan or want to take. Is it to accomplish or create something original or meaningful for the good of all concerned? Or is it to punish or to "better" someone you are in conflict with or are competing with? Or is it to run away and to avoid dealing with what is called for or what is going on?

f. The KIS List (Keep It Simple)

Diagnosing Yourself: You *know* you are living the Lower Life—operating out of the KID or the DTL if:

1. You have any big or long lasting feelings, such as sadness, shame, devastation, anger, fear, etc. and no one has recently died or is about to. (When, in fact, this is the case for you and you are dealing with serious loss, it is a different matter altogether. All new rules apply. See "Grief and Loss" under the section labeled **Other Issues of Interest in the IT Treatment Model** at the end of this Chapter.)
2. You avoid what seem to be scary, unpleasant, or difficult tasks.
3. You are impulsive.
4. You are self-indulgent.
5. You have money problems.
6. You are in trouble with:

   an employer
   a teacher
   a spouse
   the law.
7. You have addictions and are not in stable recovery.
8. You have unstable relationships.
9. You don't do your work/or you only work.
10. You "talk to or yell at" other cars on the road.
11. You play "don't rock the boat" with your spouse.
12. You feel like your luck is bad.
13. You gossip.
14. You want and/or get revenge.
15. You hold a grudge.
16. You keep a scorecard on life and friends.
17. You cheat.
18. You put on a diaper and drive across country to have an encounter with a lover's lover for some secret evil purpose.*

19. You feel sorry for yourself for more than a minute before doing something good to take care of the situation.
20. You yell at anyone.

Get the idea?

In each of us the DTL is harsh and robotic, and the KID is a KID and acts accordingly. What matters is that neither the DTL nor the KID is supposed to be on the Throne and running anyone's life. When we are children our parents are supposed to be running things and when we're adults the "Adult" in us is supposed to be in charge. Remember, the KID is a complete, intact, full part in the psyche. When either the KID or the DTL gets on the Throne, it blocks out a sense of the other parts and very bad things (sometimes small, sometimes big, sometimes very big) can happen. A child or a robot is running the show. It can be like a wolf in sheep's clothing. *Look at what Lisa Nowalk, the diapered astronaut, did to her life! She was arrested and prosecuted for attempting to do harm (murder?) to her ex-lover's lover! People who thought they knew her well have said that wasn't at all like her. No, of course, it was not like the *part* of her they were used to seeing at work on the space shuttle (which I suspect was mostly the DTL part). It was a completely different part (KID) that got full control of the entity once triggered by a love rejection and went to work with obsessive compulsion on her scurrilous plan.

In traditional (old paradigm) therapies the goal is to heal and "grow up" the "patient." The goal in IT is to calm the KID down enough to loosen its tight little grip on the Throne of your life and to "switch" into your Inspired Self. When this is accomplished the KID heals a little more each time, and at the same time you have in an instant become an adult.

"We shall be changed in a moment, in the twinkling of an eye."
--1 Corinthians, 15: 51-52

****

THREE: Provide Primary Treatment: Make the Shift

Once primary diagnosis has been achieved and you have made the assessment that you are at least in part living the Lower Life, you are ready to begin treatment.

IT Treatment Consists Of:

1. Diagnosis and assessment: Making the assessment of which part is on the Throne and which part needs to be on the Throne.
2. Primary Treatment: Making the Shift. (See Methods.) This immediately puts your True Adult Self (IS) on the Throne, and lets the KID know that a parent (the internal parent) is home and on the job.
3. Healing the unresolved issues from our past that are stored in the KID. This requires:
    a. Validation of the KID's feelings. This calls for non-judgmental recognition of how the KID feels about the past event. The KID cannot have the wrong feelings. *Whatever* feelings the KID has *are* the feelings to be validated. Remember, this is an internal process. It is between your Inspired Self and the KID only. The KID feels what the KID feels and needs to be validated! And do not let your DTL get in on it!
    b. Permission and encouragement for the KID to express those feelings to *you*. Pounding pillows, running, crying, and yelling when alone are all viable options when the KID's deep and ancient feelings begin to come up. (See Methods.)

   Both a. and b. above are necessary for the KID to calm down (become free of symptoms) and integrate into proper place in the psyche. Both are necessary for the KID to be finally seen—seen by the IS. (More about how to do this in section Four: Treating the KID.)
4. Practice the methods to make the Shift. This will grow the Inspired Self. Like a muscle, its presence in your consciousness will expand and strengthen with greater use.

> If the KID is on the Throne, always use kindness even as you are being firm.
> If the Dead Tapes are on the Throne, *Use Mental Discipline Methods to Chase Them AWAY!*

The KID in you needs to be treated at all times with kindness and firmness and is *never* to be dealt with harshly. This is the case because the KID has already had more than enough mean, shaming, angry, harsh treatment from outsiders, and from the DTL in your head, to last an eternity.

However, the DTL is another matter entirely. They are not a living creative part and you can be as harsh as necessary to get them off the Throne. The goal is to get them disengaged from the KID. When they are on the Throne they have unacceptable access to the KID and to those "out there." Just get them off the Throne! You can yell at them, laugh at them, call them names, tell them to "Shut up!" and whatever else that works to get the job done. Another name for the Dead Tapes that some people like to use is the "Shoulds." They can be very much like cackling, nasty old fairy tale witches! A great book to help you in working with the Shoulds in your head is *The Self-Talk Solution* by Shad Helmstetter (1987). It may be hard to find but is well worth the effort. Other books by the same author are also helpful. Anything that helps you get more *realistic* about them, anything that helps to *dehumanize* them and diminish their power in your psyche can be used. The important thing is that you begin to realize that just because you "think it," does not mean you should believe it. Some of your thoughts are not true. They may arrive with a gusto of feelings in tow, but they may not be true. You can challenge the ones that are harming you. You can use discernment. Guess which part in you has the power of discernment. If you guessed the Inspired Self, you would be right. In other words, by using discernment, you have made the Shift.

Note: Numbers 2, 3, and 4 can be practiced almost simultaneously, however, getting the KID or the Dead Tapes off the Throne as quickly as possible (the Shift) is the priority.

Primary Treatment

How to Create the Shift

The IT Methods

Once you have begun to recognize which part is on the Throne, and are able to discern what is appropriate, you are ready to make the Shift. In Integration Therapy, the goal is to properly integrate the parts and to thereby function consistently as an adult. Probably no human being has ever achieved perfection in this endeavor. It can be very helpful to realize that the task will never be complete. It can be helpful to look for progress and to avoid the expectation that perfection is attainable. The KID will always make an occasional unbidden appearance onto the Throne. The DTL, with some diligent work, can greatly recede to the quiet back street of your psyche, only to suddenly blast you at an unexpected moment. But it can become much less evident and more manageable and life can be a joy! The Shift itself is a black and white event. In a given moment you are operating solely as the KID, or the Dead Tapes, or the Inspired Self—black and white.

> "We shall be changed… in the twinkling of an eye."
> --1 Corinthians, 15: 51-52.

Method #1:

Talk to the KID
Always Be Both Kind and Firm

You can either be the KID or be with the KID. If you discover that the KID is on the Throne in a given situation and you want to get self-control, begin to talk to the KID. You can do this out loud or silently in your head, as you wish, and as the situation permits. If you are talking *to* the KID, you are not *being* the KID. Usually it goes something like this: You are upset and having intense feelings. It feels like it is all of you that feels this way. Then the thought pops in that maybe this is the KID. At first you dismiss that idea because you feel so justified in your upset feeling. If you do decide to believe it could be the KID part, you can begin to talk to your little inner child. You might say in your head, "You poor little thing. You feel so scared (or whatever the feeling is). I'm so sorry you feel that way. I'm so sorry you feel so alone. I'm here now. I will take care of this now. You can go and play." The moment you talk to the KID you are no longer the KID, instead, you are with the KID. In fact, talking to the KID grows your True Adult muscle. You can either be the KID or talk to the KID, *be* the KID or be *with* the KID. When someone gets "under your skin" it means they are in direct contact with the KID in you, and the KID suffers. The abandoned KID suffers. You may need to repeat many times, "I'm here now." To get the desired effect, to get between the KID and the person out there, you may need to repeat it many times. If you try this and persist you will be shocked to discover that you begin to feel calmer and calmer. *The KID in you calms down!* This is what happens because the KID is off the Throne *and* no longer home alone.

All manner of clients that I have worked with over the years could tell you that they did not want to do this. Like you may now feel, they too felt skeptical, silly, and even foolish. For many of them there was quite a time gap before they became willing to try. They had a great deal of resistance. One of my clients was a professional football player. One is a cop. Many of my most macho clients had trouble with the thought of talking to the KID. Many of the women I have worked with were equally resistant. It is understandable. But it never failed to a person, that they would each and every one of them eventually come to a session and report that they finally felt bad enough to try it and that *it worked!* They were amazed, and they became believers, and they began to get control of their lives.

Scripts

It can be important and helpful to develop scripts that you actually memorize in order to be prepared for those moments when you suddenly realize it is the KID in you that is on the Throne and being triggered. A couple of examples of scripts you can learn for those times when someone is hurtful or rude to you might be to say to the KID:

"It's not about you. It's their problem. It's about them! You don't deserve their rudeness. I'm here now. I'll deal with this insult. You don't need to worry about it." (Then from your IS you may or may not decide this is a battle worth fighting.)

Or, "You poor KID! I'm sorry I didn't protect you from that person. I'm here now. You can go and play. I'll take care of it. I'm here now."

What matters is having a script ready so that you aren't the KID stuck in the "deer in the headlights" paralysis, and so that you are making sure that the script lets the KID off the hook.

In order to make the Shift, talk to the KID.

Triggers and Rescue Missions

How Triggers Work

Let's say you realize (however dimly) that you are in what seems to be a spontaneous regression and you are functioning as a child in a given situation. You can begin to question the spontaneity of it, the randomness of it, and look for the trigger (a current event that triggers some past loss, abuse, or other devastation). Think of it this way—you overreact to the current event only because of a pre-existing deep wound. It works like this: pretend for a moment you are walking down the street and one of your arms is healthy and normal and the other arm has a festering sore on it. As you are walking, people are walking by you from the opposite direction. Occasionally, someone will brush by grazing your healthy arm and you barely notice it. Then someone grazes the other arm and bumps the wound. You scream in pain and feel angry with the stranger who "hurt" you! In truth, they did not hurt you. The hurt was already inside you and already needed your attention. Until the unwitting stranger bumped it though, you were able to ignore it, and maybe you were even unaware of it. The problem is the wound—not the bump. The bump draws new attention to the festering wound and gives you an opportunity to heal it. If, however, as most people tend to do, you focus on the one who bumped you as the problem, no healing takes place.

How to Rescue the KID From the Past

You must first acknowledge the old wound and you can then say to the KID something like: "I'm here now. It's not 19 _ _ (whatever year the triggered event occurred in). It's now 2011 (or whatever year is current) *and we've already survived that.* I'm here now and I love you." Repeat as often as necessary until you actually feel the KID calm down. The KID will literally heal more and more each time you do this. That trigger (or "button") will fade and be harder to push (less sensitive or sore) the next time.

I came across this method when I was a student of Ericksonian Clinical Hypnotherapy. The class was filled with professional psychotherapists, all of us adding to our skills and credentials. The instructor asked for volunteers for a demonstration. A man volunteered with the presenting problem of a habit of chewing the inside of his lip. He had tried many things to stop. All had failed. The instructor took the man in trance back to the root of the behavior and what came out was an experience that he had had in Vietnam. He had had a devastating experience with his platoon and an interaction with the enemy in a village. He had killed up close and personal. The chewing he was doing on the inside of his lip was done to distract from the memory of that horrifying event whenever it was in any way triggered so that it would not reach conscious awareness. Once the connection was made, the hypnotherapist explained that the *part* of the soldier *that was stuck in time* needed to be rescued. He instructed the man to talk to that fragment of his psyche that was still in Vietnam. He told him that it was no longer 1969, it was 1995, that he was no longer in Vietnam, but rather now in Washington, DC, and that *he had already survived that.* I realized that the fragment of his psyche that was stuck in 1969 Vietnam was a traumatized aspect of the KID in him and was causing his 1995 symptoms. In my clinical work with clients I began to use the method to rescue the stuck in time aspect of their inner child. I also began to realize it was not necessary to formally induce trance and that clients could learn to do it for themselves. It worked. People got relief and greater self-control.

The KID's Real Name

When talking to the KID it helps to use the KID's actual name. The KID in you knows its name. Once again some of my clients kicked and screamed (and some of them more than others). It can take some effort of asking and some time before the KID in you will trust you enough to tell you, but with persistence eventually you will learn the name. Some people just intuitively know the KID's name (even if they don't want to admit it). But once again everyone who has ever tried to find out has eventually discovered the name. Don't believe me? Then go ahead and prove me wrong. To prove me wrong, you have to give it a sincere try of asking the KID for its name and you must persist. Read *Running From Safety* by Richard Bach. Watch the Disney movie *The Kid* starring Bruce Willis. Dickie and Rusty are not anomalies. You just might be surprised.

Method #2:

Talk to the Tapes

The phenomenon of the DTL Tapes attacking the poor defenseless KID in the psyche is extremely detrimental to the growth and development of the individual. They can cripple a person's life. It is a stilted and painful way to live. Many a fairy tale is a metaphor for the innocent child in you being abandoned to some evil and powerful authority out to do it harm.

What's in *Your* Library?

Once you have sensed that harshness is in play in your "thinking" and you are picking up that the Tapes are in control, and you have realized they need to be removed from power, you are on your way to making the Shift and it's time to act! The Tapes, remember, are ghosts from your past. They may be scary goblins to the KID in you, but really they are paper tigers. Do whatever is necessary to chase them away. This means you can *yell* at them until they recede. They have no feelings. They are dead. "Shut up!" is good to try, and "Go away!" Repeat as necessary until you feel calm. Calming down will tell you that the Shift has occurred. You can also use IT Truthink to displace the negative, aggressive thoughts. (See Method #5.)

They may show up in your psyche as actual thoughts, or they may lurk just beneath conscious awareness as broad concepts.

So, again, what's in *your* Dead Tape Library—your *personal* DTL?

Lazy?
Stupid?
Selfish?
Conceited?
Weak?
Not Good Enough?
Too Late?
Always Late?
Too Old?
Too Young?
Unloveable?
Sick?
Clumsey?
Addicted?
Spendthrift?
Poor?
Bossy?
Foolish?
Fat?
Unimportant?
Irrelevant?
Invisible?

Whatever deeply stored messages of doom and gloom that you are harboring in your inner mental halls, it is imperative that you find them. To paraphrase Haanel, in *The Master Key System* (p. 85, #4), he suggests that, in order to accomplish this, you analyze every thought by asking yourself if this thought is of benefit. You must come to understand that any thoughts that do not benefit you or others are weapons in your DTL arsenal, and that they are beating you back from success, wealth, health, and the real pursuit of happiness. And it is important to realize that they are nothing more than apparitions.

Ghost Busters!

Find them! Shine the light of truth upon them. They often hide under nice or helpful sounding covers. They may at first be hard to detect—almost invisible. If you know how to look for them you will find them.

If you are struggling in any way in your life, they are lurking in the shadows. Your struggle is their footprint. Put the spotlight on them and then you must speak truth to them. If they are of no benefit they must be banished. They must be replaced. Speak with the voice of authority:

> "Poverty, be gone! I am inspired by divine ideas. I prosper!"
> "Self-doubt, be gone! I am capable, loveable, and creative!"
> "Debt, be gone! I am rich with curiosity that leads me to discovery, productivity, and abundance!"
> "Feelings of weakness, powerlessness, and hopelessness, be gone! I am strong! I have real power—personal power—to have impact on my world!"

When you do this, you have called upon the IS to banish the banshee of destruction from your life.

Amazing Grace

Once you have chased the Dead Tapes off by talking to them instead of accepting that they *are* you, or that they are delivering some absolute truth, it is necessary to also talk to the KID to repair any damage they might have done during their reign of terror or nastiness. For many people who are riddled with guilt feelings, doubt and shame from the Dead Tapes it is key to think in terms of permission. Giving the KID permission to have whatever feelings the KID has, permission to have something others may not have, permission to be and do whatever is reasonable and harmless, permission to be imperfect, permission to try and fail, permission to trust that you (the True Inspired Adult) will be chasing the DTL and all its doubts and dire threats and warnings away. If the Dead Tapes had any real power they would never allow your mere permission to banish them. They could not be banished. They have no power except that which is given to them by the KID or by the absence of the IS. They can be banished! This is very important to stress to the KID. Once again, the idea is that you have begun operating out of your IS by talking to the other part(s). You've made the Shift!

Further, when you realize you are treating someone out there with harshness that suggests the Tapes are on the Throne, the same rules apply. Get them off the Throne of your being by addressing them. Once again you may have to speak sharply to them (in your head) to get them shaken loose. If you are angry and yelling at anyone, the Dead Tapes are in charge and need to be removed. Send them away. Need more help with this? Read Shad Helmstetter! It is his specialty.

Method #3:

Choose a Role Model

Sometimes we find ourselves in situations that baffle us. We may even begin to get an inkling that we are in some way living the Lower Life, but don't know how to change it. We may find ourselves feeling powerless and in the grips of a nasty old pattern. The KID in us is stuck. We want to make the Shift to better functioning. Maybe mom and dad weren't the best examples for us and we feel stymied. People can try one of two things:

1. Ask, ask, ask your higher wiser self what to do. And WAIT… for a quiet little voice inside to answer. This can be hard to believe in, especially at first. It can be difficult to calm the anxious voices in the KID and the DTL enough to be able to hear the "still small voice." If, however, you do persist, the answer *will* come.

2. Look around and choose a role model to emulate. Then ask yourself how would s/he handle this situation/person/problem? You will be amazed that you somehow know how they would handle it. This tells us that inside each of us (in the Inspired Self part) we know how to handle it. But, due to self-doubt or anxiety, the KID can't let go enough to let us access it (the IS and its wisdom) except by looking at how a so-called more competent person would handle it. This actually proves that we know. The information is stored inside each of us under the category "What 'so and so' would do." Then once you determine what they would do, do that!

> To put it more simply, if you know how a particular "someone else" would handle the problem, then *you* know how to handle the problem. And you know how you *want* to handle the problem.

I once worked with a very attractive woman I'll call Marlene. She looked a lot like Marilyn Monroe. In fact, she seemed to have many of her characteristics. Perhaps there was some unconscious role-modeling going on, but it was no longer getting her what she wanted. She had gotten to a point in therapy where she was realizing that the KID in her was quite active and taking the lead in many of her relationships. She wanted to live a more satisfying life but found herself feeling trapped in old ways. She seemed to be a good candidate for the role model method. Both her mother and father had been very abusive parents and they frequently but unpredictably used severe and even violent corporal punishment on Marlene and on her younger siblings. Marlene did not want to be mean like them, so she became the opposite. (Freud would call this defense mechanism "reaction formation.") Like Marilyn Monroe she became always sweet and only kind to all. Because of this, it was very hard for her to be at all self-protective. She did not know how to set reasonable boundaries, and so she basically set none. Having been raised by two abusive parents, she took a black and white view of saying no. She just said yes.

Of course, her real feelings did not go away. Unfortunately, her usual way of dealing with them was to build resentment often even unknown to her conscious self, and to then begin feeling very justified in being silently (secretly) angry with those who had "offended her." Then she would passive-aggressively act out her anger and soon regret the way it blew up in her face. She felt genuinely surprised when it did. Or, she would just "go along" for a while and then become withholding. She felt powerless in her relationships and powerless to get the KID off the Throne with other methods she had tried in therapy. In her own eyes, she was deeply convinced she was just a powerless victim even in her contemporary relationships of their "evil" ways.

Try as she might with other IT methods, she found that at times she was just stuck. So, we tried the role model method. She chose a person in the world that she really admired and asked herself what would that particular person do to handle this particular situation. She chose Michele Obama. What amazed her was that *suddenly* she did know exactly what to do to set reasonable boundaries for herself and to have reasonable expectations of her loved ones. It came out of her own brain categorized under "What Michele Obama would do!" Suddenly Marlene found her own voice in the relationship and in the situation. IT would say she got the KID off the Throne and her "better angels" (the IS) could take over. Her life got better and she found that reasonable happy medium that allowed her to be kind *and* self-protective.

Another woman that I worked with, who I'll call Evelyn, is now in her sixties. She chose Kathryn Hepburn as her role model. As she worked with her view of Hepburn, she was able to successfully take care of the abandoned KID in her by finally leaving an abusive husband after many years of humiliation and suffering. Both Michele Obama and Kathryn Hepburn are beautiful examples of feminine women who have been known to speak their minds.

The truth is that all along, inside each of us, we do know what to do. We just don't know it, or we just don't dare to give ourselves permission to know it and to then do it. The KID is afraid that the DTL will over do it, or will punish the KID for speaking up, or that dire punishment will come fast and furious from without. When structured in the mold of a role model, the KID can let go and trust that the limit will be set in a reasonable and protective way. It does not matter what the truth may be about the chosen role model. What matters is that by taking on our perception of their persona—their mature behavior—we can begin to function better. It demonstrates that inside you, you do know how to take care of yourself. The role model temporarily becomes your backbone, so to speak, until you can grow your own.

Method #4:

Stand by Your KID

How to Stand Between All Others and the KID in You

How to Keep Your Cool

Become your own bff (best friend forever). This is the part about how to keep your own power. This is the part about how not to get triggered. This is the part about when dealing with those out there (such as bosses, spouses, friends, so-called enemies, competitors, etc.) how to keep your cool. This is the part about how to prevent others from stirring up your DTL to respond to those out there and/or attack and stir up the KID in you. Here is the secret. (Does Barack Obama know it? It seems that he might.)

The Secret Is

Align *immediately* internally (in your head) with the KID in you *whenever* anyone attacks you in any way. Do this even if they might be right. It isn't about who is right. That isn't the point. The point is it is not about the KID in you, it's not the KID's problem. Protect your KID from all outside and DTL opinions by aligning with your KID. How? Internal dialogue. Talk to the KID.

Objectives

1. The KID is protected and can remain calm.
2. The KID is kept from hopping on the Throne.

Internal Dialogue

To align with the KID in you let the KID know that you are not judging the KID. Say, "I'll deal with this. You can go and play. You've done nothing wrong. This is adult business. Not your job. Go play. I'm here now. It is my job to deal with this." A private joke can help. Perhaps you verbally respond to the person who is attacking by calmly saying,

"AH." Inside your head the KID and you know that is code for "Aw Hooey!" (or anything else you might think of to make "AH" mean.) By making that private joke you have stepped between the vulnerable and innocent child in you and the provoker out there. You are developing your internal relationship and heading toward Self Mastery. You are using mental discipline.

During the time of slavery in this country the slaves that fared the best kept their self-esteem and dignity despite inhumane treatment by shuckin' and jivin' the Massa'. They did not believe the Massa' deserved more respect than they did. It was a wonderful and well-developed survival skill. They showed a face of respect to the Master and they obeyed him because the master had all power over them. But in their minds they were free to jeer and insult him. In this way they did not abandon themselves. In their minds they were free. They aligned with themselves instead of with the abusive slave driver. If someone is attacking you, they are abusing. If they are your boss or teacher and they are attacking they are abusing power over you. You owe your allegiance to the truth, and that means to yourself.

Stop allowing others to control your mood. Keep your right not to be offended. In your internal dialogue remind the KID that "it" is not about the KID but rather speaks volumes about the offender/judge. When you let others get under your skin you have not stood between the offender and the KID in you. You have abandoned yourself to the offender. Ouch! Getting angry gives away your power because it means your KID has hopped on the Throne and is relating to outsiders and speaking for you! The KID has no real power. Only the True Inspired Adult in you has power. By letting the KID "out" you have given your power to the other guy. This will cause you to be viewed as childish or worse. You did not do your duty. You abandoned the powerless KID to the wild, wild world.

Once you have gotten the KID off the Throne you are free to deal with the situation as an adult. That means you accept responsibility or set boundaries as needed. By aligning with the KID you have Shifted to the clear-headed IS and will naturally know how to handle the situation.

Write and Learn Your Scripts in Advance

At first you need a strong inner dialogue. Over time it becomes more automatic and you may not even need the words. But at first it is best to write your scripts in advance and have them rehearsed and ready. It's hard enough to figure out that it is the KID in you when you get stirred up, let alone to try *then* to figure out what to say in your head in order to get mastery. Have it ready and rehearsed.

When you feel the first signs of big emotions, some great tried and true inner dialogue lines are: "Let go and let God." "Mind your own business." "It's not about you!" Remember it's only their problem unless you let them be in direct relationship to your KID.

No one can afford to allow another person to define them. So, it is your job to stand between their opinion of you and the KID. In fact, their opinion of you is none of your business. Let them have whatever opinion of you they have. Who cares? It is just their opinion. As long as you are within the law and do no harm, their opinion is their problem. Just do not adopt it. *Do not ever let anyone else define you.* Keep your power. Do not be tempted to give it to them. Do not abandon yourself.

From "The Good Book" we read, "Blessed are the meek, for they will inherit the Kingdom." Meek does not mean weak. It takes strength of character (IS) and builds strength of character (IS) to live detached (IS) from the provocation of others. To live detached from their opinions of you is to live in truth. It is to live in reality. It is to live in the now. It means you are operating out of your strong self. It allows you to have access to your brilliance. That's power! It gives you Self Mastery. Self Mastery will give a person the edge in any situation.

Interpret for the KID

Read between the lines when others attack. Are they jealous? Are they feeling less than? This is not your problem unless you react. What such a person calls out for is sadness for their sense of lack. Be appropriately sad for them and stand between them and the precious KID in you.

1. It is not ever the KID'S fault.
2. It is not the KID'S job.
3. It is not about the KID. It is about the attacker.

4. It is not the KID'S business.
5. It is not the KID'S problem.
6. "They" are wrong about the KID. "They" can't define you!

Let the KID Have and Express Feelings to You

As you become more available to the KID, your feelings will begin to come up. Accept all feelings. When alone in private allow the KID to vent. Let the KID cry, rage, pound pillows, etc. Let the feelings (old or new) come up and assure the KID that you will not allow them to act out on others out in the world. Over time even the long buried old feelings will be spent.

Method #5:

Truthink

"Think truly, and thy thoughts shall the world's famine feed;
Speak truly, and each word of thine shall be a fruitful seed;
Live truly, and thy life shall be a great and noble creed."

--Horatius Bonar
1801-1889
A Scottish Minister

In IT, Truthink (positive affirmations) can be used to break a negative pattern of thinking and to get you into a more positive and more realistic frame of mind. IT labels this method "Truthink" because IT teaches that these positive affirmations are much closer to the truth about you and the universe you live in (True Thinking/Thinking the Truth) than the many negative affirmations that hang out in the Dead Tape Library. Truthink phrases can be memorized and said aloud or repeated silently. To affirm means to make firm, or to bring into solidity. Once again, with this IT method, the result can be that you actually Shift into your Adult part. The actual speaking of the Truthink activates your IS, and also the message of the affirmation can replace (displace like water) the outmoded Dead Tapes. Truthink when used regularly can flush out many of the old negative messages—can dilute the "dirty water" in the DTL. Truthink remodels your stuffy old Library and overrides and replaces unwanted works. Making a habit of Truthink is a very important and necessary method for replacing the nasty outdated volumes and Tapes and properly integrating the DTL.

It is important to recognize what you are doing well and to endorse yourself regularly. Speak words of encouragement in your head as you would to a child out there. "Good job!" "I'm proud of you!" "I love you!" Use Truthink consistently, rather than lapsing unnoticed back into your old habit of worry, criticism, fear, and doubt.

In a Word

Focusing on even just one solitary positive word can often break the hold that the frightened or angry KID has on the Throne. In fact, one word may be easier because it doesn't carry the belief issue that a statement can. Choosing a word such as "God," or "Bliss," or "Joy," or "Abundance," for example, and just allowing images or the meanings of that word that are personal to you to fully fill your consciousness can change your mood. It can be a wonderful first step in Truthink.

Truthink Will

1. Calm the KID and increase your self-esteem.
2. Displace the nasty Dead Tapes in the DTL.
3. Create the Shift.
4. Grow the Inspired Self muscle.

More Good Examples of Truth to Make Firm Include

"Every day in every way I am getting better and better."

--Emile Coue'

Emile Coue' was born in the late 1800s in France and he practiced what he called auto-suggestion. His reputation grew rapidly as people marveled at the effect his simple generic prescription (quoted above) had on patients suffering from a variety of ailments. I highly recommend the latest edition of his book, *My Method.* In the forward, Arthur A. Leidecker, CH, explains the powers of the simple statement thusly:

The subconscious mind, or our higher self if you prefer, knows what we need. There is no need, in fact it is inadvisable, to add specifics to our auto-suggestion. The awesome power of the subconscious mind enables it to know far better than we consciously do, exactly what our needs are.

Emile Coue' recommended reciting it aloud quietly at least 20 times as you drift off to sleep rather than indulging in the usual habit most of us suffer from of going over what went wrong with our day.

In IT language the KID is blocked from worry and complaints and the Inspired Self is invited to do whatever may be called for to improve your life. Keep in mind that wise old saying from a galaxy long ago and far, far away…

"Your focus determines your reality." --George Lucas
Star Wars

"Breathe in God. Breathe out ego."

In using this particular affirmation you can think of ego as the KID and the Tapes. To breathe out ego is to breathe out all fear, problems, doubt, anger, etc. You can substitute the word "Good" for "God" if that works better for you. Concentrate on and follow your breath slowly while repeating the words until a sense of calm ensues. You can do this with your eyes closed and envision the worry leaving your body as you exhale and picture a beautiful light filling your being as you inhale. This can also work while you are wide-eyed, alert, and driving through traffic. The point is to repeat until the Shift occurs.

"Everything I need and everything I need to know comes to me or through me."

This one got me through my Masters Comprehensives many years ago. As I looked at the exam paper my mind went blank and I felt paralyzed. It was the first time I had had that kind of test anxiety, but it had me in its grip. When I remembered the affirmation and began repeating it over and over I began to calm down and suddenly my mind opened up, answers came like a river flowing, and I wrote furiously and was one of the first ones done!! I realized years later that I had effectively gotten the panicked KID off the Throne with that affirmation and the Inspired Adult Self in me had taken over.

"God Is Here!"

This can be very powerful for a person of faith. It can be equally powerful for a desperate person willing to experiment!

My personal experience with this one came one dark night driving south on the I-95 corridor just north of Baltimore, MD. There was a lot of construction and traffic had been restricted to one narrow lane bordered by jersey walls on both sides. There was no shoulder and no give room at all. Traffic was racing along going at least 70mph! There was a semi behind me and I was racing along to keep up and ahead of him. I knew that the McHenry Tunnel was a few miles ahead and I remember hoping the lanes would break open soon. Then it happened. My right back tire blew. The car with two precious passengers began to wobble. The situation seemed desperate. I had to keep up or be hit from behind by the 18-wheeler. I hit the flashers, but intuited that to brake might cause the car to wobble or swerve into the jersey wall. I had to keep it straight or hit the wall. I could feel the entire tire eroding as we sped along. The sound was hideous as metal hit the pavement. There was no end in sight of the jersey walled lane as I looked ahead. I began to say the above affirmation with absolute focus, concentration and determination. I repeated it louder and more firmly each time as we raced to meet our fate. The two passengers became still and sank into their seats as they realized our dilemma. I continued repeating the words, all the while expecting deliverance, when suddenly the way opened up and we were able to shoot across at least 4 lanes and come to a stop on a very wide shoulder. There was not a drop of rubber left on the tire, but the rim was perfectly intact! A nice state trooper came along and changed the tire and we were back on the road and on our way home in a very short time. What had occurred? At the very least, I had Shifted into a part that kept its cool and drove us steadily to safety. That part in me was physically strong enough to keep the car perfectly straight at a very high rate of speed for a significant period of time while riding on the rim. How do you interpret that?

"Let go and let God."

This is a motto from the A.A. Twelve-Step Program. What happens, as observed through the lens of Integration Therapy, when a twelve-stepper (or anyone) prays that little prayer? Some would say that they turn whatever their concern is over to their "Higher Power" to handle it. In IT one might say that the KID is being relieved of a duty and a pressure that was never meant to be on the KID in the first place and that the Inspired Self is now being invited to handle it.

This petition, "Let go and let God," goes well with A.A.'s Step 3, which reads, "We made a decision to turn our will and our lives over to the care of God as we understood Him." In taking this step, the KID can be said to be making the proper use of the KID's free will to exit the Throne and to invite intervention: discipline, protection, and nurture by the higher, wiser part.

In the A.A. "Big Book" there is some discussion of a psychic change that takes place and enables the individual to stop drinking. On page xxix in the section called *The Doctor's Opinion*:

> *...once a psychic change has occurred, the very same person who seemed doomed, who had so many problems he despaired of ever solving them, suddenly finds himself easily able to control his desire for alcohol, the only effort necessary being that required to follow a few simple rules.*

In this quote the words "suddenly" and "easily" are of special interest here.

And on page 27 in the section called *There Is A Solution* Carl Jung is quoted:

> *...Exceptions to cases such as yours have been occurring since early times. Here and there, once in a while, alcoholics have had what are called vital spiritual experiences. To me these appear to be in the nature of huge emotional displacements and rearrangements. Ideas, emotions, and attitudes which were once the guiding forces of the lives of these men are suddenly*

cast to the side, and a completely new set of conceptions and motives begin to dominate them.

Again, note the word "suddenly." These quotes from *Alcoholics Anonymous* seem to provide compelling evidence of a sudden and complete Shift from an immature part (the KID) to an emotionally mature and wise part (the Inspired Self).

> "We shall be changed…in the twinkling of an eye."
> --1 Corinthians, 15: 51-52

In my own life I've had such sudden experiences, and one was in reverse. It was about 1982 and I was living with my husband and two children in our chalet in a quiet mountain top community in West Virginia. I had been a student of the Twelve Steps and in recovery for a number of years and had developed a wonderful sense of balance in my life. One day as I was standing in my kitchen putting dinner on the table for my family something happened. I don't even remember what it was now, but it displeased me greatly at the time. I suddenly felt anger rise up in me from somewhere unbidden. With it came a host of old negative feelings, thoughts, and attitudes and I felt like having a tantrum! The observer in me (the part that I now call my Inspired Self) caught my attention and *I saw it.* I was able to stop myself from acting out because I was able to detach. That moment and the insight that it delivered changed everything for me because with it I instantly realized that all those old immature feelings, attitudes, thoughts, and behaviors that I had thought I had outgrown were still intact in my psyche. I Got It. We must be parts. I realized that there was a "KID" living just under the radar in my psyche even when I functioned as an adult. And I realized that she was still Mad! Mad! Mad! In other words, I realized in my bones that the child part in me had never grown up despite all that I had learned in recovery—despite all my "adult" knowledge and awareness. I got it that my maturity was dependant on whether or not I maintained operating out of my higher wiser part.

"Live and let live."

This gem comes from the wisdom of the program of A.A. In plain English, Mind your own business! Boundaries are sacred.

Other Methods that Can Be Used to Create the Desired IT Shift

Method #6:

Gratitude

It has been said that it is impossible to be grateful and fearful at the same time. It is impossible to be grateful and angry, or depressed, or anxious, or whatever in the same moment. Gratitude, when it takes hold in the psyche, blots out all the negatives. Therefore, it can be said that gratitude creates a Shift from the Lower Life to the Inspired Life. Two good techniques for evoking an attitude of gratitude are:

1. Make a Gratitude List. Just begin listing in your head, out loud, or on paper everything you can think of that you are genuinely grateful for. At first it may be difficult to think beyond the thing that is making you miserable at the moment. But with mental discipline, with determination, the ideas will come. And as the ideas come gratitude will set in.

2. Just say "Thank You!" over, and over, and over, and without trying to think of things to be grateful for. You can say "Thank You!" even while being stuck in your misery. But it must be repeated and repeated until you actually begin to feel grateful. Once that occurs, the Shift is a done deal and the KID has lost its grip.

Method #7:

Music

Music can change the mood in an instant. A melody, movement, or song can be used by you intentionally in order to change your mood. You can thereby bring about the desired Shift. Anything that breaks the pattern of thought (the KID's thoughts) and releases the grip shame, fear, anger, or dread, etc. has on you is a pattern changer. Breaking a negative thought pattern (when life and limb are *not* immediately threatened) creates the Shift from upset KID to calm and reasonable Inspired Self.

Method #8:

Meditation

The purpose of meditation is to release you from the grips of what the Buddhist would call "the chattering monkey," or what in IT would be called the "Lower Mind" (the KID and the Dead Tape Library). In other words, meditation is a practice of Shifting into a higher state of consciousness. With meditation a person learns to observe and detach from the thoughts that continuously float or race through the head (thoughts from the KID and the DTL). This act of observing with detachment the thoughts as they appear immediately Shifts the person into the higher mind. It is an exercise that weakens the power of the random thoughts that tend to otherwise control us. You can either be lost in the thoughts or observe the thoughts. This is much the same as the phenomenon in IT that says you can either *be* the KID or *be with* the KID. The observing mind in meditation is the IS. By meditating regularly a person actually grows the Inspired Self muscle. This makes it less frequently necessary to Shift because the person is operating more often as an adult. Further, it makes it easier to make the Shift when needed and desired either automatically, or by using any of the aforementioned methods. Even Mother Theresa recommended meditating for at least 20 minutes a day.

Method #9:

Medication (a last resort or a first requirement)

Medication can be helpful and maybe even necessary when the KID's grip on the Throne is remarkable. This can be the case due to organic causes, high sensitivity, or when the type and severity and the duration or frequency of abuse, trauma, or neglect is profound. Of importance here is to be aware that the illness is in the child part only and medication does not medicate the Inspired part.

A wonderful movie that illustrates this is *A Beautiful Mind*, directed by Ron Howard. In it the main character played by Russell Crowe is based on John Nash, a real person and a brilliant mathematician who suffered from schizophrenia. John grew up in West Virginia in humble circumstances. He achieved a scholarship to Harvard and was able to create a successful life of achievement for himself despite his "illness." He was the recipient of the Nobel Prize in Mathematics. With great effort over time he was able to learn to manage his hallucinations and delusions (coming from the lower parts) by detaching from them. He became the observer self that in IT would be called the Inspired Self. He continued to have the visions because he decided against the medications that would have helped suppress the symptomatic KID. With great effort and determination he was able to learn to discern what was real and what was imagined (the KID and the DTL). He took the KID in him off the ruling Throne in his psyche. This could be said to be a personal achievement that rivals what he accomplished that earned him the Nobel Prize. For many people with this condition, medication is necessary to blot out the activity of the KID and free the person to function. John Nash's accomplishment in his own mental life is a demonstration of the power of the Inspired Self. He, not unlike William James, used the power within to overcome the grip of the KID on the Throne of his being and was able to return to vital life. For many of those suffering such, medication makes sense, especially if they have no awareness of the parts in their psyche and the power in the IS.

Method #10:

Hypnosis

There is a growing body of documented clinical evidence in the field of hypnosis that suggests that with hypnosis people are able to access their higher, wiser part. This part is generally accepted to be their subconscious mind. It has been documented that people under hypnosis have created symptoms such as actual blisters on the skin that have then been dissolved again under the direction of the hypnotist. Also, by accessing this part of their psyche, they are often able to break old, entrenched habits such as smoking and overeating. Even with self-hypnosis techniques people are able to reduce stress and gain other such wonderful and lasting results. Are they making a Shift to a more powerful part? It is possible.

Method #11:

Journaling

Keeping a regular journal is a powerful way to get to know your True Self. There is an old saying, "Out of the lead of pencils lies do not flow." By writing on a regular basis you can begin to discover your emotional patterns, your real desires, and your motives. After some time your real dreams can begin to emerge. By learning your patterns you can become more adept at recognizing which part is most often on the Throne and thereby strengthen your ability to make the Shift as needed.

Method #12:

Laugh

Give yourself permission to laugh. Find something to laugh about or just start laughing. Laughter breaks the spell of the DTL and tells the KID that there is nothing to fear. Laughing promises that all is well and the KID is safe.

Sometimes, however, the KID in you will laugh even as you are speaking of what sound like painful truths. That is defensive laughter. It is a survival technique meant to keep you in denial and to keep hard feelings at bay. Don't fall for that laugh. You can handle the truth today when the IS is involved.

In general, however, laughter is good medicine and takes you from memory (past) and dread (future) to fun, peace, and joy (present). Norman Cousins, who became a well known author and proponent of the power of positive thinking, once cured himself from a physical illness with a poor prognosis after getting a bad medical diagnosis. He did so by locking himself into a hotel room and literally laughing for days! Laughter is good medicine. It releases good chemicals throughout the human body. It boosts the immune system and lowers blood pressure. Laughter releases the body's natural tranquilizers from the inside out. People who live the longest are people who laugh and feel joy. Laugh. Laugh often.

Method #13:

Breathe

Breath and memory are connected. If you want to memorize something hold your breath to the count of 4 and you will remember it. When trauma occurs, one of the reasons we get stuck is because at the moment of trauma we do hold our breath automatically. Breath can also be utilized to release and cleanse the sharp edges of a memory. Breath can be used to loosen the hold it can have on the psyche. Just consciously and purposefully taking a deep breath and releasing it slowly can give you the opportunity to reassess the situation and make the Shift.

Method #14:

Yoga

Yoga is a process that helps the practitioners to fully inhabit themselves and their life—to come home to themselves. Through breath work, asana (poses) practice, and meditation people develop a holistic experience of body, heart and mind. Through sustained practice they are led to simple presence and deep peace within (the IS).

Anyone who has practiced yoga for any length of time can attest to its ability to gently create a Shift in mood and outlook. In IT terms practicing yoga can lead to a realization of the Inspired Life.

Method #15:

Transformational Prayer

Devotional prayer, unlike anxious prayer, is not fear based. It is prayer that is based on faith and devotion and perhaps on awe of the Almighty. It has the power to lift the supplicant into a higher state of consciousness. Faith-based prayer can help the KID to let go of the Throne.

I once worked with a woman I'll call Jane, who was painfully unhappy with her new husband's behavior. Over the long haul in therapy Jane actually came to appreciate him, but at an early juncture in the process she was in her word "beside" herself with angst. In a way that seems rather insightful and almost possible when you think of such a phenomenon in IT terms. In my office one day she began reciting a prayer in trance-like and ever more anxious tones. This she did after reporting a particularly frustrating exchange she'd had with her spouse. It took me quite by surprise and I was suddenly privy to her "at home" ritual for dealing with frustration. As I observed (only for a nano second before I intervened) she began working herself into a frenzy that verged on a panic attack, and all with the words of a prayer! Once I grasped what she was doing to herself I intervened by saying her name sharply, and then saying "Stop!" She looked startled and snapped out of trance. We were then able to process her behavior. She reported that sometimes the more she "prayed," the more scared she became that she was trapped and that her prayers would never be answered.

What part of her do you think was praying? Let me be clear. There was nothing wrong with the prayer itself or with praying. But the KID in her was getting the bejesus scared out of her by the DTL with the whole process! Be wary. You might want to make sure any prayer recited is prayed not out of fear, but in faith.

FYI: A notable difference between prayer and meditation: prayer is talking to a Higher Power; meditation is listening for Higher Power.

Method #16:

Move/Dance/Walk/Exercise

We were built to walk. Any exercise will have an effect on brain chemistry and mood. It will therefore have an effect on outlook. The right amount of exercise can get the body virtually humming and a Shift to expanded consciousness can occur. Just ask someone who runs regularly. It can create what some call a runner's high. It is a Shift into feelings of wellbeing and empowerment.

Method #17:

Read *The Power of Now*, by Eckhart Tolle.

You can only live in the present when and if the Inspired Self is on the Throne.

Method #18:

Read, Learn, and Practice the Third Step of Alcoholics Anonymous.

Turn "it" (whatever is bothering you) over. That never means you don't do what you can. It just means that by getting the scared or angry or ashamed little KID in you off the Throne you can be freed to take appropriate action and let go of what is clearly beyond your apparent control. Once the KID and DTL are off the case, watch out! That is when miracles can (and often do) happen.

Method #19:

Creative Visualization

Read and Practice *The Master Key System,* by Charles Haanel.

First published as a correspondence course in 1912, and later (1917 and 2007) as a book, this system takes the reader through practical steps to harness the power of their thoughts and imagination.

"Imagination is more important than knowledge." --Einstein

****

FOUR: Treating the KID: Dealing with Symptom Clusters

Treatment Goals for Healing the KID

It is important to note that Personality Integration Therapy can be helpful "on the spot" in any given moment for acute situations and symptoms by making the Shift. It is also beneficial for long-term resolution of deep wounds and for untying the underlying knots in the KID that bind us. Over time the acute sensations and symptoms can recede, resolve, and even diminish almost entirely. Self Mastery and the freedom that comes with it is the goal. This can only come about with determined hard work and diligence—i.e., mental discipline. For those now living the Inspired Life it has been well worth it.

A Case for Dropping the Label and Dealing with the Need

With IT, it is important to avoid over-all labeling of the individual with the commonly used old paradigm mental illness labels. IT is not the first new paradigm theory to realize the powerful negative significance of such a practice. IT makes use of such medical descriptions only when dealing with the symptom clusters found in the KID part.

The following are important examples of new paradigm personality theories that do not use the American Medical Association's labels that can be found in the *Diagnostic and Statistical Manual of Mental Disorders,* the DSM-IV-TR to categorize the "patient" as mentally ill.

A. Reality Therapy (RT) and Control Theory

It was the noted psychiatrist William Glasser, author of *Reality Therapy* and *Control Theory,* who proposed that there is an influential impact of diagnostic labels, both on the thinking of mental health professionals and on their subsequent treatment of the "patient," and then, of course, directly on the patient as a result. During his psychiatric residency, Glasser began developing his theory and methods for treating the hospitalized patients under his care. When he began seeing them not as sick, but as needing to take responsibility for themselves he began to get amazing results. It is Glasser who points out that people have much more control of themselves than they may realize or admit. He gives the example of the person who yells at people in the home environment, but would never let that happen in public—in a movie theatre, for example. The person has the ability to exert control when "necessary." IT would say that the DTL could be at work, or that it could be the IS. Glasser uses that as proof that we do have control. From there he goes on to hold them responsible for behaving within the norms of society. Glasser's theory and methods have had a profound influence on my professional development. While working as a crisis intervention counselor and family therapist in an agency that served adolescents, I was trained and certified as a Reality Therapist. A Reality Therapist functions as a facilitator and assists the person in their decision-making process for their own life. As a result, the person builds confidence and hope in their own ability to have a functional and creative life. In RT terms they grow up. In RT there is a profound respect for the person's inherent desire to be responsible. In IT language, there is an underdeveloped but available Inspired Self in waiting.

B. Ho'oponopono (ancient Hawaiian teachings)

In *Zero Limits,* author and teacher Dr. Joe Vitale introduces Ihaleakala Hew Len, PhD., a master teacher of modern Ho'oponopono, to the world. In using this system for healing, Dr. Hew Len was able to heal an entire ward of criminally insane inpatients at the Hawaiian State Mental Hospital where he worked as a psychologist. According to this ancient system there are two ways to live your life. You can live from memory (what IT would call the Lower Life—the KID and the DTL), or you can live from inspiration (in IT—the Inspired Life from the IS). Once again, a doctor who disregarded psychiatric labels was successful in restoring patients to "sanity." They became self-responsible.

C. Personality Integration Theory and Therapy (IT)

IT teaches that we have the power to heal ourselves and that only one part contains the symptoms. The first step is to determine which part is running your life in the current situation. If you determine that the DTL is running the show the next step is simple: send it packing! Make the Shift. If you determine it is the KID that's in charge, three things are required:

1. Make the Shift.
2. Deal with the situation from the IS.
3. Internally meet the true need(s) of the KID. To do this work you will want to determine:

    a. Presenting symptom clusters. These may include depression, rage, migraines, unstable relationships, obsessions, compulsions, failures, delusions, addictions, and anything else that feels miserable or inflicts misery.

    b. DSM medical diagnosis if any, and only if helpful to overall understanding of the current symptom clusters and the current state of the KID for IT treatment by the IS. Determining symptom clusters in the KID can be helpful as behavior predictors and as shortcuts for creating treatment plans. They do not define the human being, however.

    c. Treatment: Determine any triggers at work and what the KID in you really needs from your Inspired Self internally (in your head) in order to calm down and properly integrate it into its true place in your psyche for the situation at hand.

All three theories: RT, Ho'oponopono, and IT, see the person as powerful and capable and fully able to get control of their own life and live responsibly and creatively. William James just might approve.

Your Personal Guide:

How to Determine the KID's Triggers and Find Solutions

A powerful way to determine the underlying cause of over reactions to today's events (what the ancient triggers are) along with what is needed for resolution serves as further evidence of the existence and depth of the spiritual dimension in you (the wise Inspired Self part). Just ask. Ask your higher self. Ask and wait for an answer. Many times in therapy a client will ask why they do this or that, or why they feel this or that, or what they should do. When I ask *them* what the answer is, they generally protest. When I persist, instructing them to just listen for an answer, one *always* comes. Often it was something they would have dismissed if they had not been encouraged to take themselves seriously in that moment. This is true because many of us have been trained not listen to or trust ourselves. We were trained by our families of origin and by society in general. When I insist, they reluctantly tell me what thought has come up. It is always the answer. Or I may ask, "What is that about?" in response to a complaint or concern, or "What are the tears about?" Our tears always have a tale to tell. But the tale may not be immediately obvious. It may be hiding in the unconscious and need a nudge to reveal itself. Again, they usually need some urging to listen within for their own answers. The answers really are inside them. Socrates knew this secret. They just need to believe it and become attuned to listening to themselves. They need to learn to take themselves seriously. They need to repair the basic trust in themselves that was broken by imperfect parenting and false cultural beliefs. When we were little, many of us were trained not to believe or honor ourselves. We were told not to cry, or that our feelings were otherwise wrong. We, therefore, did not keep the connection to our wisdom open. It can be repaired. We have an inner guide, a still, small voice that we can trust for answers and direction. By learning how to discern the still, small voice of our Inspired Self from the voices of the KID and the DTL, we learn we can count on ourselves. We begin to feel more substantial, more solid. We feel safe in the world. Fear dissolves.

Personality Integration Therapy *and* the "Diagnosed" KID

(Dealing with the Real Needs of the Properly De-Throned KID)

IT Treatment for Specific Illness Model Labels

Symptom Clusters

Example #1: IT, Alcoholics Anonymous, and the Addict

"Hi, my name is _______ and I am an ________(alcoholic, food addict, drug addict, workaholic, gambler, sex addict, etc.)."

What part of the person is speaking? People in A.A. might say it is the entire person. According to IT, it is a part. It is the KID. In IT the treatment is for the KID to let go (of the Throne of its being) and discover that the world does not come to an end, that they are not alone, and that life gets better. In IT when the KID "let's go," the KID discovers that it is not alone and that there is an adult at home that can increasingly be relied upon for all that the KID needs.

Can't relate? Think you don't know much about addiction? Here's a snapshot version—a metaphor, to help you catch up:

Picture Gollum from J.R.R. Tolkein's *The Lord of The Rings Trilogy*. Gollum is addiction personified (correction: hobbitified)! In the story Gollum is addicted to the ring of power. Re-possessing it becomes his entire life focus. In reality, the ring seems to possess him. He wastes away into a strangely pathetic, horrifyingly misshapen creature because of his obsession with recapturing the ring. Yet, there is a remnant of some decent part of himself that tries to speak to him from time to time in moments that could turn the tide for him. This he ignores and continues down the path of self-destruction, attempting to annihilate all who stand between him and his "precious." Throughout his journey he has no idea that he is not in control of himself, but rather is acting in slavery to an object. In the end he destroys himself as he blindly leaps into disaster even as he finally grasps the illusive "ring of power."

Curious? Go see the movie. Or better yet, read the books.

In examining the twelve steps of the treatment program of Alcoholics Anonymous (which have been adopted and adapted by Gamblers Anonymous, Food Addiction Recovery Programs, Emotions Anonymous, Narcotics Anonymous, and other "Rings of Power" Anonymous) we find nothing that would be incompatible with IT. In fact, it correlates closely.

Let's look at the Twelve Steps of Alcoholics Anonymous from the IT perspective:

Step 1: We admitted we were powerless over ________ and our lives had become unmanageable.

IT: When the KID runs your life addictions are common and life is unmanageable. An unprotected and unsupervised KID cannot stop running away from the pressures and mysteries of life by using whatever helps blot out reality. A KID cannot manage an adult life very successfully. The addict in you is a part of the KID in you. It is the KID in you that must realize that it is powerless and living under the illusion that it can manage your life.

Step 2: Came to believe that a Power greater than ourselves could restore us to sanity.

IT: Came to discover that we did not have to be "home alone" in our head (the KID) and that there was another part that could be called upon to develop and grow and handle adult life. That part, the IS, is a power greater than the KID (and the DTL) and is connected to and can draw from and call upon the "All There Is."

Step 3: Made a decision to turn our will and our lives over to the care of God as we understood Him.

IT: Hit bottom and decided to let go of the Throne and let the True Adult in me, the Inspired Self, run the show. This is the Shift. It takes a major leap of faith for the KID to let go. The abandoned and unprotected KID has been convinced no one else was home in the psyche and must become desperate, becoming however dimly aware of its powerlessness, and must therefore feel hopeless in order to take that leap.

In IT there is another method that can be applied to make the Shift. Talk to the KID. By talking to the KID, the KID is replaced on the Throne by the IS. You cannot talk to the KID and be the KID at the same time. It may take more than one attempt of talking to the KID before the Shift actually occurs, but if you persist in talking to the KID the Shift will ultimately happen. You will know it has occurred when you feel your insides (the KID) calm down.

Step 4: Made a searching and fearless moral inventory of ourselves.

IT: Develop self-forgiveness by coming to understand that the flaws are the flaws of a child part that was never meant to be in power in the adult world-at-large, and that there is a higher, wiser part that has never "sinned" that can set things straight. This is the beginning of overcoming shame.

Step 5: Admitted to God, to ourselves, and to another human being the exact nature of our wrongs.

IT: Getting feedback from a therapist, clergyman, or other wise and trusted person who will not judge or condemn is powerful. Confession is helpful under the right circumstances. Soundboarding with a trusted friend can help a person get greater clarity and put things in perspective. But the main healing element in IT terms is to come to really understand that past is past, that all misdeeds were perpetrated by an unsupervised child part, and that the KID must not run things any longer. This overcomes the devastation of the impact of shame. Further, it breaks the cycle of isolation.

Step 6: Were entirely ready to have God remove all these defects of character.

IT: The defects of character are the immaturities of a child and the real defect is that the KID part was abandoned by the missing in action IS. Were ready to let the IS run the show.

Step 7: Humbly asked Him to remove our shortcomings.

IT: Invited the IS to take over. Made the proper (and only) use of free will that resides in the KID and invited the Shift. Once the Shift has taken place and we are operating out of the IS, we will operate without shortcomings!! The IS in us always knows and does the right thing. Hence, the Shift removes our shortcomings as long as the KID is kept off the Throne and therefore kept from running the show. No human being has to date achieved this absolutely. Vast improvements in conduct are the goal.

Step 8: Made a list of all persons we had harmed and became willing to make amends to them all.

Step 9: Made direct amends to such people whenever possible, except when to do so would injure them or others.

IT: Are children to be forgiven? Knowing that it was the unsupervised child in us that did the "wrongs" can be amazingly freeing. Those we might have harmed may not see it this way. That is not the point. Once *we* understand this, we may find it easier to own up and square up. The shame factor can disappear or greatly fade. Then the higher, wiser part in us (which always wants to make things right) is invited to do so.

Step 10: Continued to take personal inventory and when we were wrong promptly admitted it.

IT: What is imperfect about us as human beings is that at times the wrong part will find its way to the Throne of our being, and wrongs will occur. What is perfect about us human beings is our Spiritual Nature, our Spirit, our Inspired True Adult Self. When we perpetrate some wrong we self-diagnose and Shift into the appropriate part, and then are willing and able to right the wrong. This overcomes shame.

Step 11: Sought through prayer and meditation to improve our conscious contact with God as we understood Him, praying only for knowledge of His will for us and the power to carry that out.

IT: On a regular basis performed any and all methods that promote the Shift to our IS so that we are ever more consistently operating out of all the wisdom, guidance inspiration, and love that is contained therein and ever available to us.

Step 12: Having had a spiritual awakening as the result of these steps, we tried to carry this message to alcoholics, and to practice these principles in all our affairs.

IT: Looking at ourselves through the lens of IT, and thereby gaining greater ability to operate with integrity, we have much to share with our fellows, and our lives shine.

From *Twenty-Four Hours A Day,* March 12, we read:

That's what you do in A.A. You come to yourself. Your alcoholic self is not your real self. Your sane, sober, respectable self is your real self. That's why we alcoholics are so happy in A.A.

--Walker

The twelve steps, when properly and diligently worked, like IT, can facilitate the Shift from child in charge to adult in charge in the psyche. Such a Shift sure can put a big dent in a person's shame core. That is a very good thing.

Personality Integration Therapy is not a substitute for the Twelve-Step Program of Alcoholics Anonymous (or "any addiction" anonymous). What it is, is another tool that can be used by the addict striving for recovery. IT in no way replaces the twelve-step program. The power of the recovering community, as well as the common focus found there, are just the tip of the iceberg of what is provided by the anonymous programs. But IT can make the twelve steps more accessible for some people, and may even help create a certain synergy when used as an adjunct. The twelve steps are shame busters. So is IT. Together they can make a very powerful pair. It can be a very good fit.

When a person engages in the IT process, any underlying addiction will become evident. It can't be overlooked or ignored when the IT process is pursued. It will come to light. IT does not guarantee that an addiction will be *dealt with* by the addicted person, but IT will uncover it. Through IT treatment the addiction will no longer be a secret—the client will become aware of it. Once this addiction becomes evident, the client must deal with it in order to continue IT treatment. This isn't an arbitrary rule; it is a fact. Addiction is a growth-stopper and IT is about really growing up.

Whenever I have worked with a client suffering with untreated addiction my first phase focus (if they are not already working in a twelve step program) is geared to getting them into such a program. Integration Therapy can effectively uncover an underlying addiction, but it is not the primary treatment for addiction. It can be a powerful adjunct.

In looking at the twelve steps through the lens of IT, it seems clear that this too is a system with the Shift built into it. IT is highly compatible and when added can help create synergy.

An important effect that IT offers to addicts in recovery is a better understanding of what the negative voices in the head really are, and what they are not. The negative impact that the unchecked DTL can have on mental stability and recovery can be weakened and even overcome with IT awareness and work. A boogyman uncovered loses its power to terrify and control. Further, by thinking in terms of the parts in the psyche, some people are able to more quickly begin to develop a more realistic view of themselves. With that, their *genuine* self-image improves. The terrible central culprit "shame" can be even more directly confronted and dealt with. One of the many reasons the twelve steps are highly effective for so many who once would have been considered hopeless cases by the medical community is because by working those steps the person confronts and begins to overcome shame. Addicts are known for inflated, grandiose, and entitled self-images. But that is merely a defense for a mistaken secret low self-image. As the addiction progresses and the addict behaves in more and more devious ways the gap between the secret and the public false self-images widens and shame increases. The steps provide a powerful process for dealing with shame. IT can be helpful to the addict in that process because it zeros-in to uncover blocks to working steps 1, 2, and 3. It can also be a very helpful and important part of step 4—the self-honesty step. The more quickly the person with addictions can become realistic about themselves, the more they are able to let go of shame, the more they are able to "Let go and let God." IT can greatly enhance that process.

The Dry Drunk Phenomenon

Occasionally, people wishing to break the drink habit, or any other addiction, will seek to do so on their own power. Though rare, there have been those who have succeeded in "quitting" long-term without attending A.A. or the appropriate twelve-step program. At least they seem to have succeeded. There are those too, who are members in good standing that stop using their "substance," but find little joy in the process, no matter how long they have been working at it. This is sometimes referred to as "white knuckle" sobriety. In such a case, some would say that the KID used drinking to shut out the overwhelmingly critical yelling of the Dead Tape Horror Show, and then were able to stop drinking by letting the Dead Tapes take over. That would be an example of a person with no real faith in a *higher* power choosing what would seem to be the lesser of two evils. This can be achieved by some individuals through the power of group support. IT would suggest that these rare souls are actually handling the problem by operating out of the DTL. In perhaps many of these cases, there has been no real surrender by the KID part. Too ashamed? Too scared? Too angry? Too scared or ashamed of their anger? In such a situation, the True Adult has not really been summoned. Lip service aside, the drinking/using KID seems to have been subdued by the rigid, robotic Dead Tapes. These folks are then, in fact, still living the Lower Life, rather than the life in the fourth dimension that Bill Wilson (A.A. co-founder) so deftly described, that comes as a result of "turning it over." When this is the case, the person's personality is flat, or agitated, or "all business" (GRUMPY!), and they wear the face of depression. Therapy can be helpful and sometimes a medication evaluation is indicated in just such a scenario. Bill Wilson himself took anti-depressants after becoming sober.

Narcotics Anonymous (the twelve-step experts on drugs per say) considers doctor prescribed psychotropic medications an outside issue. They do not have opinions on outside issues. They have no quarrel with drugs that have no street value (no ability to get a person high). The worst part for the person suffering so and going untreated, is that they are functioning as a pseudo-adult. There is no real adult development. They do not grow up. And often they believe that this is all there is. They do not realize that they are still living the Lower Life. They have not really dealt with their addiction functionally. They are not in "recovery." They are squashing the addict KID part with Dead Tapes rather than letting the KID off the hook. Very different. When a person has surrendered, and the KID is off the Throne, the KID is free to begin showing up in that person's life in the way that it was meant to. It does not matter whether medication was used to get the KID off the Throne or not. Whatever is necessary should be done. What matters is to get the KID off the control panel! When that is accomplished, the KID is free to be a KID and laughter and joy get sprinkled about. This can be true even if the recovering addict's life is not yet perfect.

If someone is sober and depressed, or sober and avoiding life, are they really sober? Sobriety can bring with it wonderful life changes. If someone has been sober for some time and perhaps are even in therapy, and still are not experiencing a much better life, could medication help? Maybe. As more people learn about IT and the parts and how they function with addiction, the less likely that a "dry drunk" or "white knuckle" episode will go undiagnosed and left untreated.

The Inspired Life

Sometimes when people embark on a twelve-step journey (or on a spiritual path for the first time), the life they had built during their years in addiction (or spiritually asleep) crumbles. It may have appeared to be a good life. On the surface of things it may seem almost ironic and unjust that just as they get sober their life seems to fall apart. But let's look a little more closely. In IT terms, the life that was built during the time of active addiction was most probably built *by* the Lower Life cast of characters, i.e., the pseudo-adult in them—the Dead Tape Library and/or the KID! If that is the case, the life in question was not built by the IS. Once in real recovery they have activated the Inspired True Adult in them and it is very likely that they were *in the wrong life* and the new life will be a better fit. They may have to start at the bottom, but improvements and promotions can come quickly when they are on the right track. If the newbie cooperates—avoids self-pity—they can often be amazed at the new direction of their life. When people get sober, get on a spiritual path, get the KID and the DTL off the Throne, they leave the Lower Life behind and rise to the wonder and promise of the Inspired Life.

Then There's the Pink Cloud

Eckhart Tolle (not an alcoholic), author of bestseller *The Power of Now*, tells about a profound experience he had that sounds a bit like the "pink cloud" syndrome that many a newcomer to the twelve steps may experience short-term and early on in their sobriety. With Eckhart, it seems that it never faded. What he talks about in his book is a complete ego (IT = KID & DTL) deflation experience that was born out of absolute despair. In IT terms, he abruptly stopped living the Lower Life and made the Shift. His higher, wiser Self (IT=IS) seems to have taken up what appears to be permanent residence on the Throne of his being. He came home to himself and his life changed dramatically. For most people the Shift into a more heavenly state of mind does not last long and upon reentry into "earth's atmosphere," they have to begin working at the "letting go," KID off the Throne, process one step at a time. But the pink cloud is a promise well worth remembering through any tough times that may come. A.A., *The Power of Now*, and IT are all pointing to the same payoff for the practitioner: *a way out* of the nightmare of the Lower Life. When the three systems are considered together much progress can be made.

Example #2: IT and Obsessive-Compulsive Dis-order (OCD)

In the Illness Model, OCD is graded for severity of symptoms on a continuum. On a 1 to 10 scale patients are rated according to how much they believe their OCD thoughts. From 1, wherein they know their thoughts are not real but still can't stop themselves from performing the behaviors of the disorder, all the way to 10, wherein they can't tell what is real or not real. Generally, OCD is thought to have a physical component in the brain and to be at least partially caused by a streptococcal bacterial infection (strep throat). That said, through the lens of IT, OCD and its symptoms can be greatly aggravated or minimized by certain other factors. The IT view would suggest that OCD becomes a brilliant survival technique developed by the KID. It is labeled a disorder when it begins to turn on the person and restricts their life. But its original development by the KID in childhood serves as a protection. It is of the KID, by the KID, and for the KID. It is lodged in the KID.

I first fully recognized this in a flash of insight when I was working with a very bright young woman I'll call Margo. She suffered gravely from OCD symptoms, but it soon became clear that she was very capable and high functioning at her job. In fact, she seemed to be free of symptoms in that environment altogether. However, at home with her husband, as she described it, she thought and behaved like a frightened child. When at work she operated like an adult. When at home, she had multiple, strong OCD symptoms. It became clear that in the work environment Margo was able to get the KID off the Throne (even the part of the KID that suffered with OCD) quite automatically, effortlessly. At work there were no symptoms. She functioned like an autonomous adult. It would then appear that OCD must be lodged in the KID part in the psyche and that OCD symptoms appear or increase when triggered by the particular environment or by someone or something in it. OCD is lodged in the KID.

With this concept in mind, a person seeking treatment will be assisted by the IT therapist to gain awareness of a stronger part (the IS) that can begin to deal with the clever but distressed KID in their psyche. According to Personality Integration Theory, the KID part can develop obsessions and then act out their inevitable compulsions as a distraction from what the KID is really afraid of in life. Often it is a clever way to engage the mind when it is forbidden to be mad at someone very powerful and scary. When overwhelmed with anger at a caretaker who is unable to see any flaw in themselves (i.e. a very controlling parent) what's a KID to do? OCD is a device for survival, brilliantly devised in childhood as a distraction from what is (during childhood) overwhelming and too frightening to admit or deal with. Symptoms can include various contamination worries. Unconsciously this can symbolize a sense of being "contaminated" (invaded) by a symbiotic (enmeshed), demanding, and over-controlling parent. It then becomes so powerfully embedded that medication may well be required to enable the KID in the treatment seeker the ability to let go of the Throne.

Just a Thought:
When John Steinbeck penned, "A sad soul can kill you quicker, far quicker than a germ," was he really on to something?

With medication and IT treatment the person is guided to validate and rescue the angry child of their past, and to more realistically evaluate what mom or dad was really like and how they (the person in treatment) really felt (and how the KID in them still feels) about them. An IT technique used with OCD sufferers is to recognize that an onset or increase of "OCD symptoms" is a signal to look for "Who are you mad at?" now and in this given situation, or "What (old fear, or relationship, or memory) is being triggered?" from your past.

As a part of the treatment process, when Margo's symptoms would flare she was able to learn how to manage them while working on what the triggers and underlying issues were. By "managing them" Margo was acknowledging to the KID in her that they were manageable and she had to some degree become the observer and a companion of the KID rather than just *being* the symptomatic frightened KID. Over time, Margo became clear that there was always a trigger (person or event) and she could look for it. She also came to understand the symptoms were clues to what happened to her in childhood. This greatly empowered her. Once a person realizes the onset or increase in symptoms are not random occurrences, that they are grounded in events, they become less frightening and the person feels less at their mercy. Coming to understand that as irrational as the symptoms may seem to be, they are purposeful and almost predictable can be a major relief. Secret shame can greatly fade. Further, it gives the person a functional job to do once the symptoms reassert. Margo's OCD symptoms became less severe and less frequent and of shorter duration, and she developed more and more self-confidence and mastery over them. She believed them less and less and felt far less at their mercy when they did reassert. She had learned that they did not come "out of the blue," but rather in response to some old wound being triggered. This gave her greater and greater self-control. Margo was eventually able to discover and develop her own real interests and talents and go on to live her "own" life.

IT has no quarrel with other methods, largely behavioral and cognitive behavioral, commonly used in the treatment of OCD such as Exposure and Response Prevention Therapy. IT can be useful in conjunction with such techniques and adds an empowering self-awareness piece that can greatly increase motivation and self-image in the person seeking treatment. Because IT does not just treat the symptoms, it can be extremely helpful in untying the knots that underlie the symptoms.

Example #3: IT and Depression

Depression is generally not a primary condition. It is a symptom of other phenomena, often unconscious. In the fading paradigm of the illness model of mental health, depression is a set of symptoms that take over the person. Symptoms overwhelm the patient and life is curtailed. Many normal activities become difficult, if not impossible, to perform. Thoughts become dark and brooding. Muscles become heavy and can feel paralyzed. The brain chemistry can both cause and can reflect the impact of the condition, i.e., it can become a vicious cycle. Some treatments in the old school approach include medications, behavioral approaches, and talk therapy. Those who value talk therapy recognize that there are unresolved conflicts and anger to be processed. The goal is for the person to work through unconscious conflicts and to heal.

IT would say that medication may or may not be required to calm the angry and frightened KID enough to loosen its grip on the control panel of the person's life in order to allow the emergence of the Inspired Self. However, a word of caution by noted clinical neuro-scientist and author of *Magnificent Mind at any Age,* Dr. Daniel Amen, suggests that giving everyone the same treatment (Prozac all around) is a problem in today's medical treatment model.

The IT treatment for depression would include:

- Uncovering the old wounds and mistaken beliefs, and unconscious conflicts from childhood.
- Validating the KID for any discovered trauma, neglect, or abuse once suffered (and still suffering residually). Giving the KID *permission* to be as mad as they *are*. Giving the KID permission and *encouragement* to express the anger appropriately.
- Rescuing the stuck in time part of the KID. Teaching the KID it has already survived.
- The Shift—be with the KID. The KID discovers it is not alone. The KID gives up the Throne and feels taken care of and free to be a KID.
- Internally holding the perpetrators responsible. (Reminder: It is never necessary to confront the offenders. It is a choice.)
- Referral for medication evaluation as indicated.

William James, the father of American psychology, was born in 1842 into a wealthy family. His younger brother Henry is well known as a great American writer. William, who was the oldest of five siblings, wished to be an artist—a painter. This displeased his father. After a brief attempt at art school he declared himself to be a less than talented artist and followed his father's wishes to study science instead. He went to medical school at Harvard and took up a life on the scientific path. Subsequently, he suffered from severe bouts of depression. Years later he would at times speak of a "murdered self" that was left behind in that life altering decision to leave art school. A man of great insight, and great disappointment, he deeply pondered the human condition. When James began to suffer severe depression he determined to heal by what he called returning to the vital life. He believed that through free will he could will himself back to health. And he did. He made a great study of the spiritual aspect of the person. Basically, James believed that by using his free will to access a higher power (to join with the Creator) he was able to co-create and become revitalized (return to life).

Further, according to Stephen C. Rowe in *The Vision of James* (p. 8):

Learning to "assert deepest self" and to let go of a more superficial self (that would, among other things, seek to control others) is at the center of ... William's legacy to us.

The Jamesian deepest self correlates with the IT concept of the Inspired Self part, and his "more superficial self" could suggest the IT concepts of the Lower Life and the KID and the Dead Tape Library.

Rowe goes on to state (p. 43):

...James... in effect, is making a radical distinction between two levels or even modes of self. The first and ordinary level of self...insists in its exclusive right to dominate and control. But life will "teach the lesson" and lead to the death of this self and the subsequent birth of a deeper second self, one that is identified as "will" in the writings of James. The second self is paradoxically both that aspect that is most intimately and truly myself, and at the same time the place in myself where I open or am confluent with the higher or wider vitalities of...universe.

According to James:

Every bit of us at every moment is part and parcel of a wider self, it quivers along various radii like the wind-rose on a compass, and the actual in it is continuously one with possibilities not yet in our present sight. And just as we are coconscious with our own momentary margin, may not we ourselves form the margin of some more really central self in things which is coconscious with the whole of us? May not you and I be confluent in a higher consciousness, and confluently active there, tho' we now know it not?

--James (1909/1977, p. 131)

For background understanding of the development of William's thinking Rowe points the reader to the beliefs of William's father, Henry Sr. He was a seeker after the teachings of the 18th Century Swedish mystic Emanuel Swedenborg, and according to Rowe (p. 5):

Henry believed that God is incarnate in all of humankind; that "the fall" is not a fundamental part of the human condition... but rather a result of individual egotism; and that human well-being lies in giving up egotistic pursuits by joining God's work of perfecting creation through liberating the natural divinity and goodness of human beings.

One of the great frustrations expressed by James late in his life was the fact that his psychological concepts never fully formed into a system of psychology. Many of his concepts that included the spiritual nature of man were destined to play a major part in the concepts of the program of Alcoholics Anonymous. Between the practical spirituality of A.A. and the spiritual psychology of IT, Jamesian concepts may be coming closer to finding their "system."

Example #4: IT and Bipolar I and II (Manic Depression)

The unchecked mood swings of Bipolar disorders can and do wreak havoc in the lives of the sufferers as well as in the lives of loved ones, friends, and employers. With proper medication it is possible for the swings to be effectively controlled in duration, degree, and frequency of occurrence for many who seek treatment. However, as with some of those who suffer from just depression, one of the most difficult problems with this diagnosis can be the tendency for some to stop taking medication when an upswing begins—when the person begins to feel better. Some people just do not grasp that they feel better because of the medication.

With Bipolar Disorder, depression and mania can range from moderate to profound, and even to psychotic. When a person begins to experience a swing into the manic state, one of the first things to go is their ability to judge what is reasonable. IT would say they had Shifted and now have the judgment of a child. With their judgment gone they generally make decisions that create chaos. Then, after a period of hours, days, weeks, or months, and as the person then sinks into the inevitable depression, they often experience terrible feelings of shame for their manic behavior. They feel humiliated. IT would say that the DTL is shaming the KID. Both mania and depression when left unchecked can lead to suicide.

IT teaches people to nip the highs in the bud and with that reduce the depth and duration of the depression that follows. Because IT recognizes the mood disorder with its swings to be lodged in the KID part only, the person can begin to view the phenomena quite differently than they would if they were to continue to believe that they were just a powerless victim of it. They can learn to pull in the reigns on the KID as a manic episode presents. Because the KID with manic depression has such powerfully strong symptoms, medication is extremely important, of course. But also important is the ability to understand that they can directly affect the course of a given swing with education and effort. By actively participating in the restraint of symptoms, they can greatly reduce the depth of the inevitable crash following a manic swing as well as reducing the duration and degree of the mania. Medication is extremely important for the KID with this diagnosis. IT can greatly improve the prognosis. Once again, self-esteem improves with the recognition that it is not the entire person who has the disorder, but rather it is just a part. And they come to understand that they have the power to impact the course of any episodes that may present, and the course of the disorder in their lives.

Example #5: IT and Paranoia

In the old paradigm paranoia is considered to be a psychotic disorder. The symptoms include delusions of persecution and/or delusions of grandeur. Paranoia can stand alone or, more likely, be a component of other symptom clusters. Imagine paranoia and OCD/religiosity, for example, or paranoia and depression. Paranoia can greatly intensify other conditions and make them more difficult to treat. What is it, where does it come from, and how can it best be dealt with?

You've probably heard the old joke: "Just because you're paranoid doesn't mean you're *not* being followed." The problem with that is that we tend to get what we expect in life!

Paranoia in a nutshell: A suspicion that you are not "in the know," and that there are secret, and even conspiratorial, forces at work that fly beneath the radar, and you are therefore in imminent danger and need to beware destructive events that can come out of nowhere. (Sound familiar?)

Once again, IT would suggest that the symptoms are in the KID, and are aggravated by hideous recordings in the DTL. Just what might cause the KID to develop such beliefs, reactions, and symptoms? And just where do the stored recordings originate? Let's go back to Chapters 1 and 2 and take a look at roles, role shaping, and abuse. The fourth child, the Pet, can feel all the family stress, but gets no information about what is actually going on. *Something* is going on, but no one is talking. The Pet is left alone to process the stress in his own imagination with the skills of a child. When that does not get properly resolved, the person carries the generalized sense of unspoken danger into all areas of life even into adulthood. The third child, the Lost Child, can also carry the paranoid feelings of any other family member right into adulthood. The second child, the Scapegoat, can "learn" that criticism and attacks can come at any time from anywhere. And don't assume that the Hero child escapes the possibility of becoming paranoid. His inner sense of inadequacy sets him up to live in fear of being suddenly exposed. The point is paranoia has its roots in childhood and settles into the KID, and is reinforced by recordings in the DTL.

If one or more parent or sibling is prone to sudden, out of the blue outbursts, i.e., physical attacks, tantrums, etc., the child can't predict when it is coming, from where, or how to stop it, or how to at least protect himself. The child learns he is powerless in a war zone. As a chronological adult, such a former child can carry a powerful sense of being kept in the dark about impending doom. Such an adult could have difficulty taking others at face value. Their basic trust in the fundamental goodness of people has been shattered by early shaping and horrific and unpredictable abuse in their own family.

The fact that there is a certain percentage of grown people who, due to childhood history of abuse and trauma, suffer from paranoia in varying degrees (from mild to clinically diagnosed) has become of new concern in this high-tech age of information access and internet connectedness. Those who suffer in such ways now have access to one another. They can find validation, support, and synergy for their fears world-wide. They believe the whispers and dispute the facts. They are ripe for manipulation by those who would seek to take advantage of their fears and suggestibility—by those who would exploit their vulnerability for their own ends. In fact, nationally and internationally they have sometimes become political pawns and have, as such, become actual political forces in the world.

Paranoia is difficult to treat. To directly confront the conspiracy theories by presenting evidence and facts to the paranoiac is rarely curative. This is true because those who confront the paranoid person simply become "part of the conspiracy" in their eyes. Because of this medications can be necessary to calm the terrified, delusional KID in them enough for them to be able to begin accessing a calmer, wiser part. Paranoia can make medication an issue in itself. Only by *experiencing* a sense of serenity (even just in momentary flashes at first), only by *experiencing* the calm that comes from the IS, can the paranoid KID begin to let go and begin to live in a "safer" universe and thereby find a true sense of community.

Example #6: IT and Migraine Headaches

In our current culture migraine headaches are treated primarily as a medical condition. Treatments include many new breakthrough medications.

Personality Integration Theory suggests that as with other symptoms, migraines originate only in the KID part and show up in the brain. Further, the theory proposes that they occur when the KID feels in some way trapped. If the KID in you is enraged at someone (past and being triggered, or present), and feels that it is impossible to express that rage (and even that it is impossible to be aware of the rage because it "can't" be expressed, or because the KID would be "bad" to be mad at "whomever"), the KID is effectively in a trap. What happens to the energy created by the unacknowledged rage? IT suggests that like a pressure cooker with the lid on tight, the steam builds up and results in the migraine.

The IT treatment method is to ask the KID the question "Who are you mad at?" This question is asked over and over until the answer pops into consciousness. The human brain can't not answer, or at least pursue the answer to, a question. The brain is geared to seek the answer to any question asked. If the answer exists in the unconscious, it will come to consciousness. The answer may not come out of the mouth, but the brain will have its answer!

Asking the question, "Who are you mad at?"

1. Immediately gives the KID permission to be mad.
2. Tells the KID it is not alone.
3. Pulls the true answer from the depths of the unconscious.

What is interesting about this theory is that each time it has been applied with clients in treatment the migraine is dissolved. Eventually, many clients stop getting them altogether. When one does present, they look inside for who they are mad at and feeling that they can't be. The answer always comes. They know it's the right answer because once the angry KID has been validated the migraine begins to fade and go away.

Example #7: IT and Weight Control

"Dear God, please feed my hunger and restore my right mind."
--Marianne Williamson

What we are:

hungry for,
thirsty for,
lonely for,
yearning for,
is the True Self.

What we are hungry for is us. "Us" in this scenario includes our Superconscious awareness and our connection to Cosmic Consciousness—the All There Is. Some call it the God connection.

Obesity is one of the few ways an abandoned KID (an actual child or the KID in you) has of self-protecting. Obesity is a way to "make" yourself be bigger—more substantial—stronger. It is also a way to put "something" (more flesh) between the KID and the environment. Also, food can numb the feelings quite nicely. All-in-all, it's a smart way for the abandoned little KID (in you) to deal if *you* (IS) are not going to show up and do the *required* protecting. Oh, and then there's the idea that it can take you right out of the romance, love, and sex game (especially if that is what is believed and expected). And when you realize that what is craved is mostly fun foods with sugar and flour, it becomes clear that what the obese person is dealing with is a child's palate. What most "overeaters" crave is refined sugar and white flour—no veggies, please. When the KID is on the Throne sugar is craved. When the IS is on the Throne the palate actually changes to that of a sophisticated adult. This is just yet more evidence that supports the theory that we are parts. The Shift creates an actual change in the palate.

IT works best for weight control issues when used in conjunction with twelve-step food addictions programs. IT can be a useful and even synergistic adjunct to twelve-step work for this issue. (See IT, Alcoholics Anonymous, and the Addict.) Beyond that, it can be important and helpful to use IT methods to deal with psychological issues often associated with weight concerns. These may include fear of fat, fear of people, fear of sex and relationships, fear of success, etc. The KID can be gently assisted off the Throne by developing various IT scripts to address the pertinent weight-centered issues.

> "Dear God, please feed my hunger and restore my right mind."
>
> --Williamson

By repeating the above quote by author Marianne Williamson, IT would suggest that the KID is inviting the IS: to deal with the real hungers, and to step up and be present, and take over the Throne. That is to say, Marianne's quote is yet another Method that can be used to create the Shift. By praying that prayer, the KID is inviting intervention. In her book, *A Course In Weight Loss,* (based in part upon concepts found in *A Course In Miracles),* she recommends *writing it down* thirty times in the morning and again thirty times in the evening for three consecutive days. Or, writing your own script that talks *to* the KID is also a viable option that can create the desired Shift. It is not at all unusual for people to choose a weight-loss method and to successfully get the weight off. Successful weight-loss methods can include various commercial weight-loss programs, pills, exercise, religion, and surgery. The problem is that the actual weight loss, though difficult, is not the most difficult part of the weight problem. A long-term success for most people dealing with this issue is very rare. In fact, the long-term success rate is dismal.

Most people who are able to lose weight gain it all back and then some within six months to a year after achieving goal weight. Because of this, many programs today do attempt to offer plans for maintenance, and life-style changes are encouraged. Yet, the long-term prognosis remains poor. The problem is complex. For example, in long-term studies of preemies over time (as they grow up) it has been discovered that obesity rates are higher for them than for the general population. Recent studies have shown that this can be due to nutritional deprivation in infancy. This causes a brain deficiency in the development of the mechanism that functions like a regulator to register when the belly is full. The nutritionally deprived infant does not develop the "brakes" that are required in order to have control over food intake later in life. Even so, with a twelve-step program, therapy, and a nutritional food plan, prognosis can greatly improve. IT would say that there is a part (IS) that can overcome even some physical conditions under the right circumstance. IT methods and other programs (such as Marianne's) can add to a better outcome because they address the deeper imbedded issues in the KID. They draw upon the higher, wiser, spiritual part to provide actual healing and to take control of food intake. The IS not only can stand between the "hungry" KID and the world out there, but can actually fill the KID up.

With IT methods people are encouraged to deal with the food, body, weight, and eating issues of the KID and the DTL. The process can be very enlightening and as the IS becomes engaged, the prognosis can improve markedly. When real and proper boundaries are set in a person's relationships (this can only be done by the IS), the person is safe and living from inspiration. When living from inspiration (which can come and go, especially at first) there is no reason to overeat. It is the unprotected, abandoned, emotional KID that eats addictively.

People who are living the Inspired Life are full of love, promise, curiosity, adventure, and joy. With all of that there is no room for extra food.

Hint: To stay in the Inspired Mode some people choose to avoid sugar and refined flour. When avoided altogether, cravings can become a thing of the past. Also, sugar and flour reportedly make alcohol in the gut and this can tend to get the KID stirred up.

Example #8: IT and Post Traumatic Stress Disorder

PTSD is a condition gaining much attention in our current environment of Iraq and Afghanistan War returnees. More soldiers are actually surviving serious, and what once would have been lethal, wounds. As they return from war we are seeing an increased incidence of PTSD among that population. Some of the symptoms of that syndrome include anticipatory anxiety that is worse than fearing something real. When triggered, automatic thoughts occur at the speed of light. The individual operates as if in a previous and dangerous or horrifying situation. They go into a deep trance state. For proper treatment the internal dialogue must change and the thoughts must slow down. In IT language the KID has gotten stuck in time and place and requires rescue. The severity of symptoms is correlated with the severity of the original event but also with the severity and level of abuse experienced in childhood. The more abused the sufferer was in childhood the more fertile the psyche, the more "prepared" it is, to embed the traumatic event when it occurs, and therefore, the more powerfully stuck the fragment of the psyche can become. PTSD is a severe form of triggered regression and actually blocks awareness of current time and place. This creates a severe trance state. All symptoms reside in the KID and serve as clues that can be followed backward to determine what happened and how to heal. *All Symptoms Are Purposeful. They Are Clues to Follow to "What Happened."* (And not just in Vietnam, Iraq and Afghanistan.) *They Are Nature's Maps to Healing.*

Example #9: IT and Severe Anxiety

Anxiety has been called the "what if" disease. It can stand alone or combine with other symptom clusters. IT would say that anxiety is the result of the abandoned and overwhelmed KID sitting on the Throne and unable to handle life and its various situations, or the DTL shaming and working up the KID with dire warnings and unnamed hauntings from old buried abuses, and unreasonable demands. A child doesn't have any way of knowing what is a real threat and what is imagined. A child lacks the necessary skill set to handle adult issues and problems. It is common for the family pet (role) to carry anxiety into adult years. The family pet, remember, was not let in on the actual problems of the family, but did experience all the energy of the feelings floating around. In other words, they felt the worry and fear, but had nothing to attach it all too. Life then became just scary in and of itself. Therefore, the pet is prone to generalized anxiety and unnamed fears. The lost child too can carry the anxiety of the other family members, as that child becomes the one who validates and the caretaker (carrier) for the feelings of the others. In IT treatment it becomes important to challenge the Lower Life thoughts and to use mental discipline to help the KID off the Throne. It can also be helpful to excavate old wounds that haunt. Various breathing exercises and relaxation techniques can be helpful, but becoming aware of the actual roots of anxiety and the mechanisms at play are essential in the IT process.

In the end what it all comes down to with the IT approach is that the IS needs to talk, talk, talk to the KID and the DTL!

Example #10: IT and Multiple Personality Disorder (MPD)/ Dissociative Identity Disorder (DID)

Two famous examples of multiples in popular literature are Eve White and Sybil. *The Three Faces of Eve*, first a book and then a famous movie, is based on the actual case history of Chris Costner Sizemore, a Georgia housewife. It was originally documented by psychiatrists Corbett Thigpen and Hervey Cleckley. The 1957 movie based on the book starred Joanne Woodward and was directed by Nunnally Johnson. *Sybil*, first a book by Flora Rheta Schreiber, and then a TV miniseries, is based on the story of Shirley Ardell Mason. Both Eve and Sybil are famous portrayals of the MPD/DID phenomenon and of the complexities of pathology oriented psychiatric treatment. In real life the women portrayed were never really fully recovered from their psychiatric symptoms and struggles.

What IT would offer to treatment for multiples is, once again, the awareness that all symptoms and all personality fragments are in the KID part only. What this means for the person in treatment is an immediate sense of empowerment. Rather than just being a sick person to whom things happen with full dependence on the analytical skills of the experts, they become more able to become a major participant in their own recovery process. They also become protective of the fragment(s) they are trying to rescue and integrate. IT gives them a completely new perspective on the puzzle.

Example #11: IT and Narcissism

True narcissism is the absence of the True Self. The narcissist operates as a child and sees himself as the center of the universe. It goes far beyond a tendency toward self-centeredness. This person cannot see the other people in the world around him as full human beings. Generally, all events are perceived only in the light of the impact on him. If, for example, the teenaged daughter of a true narcissist were to have an untimely pregnancy, the parent would be far more concerned about the impact on him rather on the daughter or whatever child might come of it.

Self-hate is a central aspect for the narcissist, which means that underneath all the selfish behavior is a learned hatred of the self (actually of just the KID part) that comes from severe criticism and neglect or abuse during childhood. This self-hatred has stunted any real growth in the person. Because of the self-hatred, the person must strive for great success to compensate for true identity and craves adulation and the spotlight. In IT terms, the DTL is filled with messages of loathing and is attacking the "horrible" KID, and the KID has thereby learned to hate the KID. This person is filled with an underlying seething rage at those who abused him in the past as well as those who thwart him in the present. All this he works hard to keep from his conscious awareness. Even as the KID is feeling inadequate and despicable, the KID is striving to grab at what everyone wants, which is self-esteem, love, and belongingness. This must come, the KID believes, from others out there. Pleasing them becomes everything. When that goes awry (as it often does) the narcissistic rage can quickly surface.

The IT concept of the parts can make it more possible to address the self-hatred issue and to grow the Inspired Self.

Example #12: IT and Borderline Personality Disorder (BPD)

Another term for this is "unstable personality." Some symptoms common to this "disorder" include:

- Impulsivity
- Vast Feelings of Emptiness
- Mood Swings
- Suicidal Tendencies and Gestures
- Absence of an Internal Compass
- Lack of Loyalty
- Seductiveness
- Manipulation
- Substance Abuse
- Unstable Relationships

Does any of this ring any IT bells? This is the life of an unsupervised and neglected child. This is a person with a vastly underdeveloped True Self. The emptiness they feel is for the Inspired Self (IS) and the active presence of the protected creative aspect of the KID. The terrified aspect of the KID in them is flailing around on the Throne and looking for someone to take care of them (in some perfect way that the KID secretly demands). Their unconscious immature goal is to be taken care of—and in some perfect way. This person has no real conscious sense of the missing part and looks to others for a rudder and a sense of completion. By being seductive they are able to attract suitors, but they tend to take hostages rather than be in reasonable relationship. This person is very wounded and gives off mixed messages due to their own internal conflicts. When they feel internal turmoil, they look outside themselves for the "culprit." Whoever is in range gets blamed even though the problem is inside their psyche. In reality the other person becomes a convenient scapegoat. They therefore push others away, yet don't want to be alone. Filled with self-pity, they are easily triggered to rage and act out in the above listed ways.

This person seeks treatment only when all else fails and no one is forthcoming to rescue them, or they may seek treatment just to get the other guy fixed.

The therapeutic treatment goal is to first assist the person to realize that there is a better way, and that there is much more to life than they have been able to access. In other words they must come to realize that they have been "home alone," and that both the problem and the answer lies inside them—that what they are empty of and lonely for is the True Self. Only then can they begin to experiment with what is ethically in their power to do. They begin to find real power as opposed to manipulation. They discover strength and wisdom and can then and therefore afford real concern for others. They empower themselves. They grow up.

Example #13: IT and Adult ADD

"Your focus determines your reality." --Lucas

Focus is *the* issue for the child and the adult who deals with the symptom cluster known as attention deficit disorder. Lack of focus that results in minimal ability to be organized, general distractibility, and impulsivity can make life very difficult for the sufferer. A good way to understand the usual state of mind of the untreated person with this issue is to think about how children behave when they become over-tired. They can become "wired" or hyper. Under such circumstances they are working hard to stay awake. Their brain wants to sleep, but they don't want to miss anything, so they fight to stay awake. That seems to be similar to the experience of the KID with ADD symptoms. IT tells us there is a part that is always awake. Therefore, what IT would add to the many strategies and tools available today to the adult with ADD symptoms is that there is a part of them that does not *have* ADD. There is a part of them that is always awake. That part can be grown, like a muscle, to run their life. IT teaches that it is the KID that has ADD. It is the KID that is distracted, late, disorganized, unable to focus, etc., and that the answer to Self Mastery can be to *realize* that they can learn to Shift. Diet, supplements, and medicine can enable the KID to wake up enough to make the Shift to a more consistent way of living. When they make the Shift, they have in an instant gained the ability to focus on things that enhance their lives.

****

RESISTANCE

When we decide to change and set out on a course of action to make it happen, it is not at all uncommon to develop resistance to the very change we seek. Once again, this phenomenon can be better understood by realizing that we are parts. What one part seeks, another may fear. The upshot is that we can be very creatively resistant to that which we seek. Under the umbrella of resistance many a seemingly reasonable thought can appear and throw the seeker off course and back into the comfort of old patterns. The following are examples of KID tricks and traps, and DTL deceits that have the power to stop you only if you are unaware that they are just resistance—only if you give them power by believing them.

Some of these forms of resistance have been touched upon in earlier pages of this book, but they deserve a closer look. Keep in mind which part is doing the resisting. You are catching on. (Are we having fun yet?)

Blame

Blame is a bad thing. Today no one with any integrity wants to be a blamer.

Personality Integration Therapy is never a blame game. It is never about blaming. It is *always* about dealing with the impact of what happened in order to gain mastery over it. What is blaming? Blaming seems to be about letting me off the hook because "it" is your fault. Or, blaming you can serve to make me feel superior.

To properly integrate the KID and the DTL it is necessary to hold the perpetrators responsible, but not for the sake of blame. Rather, it is for the sake of *internal integrity*, and to validate the KID in you. In getting honest with yourself about what happened to you, you can stop using your precious energy to trick yourself into believing things not true. Through the eyes of evolution and the eyes of IT, holding the offenders accountable includes the understanding that they were caught in the Lower Life. But a spade is a spade and to pretend it is anything else is a lie to yourself. *A lie to yourself*; how significant is that?

Dealing with what is rather than what "I wish," or what "ought" to be is about accepting God's creation as it really is rather than re-writing the story to make it prettier. Which part of you do you think wants to pretend?

Intent vs. Impact

People get stopped from looking at past abuse or neglect because they believe the perpetrators had no intent to harm. And if that is true, it does matter. But intent, or the lack thereof, never overrides impact. People worry that mom or dad didn't mean to hurt them. Perhaps they were ignorant, or sick, or prone to accidents. So, they feel guilty dredging it all up. Or, they don't want to get mad at a parent they genuinely like today. Still it is the *impact* of abuse or neglect that the victim is left to live with. And so, they are neglecting themselves if they ignore it. Remember the story of mom and the car and your foot? You know that she didn't *intend* to break your foot, but the *impact* broke your foot! The impact of her mistake was that your foot got broken. Would there be pain? Would you go to the doctor to treat it? Even if she didn't mean to break it? Does it do any good to pretend it isn't broken? To pretend you don't know how it happened? Get the point?

If intent is also present, sometimes people can wish to resist that fact, too. It is very painful to face the truth about a parent with that much hostility and disregard. But to ignore what the KID in you knows is true is to abandon the already wounded KID for the sake of a guilty parent. Under such circumstances your job is to help the wounded KID understand that it is not about the KID. The problem is situated *only* in the hostile parent.

Caretaking

If you were raised to care-take your parents' feelings, it can haunt you when you enter therapy. Once again, people generally don't want to disparage the parents of today. They may even feel sorry for them. The antidote to such resistance is to try to begin thinking about giving yourself *permission to stop carrying their feelings.* It is the DTL that carries the message to never make mom or dad feel bad. And the DTL is attacking the KID in you with that message. That message is not for your good. It isn't really even for their good. That message is to protect the Lower Life needs of your parents. It is a remnant from your early training. It means that they (your parents) are still running you from inside your head. The rule of thumb is "not at your expense." What that means is that if pretending you are not mad at the offenders is calling you, or more aptly, causing you to abandon the KID in you on *their* behalf, then you are caretaking them at your expense. You are (*in your own head*) choosing to be loyal to them *instead of* to yourself. If you were abused or neglected, you were trained to not admit it and to not hold the perpetrators responsible. This can cause serious resistance to self knowledge and Self Mastery. After validating the KID by talking honestly about it in your head, tell the KID to go play. Let the KID off that hook. The Inspired Self in you can take care of the situation now.

Being a Good Parent to Your Own Children

When a new client begins to get the idea that there were things mom or dad did that had negative impact on them, they will often think about their own parenting of their own children. I tell them then to think about the big pitcher metaphor. In order to fill up all the little cups you must first adequately fill the big pitcher. Aside from any abusive practices, which must be dealt with immediately, I recommend that they put the worry about their parenting of their children on the shelf for a time and give themselves their main focus. As they deal with their own issues their parenting style will change.

Don't Know for Sure (Self Doubt)

Many a client will resist holding a parent accountable in their own head for abuse or neglect because they believe they have to be absolutely, positively sure that what they *think* happened *did* happen. And they feel a modicum of doubt. It is the nature of abuse and neglect to leave the victim unsure and even feeling unworthy and deserving of the mistreatment. It is part of the abuse syndrome for the victim to question their own sanity, their own recollection, and even whether they may have caused the abuse. The antidote for the self-doubt syndrome is to ask what they think "might" have happened. Ask, "What is *your* truth about this? What belief about this are you *living* with?" They usually say they don't have a belief and at that point I tell them a truth. We live with our best guess. Whether your parent is guilty or not, what assumption are *you living with*? That is what needs to be dealt with; what you "think" is true. It sets them free. They are living with an assumption that doesn't need to be *proven*. The assumption needs to be dealt with. The KID in them needs to be validated. They are free to deal with the KID in them and hold the "culprits" accountable. Over time, the doubts tend to give way and people claim the truth wholeheartedly. Why would they think it might have happened if no such thing happened? In time, people close the gap and come to realize "it" did happen and they did not deserve or cause it. They thusly learn that they can *trust themselves*. They learn that there is an intrinsic honesty within that they can count on. Abuse and neglect is what broke that basic trust in themselves. They were trained to not believe their own instincts and awareness. By doing this work they are on the road to repairing belief in themselves.

The Taproot Effect (Melody)

The idea that no one stood behind us; that our parents were operating as out of control children even just some of the time when we were so little and vulnerable is hard to face. Survival, after all, is threatened for children when there is no adult in charge. But as adults today we can assure the KID within that all of that has already been survived. The KID really doesn't know that until we tell them that it is so, and that it is now safe to be self-honest about it.

****

A Refresher: More About Power

In every given situation (unless under some physical threat) we have power. (See IT Basic Tenets.) We may have to look for it. It may not be easy to find, and we may not like what it is when we find it, but in every situation we have power. It is one of the perfections of this universe. Maybe it is the power to hold one's tongue, or to change ourselves, or to leave a given relationship when we would prefer to change the other person or somehow change the situation. It is always our job to find the power we have (never power over others; our personal power) and to exercise it even if we would rather change someone else.

****

Other Issues of Interest in the IT Treatment Model

~ IT Treatment and Major Loss and Grief

We all, at times, experience real loss and the accompanying deep grief. The loss of a loved one through death or even through divorce, the loss of a limb, a career, or even the loss of a pet can bring on real grieving. Real losses will upset the equilibrium and require a genuine period of bereavement. There is no right or wrong when it comes to grieving. It is an individual process. It comes and goes in waves. It moves like a rollercoaster. And it takes as long as it takes.

Permission can become a very important word in the grieving journey:

Permission to feel whatever you feel—no judgment.

Permission to take as long as it takes—no judgment.

Permission to be different than you were—no judgment.

Permission to do strange things you might never have done before—no judgment.

It is the KID in us that experiences the wound of great loss and needs to be allowed to feel whatever s/he feels. Allowed, not abandoned. The DTL must be closely guarded against. What is normal for the KID to feel in such a situation? It is normal to feel angry. Angry at the lost loved one for leaving. No judgment. This is what the KID part feels at such a time. It really is an immature part that needs support and understanding. It is not the rational part of you. It does not have to have rational feelings. S/he needs to be allowed to express to you anger, fear, confusion, etc. When people don't know about the parts, they can become horrified at their irrational anger at God, at their irrational anger at the beloved one who died. So, they deny it. And symptoms worsen.

There is another part that can be there to shoulder the great burden of loss. There is a part untouched by grief—by loss, a part in you that is connected to the Divine, that can whisper to the KID through the tears, can whisper of hope, of comfort, and of the eternal nature of love. When the KID is allowed to be real to you, s/he can begin to experience that greater sense of connectedness, and s/he can begin to heal in whatever amount of time it takes.

****

~IT Treatment and Couples

Once, while on travel to a conference in NYC, I met a bright young couple from Amsterdam in a coffee shop over breakfast. They were fresh from Europe and thrilled with their plans to travel across the USA and to be married once they arrived in "The West!" They were an adorable, in love, adventuresome young couple, and full of infectious enthusiasm. During light conversation it came out that I work with couples in counseling. They quickly asked me for advice. Looking at their open, fresh, eager young faces I felt both a sense of responsibility and of opportunity. And I had one brief moment to deliver. They got my 30-second "elevator" version of "How to Have a Happy Marriage and Remain Best Friends." It all boiled down to 2 words of advice:

- Don't look too closely at each other—look together out there at the ever-widening horizon.
- Be willing to let the other go.

After a moment of thoughtful silence, they looked at each other and nodded rather solemnly. I took it as a signal of profound understanding. They then both thanked me profusely, and said that they took meeting me as a good omen and promised to heed my words. Then they were off to roar off on their motorbike into abundant, joyous, adventuresome life.

I often think of them and smile. In my mind they are happy and joyous and free to this very day.

It only takes one "mature" person in a relationship to raise the functioning of the relationship as a whole. The problem is that in our relationships today it is often the KID in me that is in relationship to the KID in you. The KID is not up for the duties, responsibilities, and other requirements of a healthy marriage, and how KIDs can trigger one another! Or the DTL in you is married to the KID in me. Oh, how I can let you make me suffer! Neither the KID nor the DTL should be running your marriage.

It is not uncommon today for couples to have a difference of opinion and even motivation concerning the state of their relationship. This can occur because what is satisfying for the KID or the DTL in one may step on the other's toes. When one is feeling the need for change but the other is unwilling to seek help, couples counselors can have little or nothing to offer.

With IT only one partner is needed to seek and effect change.

One of the great perfections in our universe (Perfection #4) guarantees that my actual boundaries will not conflict with yours. As I am learning to set mine, I am also setting yours in the areas of life where they connect.

It only takes one mature person to raise the functioning of the relationship as a whole.

The SECRETS to a happy and successful relationship are:

1. *You have to be willing to lose the other person.*
2. *Focus on what needs to be changed in you.*
3. *Look, not so much at each other, rather look at life together.*
4. *Learn and practice the ABCDs of a happy marriage.*

#1. If you are not willing to risk losing your beloved, you may find you have no leverage.

Once a relationship begins to get into trouble, the one who cares the least in that given relationship holds the power.

That does not mean that you actively seek to throw your partner out. That would be like throwing the baby out with the dirty bathwater. You do need to get your own power back and let them have theirs. They may well change, and/or your attitude toward them will change when you function as a True Adult. What being willing to lose them does is set a limit on what you will tolerate in the other's behavior. It doesn't guarantee the relationship will survive, but as you function out of the Inspired Self in you, your partner will lose any power they may have unfairly wielded over you. When you become willing to let them go if necessary, they must step up or lose *you.* At first they will most likely step up the attempt to control you, and you will probably see flashes or full episodes of their misplaced ancient rage (childhood rage at caregivers long stored). If you persist in kind ways (Rudolf Dreikurs, a student of Alfred Adler, taught "kindness with firmness" in *Children: The Challenge*) to set firm limits, they may well come around. There are never any guarantees, but you can stack the deck in favor of improvement. Your *only* leverage in such a relationship is your willingness to let them go. If you can't fathom losing them, ask yourself why that is the case. IT would suggest that you want more from them than they are meant or equipped to give. If this is the case go directly to #2!

The person who is most detached holds the power. As you function more consistently out of the IS you are less likely to try to control them. Your partner is therefore far less likely to be triggered, and is naturally encouraged to behave more "reasonably" also.

You have to be willing to lose the other person. To do that, you have to get the KID in you off the Throne and out of your marriage. Then hurry off to deal with your unmet needs yourself!

#2. Focus on what needs to be changed in you.

This is where your personal power lies. When you use your power in this way you may well have a great deal of influence on others. That can't be your goal; it can be an outcome.

Your unmet needs from childhood are not ever going to be met by your partner.

If things have seriously deteriorated from a happy courtship, you can safely assume that that is most probably what is going on. One (or more likely both) of you is seeking to get the old wounds healed by the other. Can't happen. No one can read your mind but you. No one else can calm the KID in you in long-term and meaningful ways. Your work must be done by you internally. We have to learn to meet our own needs and only then are we free to enjoy each other's company.

Harville Hendricks has written extensively on the subject of relationships. He maintains that marriage gives us the opportunity to get our childhood wounds brought to the surface, and that that is nature's way of giving us the opportunity to heal them. IT agrees that the spouse can bring it out, but stresses that you must heal your own wounds. And it is not your job to push your partner to do the same!

Old joke: God invented marriage because in it each partner drives the other to seek God!

In Al-anon people are amazed that when they begin to focus on their own life, their alcoholic partner often "magically" gets better. That same partner may even end up quitting the drink thing altogether. Similarly, with IT methods and concepts, people can begin to find their boundaries and as they change they will have impact (often profound) on their partner. As new boundaries are discovered and set, the partner will either adapt, seek to join in counseling, or leave. If the partner decides to leave the relationship it is usually with the approval of the IT client. Occasionally, the person in treatment will come to the decision to leave, but this is fairly rare. When a partner begins to operate out of the Inspired Self part in them in their relationship with their significant other, gentle change can remarkably come about. Focus on what needs to be changed in *you.*

#3. Look at the adventure of life together.

Stop focusing on the faults of your partner! When each spouse in a couple is asked to rate how much effort they contribute to the good of the marriage they almost always report that they give 95% and that their spouse gives 5%. Their spouse reports the reverse! Because we can't see what our partner is thinking and processing we can't know what considerations and sacrifices they may be making. Perceptions can't be trusted. Stop focusing on their faults.

If you do this one diligently you will have incorporated #1 and #2.

Spend 90 minutes every week together doing something new, something novel, something adventuresome and/or challenging. Science has recently discovered that when people take on a new adventure or challenge it stimulates the same brain chemicals and brain activity as falling in love. When couples share fun and exciting experiences together they bond. In effect, they fall in love again. When two Inspired Adults are in significant relationship to each other, they focus together on the journey. They look at life together and their companionship enhances their lives.

The late Ruth Gordon Jones (Ruth Gordon), a crusty old character actress, who is perhaps best known for her role in the Clint Eastwood movie *Every Which Way But Loose!*, expressed this idea very well. In the movie Ruth and the chimp (named Clyde) stole the show. One day I just happened to catch her being interviewed on radio. She was being asked what the secret to her long and reportedly happy marriage to actor and writer Garson Kanin was. They were married from 1942 until her death in 1985. She replied, "Aw, marriage just gives you someone to tell it to. You know, somebody there to come home to at the end of the day and tell it to. Life can be so hard out there and we all just need somebody at home in our corner to just come home and tell it to."

I think Ruth had the right idea. We need and want a witness to our lives. We want and need companionship.

Inspired Adults do not focus on any so-called faults in the other.

Be in life together and you will also be in love.

Oh, yeah, and remember….

"Your focus *determines* your reality." (Italics mine.) --Lucas

Star Wars

#4. Learn your ABCDs and How to Fight Fair

You might be thinking that #s 1 through 3 above are all well and good, but couples have to fight *sometimes*. So, what does IT have to say about that?

How and When to Fight

If you don't want to fight, the only answer is: don't fight! Sometimes you just have to say no and mean it. Or, you might say that you do not agree with whatever your partner wants, says, or does, and follow up with telling them that no matter what they say or do, that your mind is made up. Done deal. Case closed. And then, don't fight!

Do not explain yourself. Often couples or friends try to explain their stand or opinion in order to resolve a disagreement. The temptation to convince the other can be strong. Don't do it. Explaining actually serves to weaken your position. Explaining only serves to weaken your position. Explaining *weakens* your position! Explaining tells your "fight partner" that you really want their "understanding/agreement." All they have to do to "win" then is *withhold their "understanding."* So, when you disagree, what's a partner to do?

There is a lovely old saying floating about that could be very helpfully applied here:

Spirit never argues; it simply states the truth.

Let's adapt that to say, "Parents never argue," or "Adults never argue." To argue suggests doubt in your position, or suggests that the other holds the power. An argument is a power-struggle. In truth, each person is entitled to hold and use their own power in *every* situation. In a relationship, you have to be willing for your partner to *not* get on board with you in a given situation. It can feel lonely. But only the abandoned KID feels loneliness. By now, you know what IT says is needed. You can realize that you don't need your partner to stand in agreement with you. You can do that for yourself. If you really are not in agreement with your partner about something, so what?!? Stand firm with yourself. And let it go. If something has to be decided, then look to your boundaries and be true to you.

A Rule of Thumb

If your argument is about when to take out the trash, the solution is: He who wants the trash taken out first takes out the trash.

Perhaps you don't argue about when to take out the trash. Great. The trash is not the point.

Two Bottom Line Fight Rules:

1. Allow the other to keep their opinion.
2. Do not take offense easily.

How Not to Fight

Contempt kills closeness and love in a marriage. Respect and consideration (boundaries) keep the flames of love burning. Contempt and respect show up in behavior. Couples can decide to create loving habits. Recent studies (Gottman, 1994) have found that close couples—couples that stay married—avoid what he has labeled: "The Four Horsemen of the Apocalypse."

Gottman's Four Horsemen of the Apocalypse:

Criticism

Seeing partner as defective rather than just making mistakes is devastating to long-term successful relationship. Ascribing negative characteristics and motives to the behaviors you do not like in your spouse (such as selfishness, stupidity, etc.) are the kiss of death.

Defensiveness

This can be a common response to criticism. It signals a war-like atmosphere and fosters lack of trust in both partners. The defensive partner can become more and more dysfunctional and self-conscious in reaction to the critical spouse. According to IT, it is a natural but unnecessary response to heavy criticism.

Contempt

Judgmental statements that insult the partner and imply the superiority of the speaker kill love in both partners.

Withdrawal

Like defensiveness, withdrawal seems to make sense in a hostile environment, but it makes any resolution very difficult because the withdrawing partner has, in effect, given up.

These four behaviors are what Gottman calls his divorce predictors. Gottman teaches that couples that want to have a close relationship can and must decide to change these four behaviors—that they can learn to behave differently toward one another.

IT teaches the good news that it only takes one partner to change the functioning of the couple as a whole.

Why Some People Fight Dirty and Mean

The KID is triggered.
Low self-esteem.
We live in a win/loose culture (a Phase I remnant).

Those are the biggies; and they all work together to cause chaos and disaster in relationships. Once a person's partner says no, or disappoints in some way, or suggests something they don't want to do or that they disagree with, the KID can be triggered if they lack the esteem and/or the skills to negotiate. They just feel the wound and fear loss. And like any self-respecting trapped rat would do, they attack.

How to Fight Fair:

Set the Rules of Engagement

Even in outright war between countries, people have come to realize that rules of decency need to be agreed upon. The Geneva Convention, for example, is an attempt to set general guidelines and boundaries for fair play.

Couples are better able to think in the heat of disagreements and will feel more inclined to negotiate a resolution when they know the boundaries that they have set are being respected; when they can believe their partner values them even as they disagree. It is crucial to agree to work out the dynamics before any content is discussed. (See "Communication: Content vs. Dynamics" in Chapter 5.) The rules couples set provide a safe space to do battle, and they can be as simple as agreement to avoid Gottman's Four Horsemen and to keep the dynamics respectful.

Pick Your Battles

Once your ground-rules are in place, couples that minimize the number of battles they take on tend to fair best. Some people feel the need to defend their honor with every perceived slight from their partner. They let the little things get under their skin. i.e., they let the KID in them run the relationship. *Don't do it. Stop defending your honor!* Don't take it personally. In other words, stand between the KID in you and the "offender." If you don't ascribe to the theory that your partner is out to get you, then you can decide to let lots of things go. (If you *do* ascribe to the theory that your partner is out to get you, you either need to look within to deal with old wounds and a tendency for projection, or you need a new partner!) Assuming you believe your partner values you, you can save your confrontations for the *BIG* things that really matter. There should be very few of those in the minutia of daily living. This takes Mental Discipline. This takes commitment. This takes practice, practice, practice! Is a loving relationship with a partner worth it?

The ABCDs

Close couples exhibit four specific behaviors consistently. They can learn and consistently practice the ABCDs of a happy marriage. They *decide:*

A. To *always* say good morning before they get out of bed. (**A**gape′: love)
B. To say thank you often *every* day. (**B**less: appreciation)
C. To not interrupt. (**C**ivility: respect and interest)
D. To praise their partner in public regularly. (**D**o unto others: builds confidence)

According to Gottman, happily married couples behave like good friends and handle conflicts in respectful, positive ways, making sure they do not attribute flaws like selfishness, etc. to their partner's motives. They repair any negative exchanges during the argument.

Two Final Notes to Couples

1. About the word "decide"…

The words homicide, suicide, patricide, etc., all mean to put someone to death. The suffix "cide" actually means "to put to death." Therefore, the word "*decide*" means *to put all other options to death!*

When you operate from the IS, it is natural to *decide* to avoid Gottman's Four Horsemen, to learn how to fight fairly, to *decide* when not to fight, and to practice the ABCDs of a happy marriage.

2. Laugh often.

***

~IT and Basic Trust

Basic Trust is our connection to the Divine. Basic Trust is our birthright. If it is broken during childhood due to parental neglect or abuse, or trauma, we are miserable and behave quite badly (Lower Life) unless and until our Basic Trust is restored. Basic Trust cannot really be broken. It can only be blocked off. A major goal of IT is restoration of Basic Trust, which is synonymous with True Self development and is an integral part of living the Inspired Life.

****

Know Thyself

Untangling the Web of Self Deceit

It turns out that we are the wizards and only we (which includes our Spirit and our connection to the All There Is) can heal ourselves. Personality Integration Theory and Therapy can be used to enhance our self-understanding. When used alone or in conjunction with various other Maturity Model systems and spiritual practices of the new paradigm, a new era of integrity can emerge and we can become integrated and whole. We will then be free to create.

Just a Reminder

Personality Integration Theory is a theory. There is no claim that it represents absolute truth. If that were a pre-condition for personality theories, not even Freud himself would be worthy of study and consideration. William James spent energy and effort in the hope for a more scientific system to emerge. In the field of psychology today there are two schools: the clinical psychologists and the research psychologists. They have been at great odds at times in the short history of the discipline. Both agree that there is no exact science of the human mind. Yet, both struggle to provide working theories that enhance the lives of human beings everywhere. So, again there is no claim that this theory represents absolute truth. What is claimed is that people who have honestly and consistently applied the concepts of IT Theory and Therapy to improve their own functioning in their lives have improved. In large numbers and to high percentages they have improved and improved dramatically. They have achieved greater Self Mastery. Many have gone on to develop a creative side they did not know they had prior to therapy. In other words this is a functional theory. Whether it answers to absolute truth absolutely is for another day to determine. But for this day and time it is a great aid for many to improve their functioning and therefore their lives. But be forewarned, it is not a pill. There is no quick fix. It requires dedication, resolve and diligence. The rewards are genuine (you, fully you, you, genuinely you). The rewards can promise freedom.

Q and A

Ask Yourself

1. Q: Am I willing to strive for Mental Discipline?
   A:

2. Q: How often do I abandon the KID in me in relationships today?
   A:

3. Q: Do I believe every thought I have just because I think it? Or am I now more able after reading this book (and Shad Helmstetter?) to challenge the dysfunctional thoughts that used to rule me?
   A:

4. Q: Can I recognize and describe the experience of operating out of my higher, wiser self?
   A:

5. Q: What percentage of my time is spent in calm, peace, and joy?
   A:

6. Q: Am I creating from and for pure joy?
   A:

7. Q: WHO R U?????
   A:

Summary: How IT Works

1. STOP believing every thought that you think! Just because you think it doesn't mean it's true. You can start using discernment. You must activate your Inspired Self to do this, and doing this activates the Inspired Self. (A paradox.)
2. The Inspired Life
   The goal of IT is to grow your Inspired Self (the True Adult) and to operate out of it more and more consistently. Personality Integration Theory is *a breakthrough theory* of personality that *takes into account our spiritual dimension*. Personality Integration Therapy puts our spiritual nature and the seat of our spiritual nature into context in our psyches and in our lives, and provides a plan for accessing it, profoundly growing it into our lives, so that we are ever increasingly functioning out of it.
3. The True Self
   The goal is self-control. This requires personality integration, which means that the parts in the psyche are properly oriented to one another at all times. The fully integrated self is the True Self.
4. Internal parenting replaces current abandonment.
5. Practice discernment and self-diagnosis. Who is on the Throne?
6. Impact trumps intent.
7. With ever-increasing competence, use any and all available methods to make the Shift from one part to another when it is called for.
8. Remember that only the Inspired True Adult Self is to be in relationship with others both inside and out! This is how to keep your power.
9. The human condition is on course and in process of changing from survival mode through self development to joy!

Chapter 5

The Change: Working IT

"Greater than the tread of mighty armies is an idea whose time has come." --Victor Hugo

Making Change

The New Planetary Commission

Critical mass is a phrase that I first heard about in the 1980s. The concept behind it is the idea that when enough people believe in a particular idea, it will come to be. Another term for critical mass is "the race mind." It is exemplified by the "hundredth monkey" story as follows:

There once was an island populated by monkeys. The favorite monkey food on that island was sweet potatoes. On that island all the monkeys would dig up the root and eat. One day one monkey went into the surf and washed her sweet potato. Monkey see, monkey do. So, soon other monkeys were also washing the grit off the food before eating. As the story goes, when the hundredth monkey washed his food in the surf, all the monkeys on another island far, far away, started washing their sweet potatoes too!

In the same vein, it is a known phenomenon that many major breakthrough ideas throughout history have occurred in completely different parts of the globe at precisely the same time.

On a similar note, each year since 2007, in the month of March, various cities around the world participate in a project designed to encourage unity and concern for the planet and to raise consciousness. They provide a powerful global demonstration of energy conservation. Project Earth Hour originated in Australia and has grown to include more cities and more countries each year. In 2009, for example, nearly 4000 cities (including Las Vegas) in 88 countries turned out the lights for a rolling hour (8:30 to 9:30p.m.) from time zone to time zone around the planet.

On March 22, 2008, The Urban Playground Movement held what they named National Pillow Fight Day in Amsterdam. Feathers flew. Laughter ensued! The 4th annual "international flash mob," as it's called, was held on April 2, 2011. More cities every year, and more happy people. The message to the world? Start Enjoying Life.

Does the collective consciousness, sometimes referred to as the race mind, impact the environment and the affairs of daily life for the human race? There are many who believe it is possible.

The concept is even showing up today in well researched popular fiction. To whit: Katherine Solomon, a character in Dan Brown's bestseller, *The Lost Symbol* (2009), is a scientist at the Institute of Noetic Sciences (IONS). Noetic Science is the study of human thought and the potential of the human mind, and an important part of the novel is her work in the science of noetics. The popular work of fiction is introducing readers to cutting edge research in what has been a fairly obscure field of study.

With these concepts in mind, an actual experiment was set up in the 1980s by an organization called The Planetary Commission. It was run by author John Randolph Price and his wife, Jan. They devoted much of a decade to it, sending out invitations inside his books to any and all. The invitations went around the globe to commit to pray a specific prayer for world peace all at the same moment. The date and time were set for December 31, 1987 at 7am EST. All through the 1980s invitations in his books as well as other fliers were distributed and were everywhere to be found. People would fill them out, making their commitment to the project, and send them in to John and Jan Price and the Planetary Commission in Berne, Texas. By the time the day came, people had organized to gather in homes and churches all around the world, and in one voice the prayer for planetary peace was prayed. It has been repeated each year since by ever larger gatherings of people. Less than two years later, on November 9, 1989, the Berlin Wall came tumbling down! The Cold War was killed. Was this event connected to the two annual mass peace prayer events of the Planetary Commission? In a documentary recently released it seems that the series of strange and seemingly random events that occurred to bring it about created some kind of perfect storm of coincidences and "mistakes" that were beyond the control of the individuals in charge. In other words, "it" just kind of "happened!" Do you wonder? Many who participated in the world-wide moment of communion and prayer believe that mass mind in prayerful unison played its part.

If that is possible, the question then becomes, how many True Adults will it take on this planet, how many people operating mainly out of their higher, wiser self, how many people living from Inspiration will it take to reach critical mass for our species? Would reaching critical mass mean that Phase II, the Self Development phase, has been completed? One can only do one's own part. Or, one can be the 101st monkey and just wait for the majority to hopefully hurry up and get the work done. Which group would you want to be in? Which part of you is reading this? Let's get to it! Chop! Chop!

What Would Life in a World Run Only by Adults Look Like?

18 Characteristics of an Adult

1. Adults Pick Their Battles.
   Adults *choose* which battle is worth engaging in (usually life and death matters and matters of meaningful loss or serious harm only) and which to ignore. Adults do not have to defend a bruised ego because their ego (KID and DTL) is not bruised. A bruised ego is a phenomenon of the Lower Life. Adults stand between the would-be bruisers and the KID inside. The KID has no reason to act out and the DTL is contained. True Adults have the power to choose.
2. Adults Have Compassion and Generosity.

Adults do not have to worry about being taken advantage of because they have all the wisdom of an adult to assess life with.

3. Adults Do the Next Right Thing.
   Adults function responsibly. Adults have integrity.
4. Adults Can Be Appropriately Playful.
   The properly integrated KID is safe, unworried, and free to add fun when appropriate.
5. Adults Speak Softly and With Respect (even when they are setting a boundary).
   Adults can avoid shouting because they have confidence in themselves to take care of themselves.
6. Adults Know They Can Count on Themselves.
   Whether they learned to listen within for guidance from mature parents who respected them, or worked to raise themselves later in life, adults know the secret to joy and success. They have all the strength, wisdom, and inspiration that they need within.
7. Adults "Live and Let Live."
   Adults live by the A.A. slogan that teaches about boundaries. Adults have, keep, and set clear boundaries, and they respect the boundaries of others. No manipulation. No controlling nature. No criticism. They mind their own business.
8. Adults See and Focus on the Good in Others.
   They don't judge or gossip.
9. Adults LOVE.
10. Adults TRUST The Universe.
11. Adults Are Patient.
    "Patience is easy for those who trust." --*A Course In Miracles*
12. Adults Are Inclusive.
    Adults have the wisdom to see the value in everyone. Because they know there is no need to compete for resources, because they do not have a lack mentality, because they have boundaries that prevent others from wielding power over them, they are not threatened by the inclusion of others.
13. Adults Live in Gratitude.
    Their lives are rich and ever growing richer.
14. Adults Are Functional.
    Adults accomplish good stuff.

15. Adults Accept Reality on Reality's Terms.
    Adults do not attempt to single-handedly hold back the ocean.
16. Adults Live in the Present.
    They plan for the future, but focus on today. They live from Inspiration, rather than from memory or anticipation.
17. Adults Are Curious
    They are driven to discover, to understand, and to know.
18. Adults Are Creative.
    Adults live free.

The characteristics listed are about maturity. They are not personality traits. They are the characteristics that all people operating out of their integrated True Self have. Adults don't shame others or feel shame. Adults have very little to feel guilty about. Adults can make mistakes, but take responsibility for themselves and their actions. They right wrongs quickly when they occur. In a world run only by adults many of our current woes would not be. What a different planet this would be.

If you or those you know are not generous, playful, respectful, curious, courageous, confident, always loving, inclusive, and grateful, why not? If you are impatient, worried, defensive, avoidant, afraid, and lazy, why is this so? And what about the various negative elements we do still find all around us today? How do we apply IT to better our world? The following article was written for my unpublished novel *The WindWalkers* in 1994 or 1995. After making a few minor tweaks, it seems relevant to add it here …

IT and Power, Control, and Boundaries

We seem to be learning, as a species, the value of avoiding martial conflict except to set and protect our boundaries for freedom. Aggression is no longer tolerated by "civilized" countries as an accepted practice for the mere sake of aggression or acquisition alone (certain exceptions aside). And we seem to understand on the personal physical level the rights of self-protection and ownership. We've come a long way from the world of our cave-dwelling and tribal ancestors. Yet, we have to ask, what about the subtler realms of the mental/emotional world? What about beginning to understand and set our interpersonal boundaries?

It seems clear to most in this day and age just where the physical boundaries are for a people, for a family, for a city, for a person. If a violation occurs, most citizens of our popular culture can readily agree that it is a violation. How that violation is dealt with may be open to debate, but we seem to have defined most of our physical boundaries (certain complex moral issues aside).

In the realm of the psyche, however, in the world of relationships, our species remains confused. What are our emotional boundaries? How do we set them? Why is this important? And how important is it?

It seems that it is time in the grand evolving scheme of life for humankind to know itself at a deeper level (Phase II). We seem to be ready to hone in on, to fine-tune our personal emotional and spiritual boundaries. It is drastically called for.

Boundaries Are Sacred.

Just as they define nations and make it possible for them to interact peacefully, profitably; they define the soul in each of us. More accurately, our souls already exist for each of us, our souls are already defined, but they need to be discovered and respected. At this stage in our evolution our personal relationship boundaries have not been understood by our developing culture. Many are living the Lower Life unawares.

What are our boundaries? Where do I stop and you begin? What are my rights in relation to you? Until recently we were busy in the culturally accepted business of controlling and manipulating each other because we lacked a clear sense of our individual personal power. That is not working for us anymore. Our human cultures are in transition. Relationships are struggling as we try to understand power on a personal and interpersonal level. Something pushes at us and we are unhappy with one another. We are divorcing. We are striking for our greater good—to protect our rights. We are revolting—overthrowing dictators and entire regimes. We twitter. We connect on Facebook and the world wide web. We are distressed. Understanding power on the personal level has the power to redefine us.

Each one of us must now come to understand our own powerfulness and how to use our power as we find it. We can learn how to develop power-equal relationships. It is time.

Who are we really? We have heard so much and seen so much in these turn of the millennium years about admitting and accepting a certain powerlessness in our lives. (Here I refer to the Twelve Steps of AA.) Does this conflict with what is being said here? It seems not. But it does seem that the application of the term can be confusing for some. Powerlessness as used in the context of A.A. and according to IT, actually refers to power over others, and the powerlessness of the KID in certain situations. In that context, people are being encouraged to grasp the futility and dishonesty inherent in their inappropriate and fear based attempts to control others and to control that which is not theirs to control.

Power-Over vs. Power-Equal.

Finding our true power, our personal power, as it applies to our relationships, our loves, our lives, our governments, allows us to come together in true connectedness. Power-equal relationships are a cause and result of living the Inspired Life.

Let's get to IT!

Applying IT to Everyday Issues in Our Current Culture

"We must become the change we want to see." --Gandhi

It's all well and good to analyze and study the fundamentals of a theory. But let's see what happens when the rubber hits the road. Will it hold up in our everyday lives? And can we really change? What are some of the more dysfunctional issues that we face in this modern world of ours? Let's take a few such concerns and troubles head on and see what comes of it! (Which part of you has your fingers crossed?)

It seems a good idea to begin this section with an issue that we can carry forward as we consider each of the other issues covered here. Let's begin with Courage.

Courage

We each need access to our Courage—at times of great trial especially, but also in our everyday lives. Courage, that cousin to Confidence, can carry us through the very thin air of great and small leaps-of-faith. Life without risk would hardly resemble life—that vibrant force that always includes change, newness, and adventure. Life without risk would be dull, sad and empty indeed. Life without Courage would be colorless and grim. Yet, many of us have difficulty finding our Courage. We find instead that out of our *dis-Courage-ment* we have created riskless and dull patterns of existence. Where does that sad and restricting force, dis-Courage-ment come from?

For many, the roots are buried in a childhood that may have lacked a wonderful and supportive, *en-Couraging* environment. And remember, when parents or other caregivers are caught up in their own patterns of dis-Courage-ment; in their own web of unmet needs, their own fears, pains and projected failures; they can be too afraid or otherwise unavailable to en-Courage their small charges. Instead, it becomes important to create in the child a rigid compliance to a great many rules (which are often grossly unreasonable). These sometimes clearly stated and sometimes never stated rules, rule the family life, rule the growing child, and then inevitably rule the adult to come. They make up the long list of shoulds that so many of us find hanging in our mental closets. They become the bulk, the vast unwieldy rows of moldy, dusty volumes that load up the Dead Tape Library—musty old outdated volumes that can come to run our lives and fill us with dread and worse. These Dead Tapes that rule us can be robbers of our vital creative energies, of our Courage to risk, of our Courage to be spontaneous and free, of our individuality. They crush the KID.

Courage is our inheritance. It cannot be stolen from us, but it can be deeply buried. We can lose access to it. If mine seems lacking, if I seem unable to summon up my Courage when I need it, I may want to examine the Tapes that are running through and ruling my mind at that moment. As they present themselves boldly and with "authority," I may want to question.

I may want to challenge their right to rule.

I may want to follow them back to their roots to see if they are valid, to see if they are necessary. I may want to see if they serve as friends to aid me on my journey, or to discover if they are empty, like some old dark vision of a long-dead soldier of yesterday's war. Such empty shells can be discarded, released, and buried with praise for past achievements. Some of those faded soldiers may have helped me survive a battle that ended long ago in a faraway land. They may no longer be useful or needed, and in fact, they may be harmful to me today. Only the Inspired Self can perform this screening-out function.

Courage is our natural inheritance. We are born with Courage. If mine seems lacking, I may want to fill up my Library, my mental closets, with new, fresh words of en-Courage-ment. I may want to speak volumes of Truthink—affirmations that reflect a brighter, more honest, more positive view of a safer universe and my place in it.

To clean a glass of dirty water, there is no need to pick out every piece of dirt. One only needs to pour fresh, clean water in until the old water is replaced with the new.

As I discover and release my Courage from deep within my Inspired Self, as I find those words of en-Courage-ment and integrate them throughout my psyche, and then as Courage surges forth, its cousin, Confidence, building with it, I may find that not only am I facing trials, decisions, and difficulties with Courage, I may find myself embarking on true adventures and questing after joy!

Courage serves us well.
Courage is our natural inheritance.
Adults have access to their Courage.

Fear

"The opposite of love is fear…" --*A Course In Miracles* Introduction

A Course in Miracles teaches that all emotions boil down to two—love, and its opposite—fear. All other emotions, according to the *Course*, emanate from just those two. Fear, it further teaches, is not real. Everything that is built on fear can therefore be overcome with efforts based on love.

This is good to know, because we certainly tend to do a lot of our living based on the rule of fear.

Fear does seem to be the root emotion underlying the other unpleasant feelings. We are living in a fear-based world. (Just ask the media.) As you read through the other issues presented in this section ask yourself if fear does indeed serve as their foundations. If that is so, and if the *Course* is correct, then the negative emotions may be going the way of the dodo bird. Or, wait, was that bird just an illusion to begin with?

Bottom line—fear is putting your leap-of-faith energy into the negative that is as yet unseen. Why not put your leap-of-faith energy into what you want to see happen? They are both just potentials. What you fear is *not* more likely to come about than what you want. So why put your faith in your fears?

"The opposite of love is fear, but what is all-encompassing can have no opposite." --*A Course In Miracles*

Adults don't live in fear.
Adults operate out of love.

Shame

The history of shame in various human cultures throughout civilization is long and bloody. Shame has been a root cause of infanticide, murder, suicide, rejection, family destruction, personal devastation, and revenge. Avoiding personal shame and avoiding bringing shame on the family, have been high values in many cultures and families throughout the ages. According to Fossum and Mason (p. 22), "The origin of shame is in the violation and diminution of personhood." They further state (p.87), "The abuse of the past often exists as the shame of today." Shame has been one of the most painful and destructive forces in our world. It can motivate people to do *anything* to avoid feeling it! That being said, let's take a look at what shame really is. Simply put, shame is nothing more than the act of mentally turning against the self.

Shame is the act of turning against the self.

Shame and its cousin, embarrassment, are nothing more than anger at the little self (the KID). When we feel shame or embarrassment it is because the DTL or someone in the outer environment is attacking the KID. Anytime we cringe, that is what is going on inside the head and the heart.

Avoiding and relieving that horrible feeling of deep shame have served as motivation for many a horrific act. Many of our families today are what we call shame-based. If you grew up in such a family it is *always* important to find the one at fault—to find who is to blame and to exact some punishment upon them. It is important to shame them. This is very dysfunctional (gets nothing accomplished except finger pointing, inflicting shame, and creating the chaos of devastation), and it can become an absolute priority.

Shame is about what others think of me (which we now realize is their problem and none of my business). Life then becomes about judging myself, accepting the judgment of others, and/or it becomes about hiding my shame, my flaws, mistakes, and failures from others, while carrying the secret shame of knowing the "truth" about me. Self-hate is born of this. Self-hate is the Dead Tapes dumping hate messages on the so-called shameful and bad little KID! And the KID really feels it and cringes. So, shame is about letting others decide my worth and maybe even determine my fate. And it is about letting the old Dead Tapes rule. And get clear about this—it comes from being raised by children!!!

In such toxic, shame-based environments it is impossible to experiment, play, and brainstorm. It is impossible to gain a realistic appreciation for oneself. And a child raised thusly will lose its real possibilities in layer after layer of fear, self-deceit, and defensive lies.

Shame serves no useful purpose, and shame cripples.

The answer to shame is not, as so many may believe, to get better, be better, behave better. The answer is to stand up to the horrible shaming thoughts in your head that are attacking the defenseless KID in you. The answer is to give yourself permission to make mistakes and to be imperfect. The answer is to come to understand that mistakes do not detract from your value as a human being. The answer is to stand between the world "out there" and the KID, between the DTL and the precious KID in you. The answer is to send those nasty Dead Tapes packing!

Shame is insidious. To shame a child with tone, neglect, slap, or words is to teach that child self-hate. Shame cripples the one who shames and the shamed.

Shame cripples.

No True Adult shames others.
No child should ever feel shame.
No True Adult does.

Guilt

There are three types of guilt:

1. Guilty feelings.
2. Guilty doings.
3. False guilt (feelings and doings).

Guilty feelings can come from guilty doings. That is appropriate and can help deter harmful actions. However, guilty feelings born of an overextended sense of responsibility or a generalized sense of guilt are not realistic and can be harmful to all concerned. Life can become about constant confessing. Constant confessing can become addictive in and of itself when it is performed simply to avoid pain and punishment and is born of fear. The medieval religious leader, Martin Luther, was known for this tormented way of life. Reportedly he would spend hours on his knees in the confessional confessing the minutest detail of any and every possibility of a "sin" that he "may" have committed. Then upon leaving the confessional after such a session he would be seized with the thought that he may not be absolved because he might not have had enough remorse. Or he might have missed some obscure "sin." He was apparently not ever fully convinced that he had met the requirements necessary to avoid eternal damnation. He feared he would therefore be bound for a hellish eternity. Because of this he would often return to his confessor for yet another extended, agonized session on his knees. It would appear that he so feared punishment by God that he grossly over-reacted. His seems to be one case where it probably was not "better to be safe than sorry."

Some think it might have been his confessor that recommended he take his now-famous trip to Rome. Once there he was reportedly horrified to see the immense corruption in the Vatican. That shock and disillusionment ultimately resulted in the first religious break from the Pope.

Today we might say that it appears that Luther suffered from an anxiety condition referred to in psychology as religiosity, or religious scrupulosity. Today he might be diagnosed with Obsessive Compulsive Disorder (OCD). Scrupulosity is a term used for a similar anxiety condition minus religion at the center of the exaggerated sense of guilt. A person who suffers from general scrupulosity agonizes over a need to always do everything perfectly right in order to avoid an excruciating sense of guilt and any potential imagined punishment. One of the unconscious aims of such a sufferer can be to try to punish oneself enough so as to be able to ward off punishment from some external authority (real or imagined). These people suffer from what is called a rigid conscience. And they bring suffering not only upon themselves, but on those around them as well. They are rigid. Can you guess how IT might diagnose these conditions? The DTL is crushing the devastated KID and often punishing those "out there" as well. Sufferers such as these are not functioning as adults. They are living one of the many awful faces of the Lower Life. An exaggeratedly guilty conscience can be a torture chamber for the unprotected, abandoned KID.

Once Martin Luther became convinced that the authority of the Pope was fallible, he began to study scripture for his own answers. He found what he was seeking. In scrupulous study of the Bible he came upon a passage in Paul's *Letter to the Romans* that gave him the realization that it is through *faith* that one is saved. He thus came to believe that he did not need all the traditions and rituals of the Catholic Church in order to be saved; that what was needed was a powerful individual relationship with God. With the power of that concept, scales of fear and guilt fell from his eyes. The terrible guilt-hold of religious teachings that had strangled his mind for years was cast aside and he was free of the rituals and free of the old guilt, and free to develop his personal relationship with God. With that, he freed himself and offered the same opportunity to the masses. In the language of IT it could be said that he took the terrified KID off the Throne, hushed the threatening DTL, and began operating from Inspiration. It seems that he "suddenly" *matured.* Freed of his irrational terror and suffocating guilt, his great intellect was then able to flourish and an apparently calmer, wiser, more reasonable, inspired Luther penned the following:

This life therefore is not righteousness,
but growth in righteousness,
not health, but healing, not being but becoming,
not rest but exercise.
We are not yet what we shall be,
but we are growing toward it;
the process is not yet finished, but it is going on;
this is not the end, but it is the road.
All does not yet gleam in glory, but all is being purified.
-- Martin Luther

Yet another famous figure from history took refuge from the torture of his own guilt *in* the Catholic Church. After a youth spent in debauchery, St. Augustine found peace and forgiveness at last in the religion of Rome and in scholarship. He summed up the dilemma of the un-Inspired sufferer thusly:

"Where was my heart to flee for refuge from my heart? Whither was I to fly, where I would not follow? In what place should I not be prey to myself?" -- *The Confessions of St. Augustine*

A True Adult, a reasonable adult, an Inspired Self, can save the inner child from terrible mental anguish and sometimes even from self-inflicted physical abuse.

I remind you again of the words of my grad school professor, Dr. Bob Smith, "Punishment teaches *only one thing*—avoidance of the punisher!" Imagine the pain going on inside a person who is both the punisher and the avoider! (See St. Augustine quote above.)

People do all kinds of things in relationships both business and personal because they feel guilty about something that in reality they are not responsible for. Once again, this is called an overextended sense of responsibility. It means that there must be one or more Dead Tape in their head (from their Dead Tape Library) that has recorded messages from some past authority that incorrectly shouts, "GUILTY!" even when it is not the case. Or, when severely neglected, an abandoned child may bring in the Dead Tapes to create rules. These "manufactured" rules tend to be extreme and they create guilty feelings in the KID inappropriately. Basically, the KID looks around and tries to figure out what an adult would require or do. But the KID is not an adult and can only guess at it and ends up with a rigid set of rules drawn from the DTL to go by. This is a survival technique that can save a child from languishing in neglect during the childhood years. Such a child can be viewed by the world as being very mature for his age. But really the child is a pseudo-adult, and all this can backfire once the child reaches the age of adulthood. In such a case, there is very little if any real adult development.

In either scenario, remember, the DTL gets triggered or cued by events and has no power to discern. In a person with real adult development, the Tape selected is meant to be reviewed by the Inspired Self before being used, or rejected and re-shelved. When the Inspired Self is underdeveloped and underutilized people do not have enough of a sense of boundaries to know when theirs are being crossed. They are unable to assess their true responsibility in the given situation. In other words, the DTL and the KID, the Lower Life, are running the show. Neither of these parts can discern the truth. The part with real power of discernment is missing in action.

A man I once worked with, who I'll call Fred, was trying to adjust to a painful divorce. He and his ex-wife had been living apart for some time and all matters including money had been legally settled. However, his ex would regularly ask for more money for "this and that." And it seemed that when she said, "Jump!" Fred asked, "How high?" This bothered him, but he found that he could not say no to her. He said it made him *feel* too guilty. Upon analysis it became evident that in his relationship with his mother Fred had rarely been able to please her. Every time he displeased his wife during the entire marriage he would feel shame and guilt. When he was able to realize that the guilty accusing thoughts came from his DTL and were not some form of "absolute truth," and that they were attacking the innocent KID in him, Fred began to stand up to his "inner accuser." He began to hold his mother responsible in his psyche for her unreasonable treatment of him. He told the KID in him, "That was about her. That was never about you! You deserved much better treatment from her, but she just was unable to give it because there was something wrong with her. That was *only* about her! That was a reflection on her and not on you." And he began to say no to his ex-wife. His life got better. He felt better about himself.

Excessive and inappropriate guilt squelch growth.

Adults take responsibility for their behavior.
Adults deal with mistakes (their own and those made by others) appropriately.
Adults squelch unrealistic guilt.
Adults do not punish.
Dr. Bob Smith is a great and wonderful teacher.

Guilt vs. Shame

It is not uncommon for people to use the terms interchangeably in conversation today. But, as you have just read, they are, in fact, very different. The distinctions are important ones, especially when trying to help the injured KID to get over the impact of abuse and develop a more realistic self-image, and to come to understand and claim their true inherent goodness.

The difference between guilt and shame is that shame is about who you are and guilt is about what you have or have not done. Reasonable guilt serves a purpose in our civilized world. It helps maintain boundaries. Shame is dysfunctional and causes mayhem. Shame is about your self-identity and guilt is about your behavior. Guilt is about helping you avoid crossing another person's boundaries, or about having a scorecard where you can unfortunately rack up points for some punishment or discipline to come. Shame is about mentally punishing yourself out of self-hate and humiliation. Guilt can create shame.

Guilt is a fear that "they" will get you and maybe even annihilate you. Shame is about wanting to disappear and maybe even to annihilate yourself.

The Three Furies

In ancient Greek and Roman Mythology the Three Furies are Fear, Shame, and Guilt. They are the three terrible winged goddesses who pursue and punish evil-doers. They punish. By now we know what punishment does for rats, evil-doers, children, and all others. Need a refresher? Dr. Bob Smith says it teaches only one thing,

____.

(Fill in the blank.)

Also, let's be aware that both shame and guilt make us much more vulnerable to fear.

"The opposite of love is fear, but what is all-encompassing can have no opposite. Herein lies the peace of God." --*A Course In Miracles*

Remorse

A quick word about remorse is in order here. Remorse is about genuine sorrow for a wrongful deed. Though it generally includes guilt, it includes regret, compassion, and pity as well. The focus is on sorrow for the victim of the deed. The sorrow is more for the victim, and not just sorrow for having gotten caught.

Spiritual Abuse

I never met an atheist I didn't like. I've personally known many an atheist over the years, and generally speaking, their history is often quite interestingly similar. Often they seem to have been raised in fundamentalist religions. They left the church at about the age of puberty (at least in intent), and argue to this day against the existence of basically that one definition of God that they got from that one religion they were raised in; the punishing God from their early religious training. It is almost as if they were fixated on that one concept of God, a God that they would rather believe does not exist. In their fixated state (both then and now) it *could not* occur to them that that was just one set of opinions about the unknowable. Could their atheism be a way of just whistling in the dark?

Or, they grew up with no religious training at all and developed very little in the way of a definition of God, and along with that a rather deeply ingrained general skepticism.

Then there is the agnostic. The agnostic can't say for sure what is true, so they tend to put the matter aside. Both the atheist and the agnostic can make gods of their baser, Lower Life desires, such as food, alcohol, money, other people's opinions of them, etc. This can also be true of those who consider themselves (or at least strive to be) devout believers.

I worked with a person, I'll call Joe, from a fundamentalist religious background who reported having gone through a period of putting the God of his childhood into a big, deep, locked closet. In other words, this man too tried the atheistic route. But he was forced to open that closet door when he hit bottom in his life due to an alcohol addiction.

After a few months of struggling with sobriety in A.A., Joe reported that he realized that he had to give the God concept another look. He had to consider a broader and more benevolent definition of God or he knew he would not stay sober. Joe came to believe through Integration Therapy that his atheist stage (which could have lasted his lifetime had he not been an alcoholic) was, for him, a way to run from a view of God that was the view of a child. What that God of his childhood looked like through his immature eyes was not pretty!

In working with IT concepts he came to understand that the God of his childhood resembled his abusive and powerful father. That was a God who was very capable of doing terrible things. That was a God he was running in terror from. That was a God he did not like! It is not at all uncommon for the powerless, innocent child to associate the powerful parents with a developing concept of God. This is true whether the parents are benevolent and mature, or are inconsistent, cruel, and out of control. If one or both of the parents were abusive, the God of the child's understanding would naturally be a harsh, inconsistent, and punishing God.

As Joe worked on rescuing the terrorized, abandoned child in him, he was able to open more and more to his actual spiritual nature (the IS), and to broaden his concept of God. Over time the childish definition of God, that was the only God he could see from the eyes of his traumatized inner child, dissolved. Even though he had lived for years not realizing he was afraid of God, Joe came to understand that the fire and brimstone deity of his youth had been pursuing him every day of his life. He was whistling in the dark and he was in denial about the grip it had on him. Today Joe is sober, free, and enjoys a spiritual life with a much kinder, wiser, "more grown up" God.

Adults do not live in terror of a punishing God.
Adults do not fear or deny their spiritual stirrings.
Adults do not define God for others.

Forgiveness

"The mark of ignorance is the depth of your belief in injustice and tragedy. What the caterpillar calls the end of the world, the master calls a butterfly."

--Richard Bach
Illusions

It is in the Dead Tape Library that we store all the criticisms and judgments about our fellows. It is in this hall of records and opinions that we store our false sense of superiority. It is here that competition reigns high. It is here that all messages and most justifications for war are waiting. Forgiving from a place of superiority is a false act. A better word might be "release." To release another from our judgment of them is to release ourselves. Forgiveness from this more honest stance *frees the forgiver* from the suffering of a harbored grudge.

This is not to say that the KID inside should not be angry. The KID is a child. The above statements apply to adults only. The KID needs to be validated for whatever the KID feels. But again, the KID should not get the opportunity to act it out. When there is an adult at home the validated and guided KID can begin to let go the old hurts and grudges.

The DTL does the same kinds of things to people in the outer environment that it is doing to the KID inside. If the DTL in you is hard on the KID and unforgiving in its attacks and judgments, that is how you will tend to treat others. If the DTL functions unchallenged by the Inspired Self it will be a heavy-handed force in the world. The DTL must not rule, or lack of forgiveness will be the rule all around.

"If we could but read the secret history of those we would like to punish, we would find in each life a sorrow and a suffering enough to disarm all hostility." --Henry Wadsworth Longfellow

And what about being forgiven? It is the KID that can feel undeserving. That is a miserable way to live. It is a very common condition for many of us even if we are unaware of it. It is up to the Inspired Self to change that mistaken notion. Only the internal parent (the IS) can accomplish this most sacred task. And it is required.

"...all forgiveness is a gift to yourself." --*A Course in Miracles* W103

Adults don't harbor grudges.
Adults live in the present.
In the newness of the present there is nothing to forgive.

Communication: Content vs. Dynamics

In our outer relationships today people can be focused on the wrong things. We can unknowingly be sending double messages. One message is in the content. This is the message we think we are sending. It consists of information. The other message is embedded in the way we say it—the dynamics. Content is the substance of what we are communicating. Dynamics are the way we communicate that substance. Dynamics are always more important than any content that is not about life and death. The receiver of the communication on some level knows this—feels it—and will respond to the dynamics much more strongly than to the content. The receiver receives the dynamics message loud and clear. Dynamics trumps content. The sender can be unaware of the dynamics they are using! But the receiver always gets it. That is why a person can deliver a message that seems fair and reasonable to them only to be shocked at the response in the receiver. The receiver tends to respond to the message in the dynamics first and foremost. That is generally the most meaningful message. Dynamics trumps content. If the Inspired Self is the part delivering the content, it will be done in a fair and reasonable manner. If the DTL is the messenger, it can be exaggerated in importance and intensity. Sometimes it can be downright nasty. If the KID is the messenger, fear or minimization can become complicating factors. Dynamics always communicate the nature of the relationship itself. Content is just the facts, just information. Information can carry an emotional component, but the dynamics can muddy the waters. Communicating in our outer relationships can be confusing. If there is a confrontation, getting triggered is not unusual. We are not taught by our culture to negotiate. Rather we are taught to compete and to win, or that we lose. The KID in many of us can be quickly confused and triggered.

It can be helpful to real communication to think in terms of content and dynamics. Dynamics are by far the more important of the two to the quality of the relationship. Content is just the information to be exchanged. Dynamics are about dominance or respect, control or concern. Many a tyrant controls by tone, inflection, and harsh facial expressions. Until the dynamics are respectful, there is no real equal exchange of any kind. To discuss content when the dynamics are negative is to invite coercion rather than resolution. It is the person living and operating out of the DTL that will use domineering dynamics in a relationship. When that occurs it is not unusual for the KID in the other to be triggered and intimidated, or to compete for dominance.

For real communication to take place ground rules are needed to guarantee equal footing for participants. Dynamics are the hidden determinants of the relationship. Look for the nature of the dynamics. If they are not to your liking you can set new guidelines for communicating. If you discuss content before acceptable dynamics are in play the outcome will be skewed.

To change the dynamics when they are disrespectful "I statements" can be useful. "I don't like it when you talk to me that way." "I feel upset when you yell." "I can't think about what you are saying when you sound so angry at me." "I could hear you better if you tone it down." If the other person continues with negative dynamics and this is a regular pattern, you may want to rethink why you are with them.

In adult communication, dynamics matter more than content.

A good example of this is in our current politics. President Obama operates from this principle. He tends to communicate in even, respectful tones. Even when the other person behaves with big emotions (the KID or the shaming DTL), Obama (from the Inspired Self?) seems able to stand his ground and he maintains a calm and reasonable manner. He is often the one who gains the most in respect and meaningful outcomes when dealing with opponents and he is able to serve up rather bitter content for others to swallow when he feels it is necessary. And he often comes away with his popularity and political clout in tact. Dynamics matter far more than content in establishing the nature and quality of the relationship.

Adults always speak in respectful tones and terms.

The Comfort Zone (CZ)

Change is the status quo. It is a law of this perfect universe. In fact, it is the number one law of this perfect universe. Change is Perfection #1! (Were you looking for #1? Were you wondering if it was going to be disclosed? Were you wondering if it had been forgotten? Mistakenly overlooked? Well, look no further! Here it is. Feel better? Perfect!)

The Number One Perfection in this Perfect Universe of ours is this: Change is the only constant! Everything Changes. So, why do we fight it so hard? Why do we feel so uncomfortable about it? Since change is a major force in this magnificent, orderly, and benevolent universe, it must be for our good. It is natural. It is Nature itself. It must therefore follow that going with the flow of change is the only way to be happy. Since change is always occurring, all our happiness must lie outside the zone of comfort. Since all our happiness lies outside the Comfort Zone, why do we struggle to stay put?

Many people attach danger to change—attach danger to the unknown. Seeking the so-called "safety" of the CZ is just one more way we can get stuck living the Lower Life.

The CZ has its place. After a difficult experience it can be good for the soul to curl up and cocoon—for a time. But to live there exclusively, or even just most of the time and avoid new experiences is to be dying, shrinking, diminishing. To live there is to become entombed. The living dead are very comfortable—except for the tiny itch from their "still small voice" that warns of ever shrinking territory.

For the food addict, food is God *because* it helps him be comfortable in his skin. For the alcoholic, alcohol is God—same reason. So, it turns out that *Comfort* is the real God. For the person suffering with OCD, comfort is the *only* God! And for most others comfort is at least a lesser god.

Comfort is the goal of sad, lonely, and frightened people. Comfort may be the *only* goal of sad, and lonely, and frightened people. Sad, and lonely, and frightened people who are not dealing with an acute crisis that is causing those feelings are probably shame-based people. Shame and fear of being shamed are life's big deal breakers! Comfort is the God of the Lower Life Realm.

What is the Comfort Zone? It is the familiar. It is the Zero Risk Zone. It is a coffin where new interests, and unspoken dreams go to die. No sun shines in the Comfort Zone. Yet, prize it, we do.

There is no standing still in life. Life is change. (Perfection #1.) You are either growing, or you are dying. Your CZ is either shrinking or stretching. Even when it is stretched, you've got to stretch it further! *All* your happiness lies outside the CZ. We have to keep stepping outside it, yet, cling to it, we do.

What's in your DTL? It is the Dead Tape Library that holds back the KID in fear. The DTL is the gatekeeper for the Comfort Zone. Shame, boogymen, lions, and tigers, and bears! Oh MY! You must give yourself *permission* to try "this or that." By now you can guess what part is needed to open the gate and free your curious self to explore new worlds and new ways—the Great IS! The Comfort Zone is a mechanism of the Lower Life.

A program called Recovery, Incorporated was developed in the middle of the last century by a very wise psychiatrist—one who obviously cared about his patients and about human suffering. Abraham Low, M.D. developed a system for what he referred to as nervous and former mental patients. It was designed to help its followers to deal with the horror of the Comfort Zone. Through Recovery, Inc., Dr. Low teaches that we impact our moods and behaviors with the language we choose to use to describe our environments (inner and outer). For example, rather than saying, "I'm depressed," which suggests that I am passively struck and stuck with a condition that has been thrust upon me, Recovery suggests that I say, "I have lowered feelings." Having feelings that are lowered seems to offer more hope than "being" something awful. Having is less powerful than being. With this concept of choosing our language carefully in order to send a more positive message to the unconscious and to offer more hope of self-control, he suggests that "patients" say to themselves, "I have the will to bear discomfort." It then can become a matter of choice. Unpleasant? Maybe, but a choice! (Remember which part can make a real choice? Hint: Not the KID! In effect Dr. Low's system of language helped calm the KID and actually created a Shift to a calmer part.)

Do you have the will to bear discomfort? What do you give up when you don't? When you look around at the people moving about in your world today what do you see? Are they wearing their coffins? Do you ever smile at them? Say hello?

I believe a world of adults, each of them operating primarily out of their Inspired Self, would be a friendlier place, less self consciousness, and less concerned with being judged and judging others. In various sales training classes they teach people the "three foot rule." The rule is to get a new habit of talking to anybody who comes within three feet of you! People are instructed to start off with just a smile and hello and to expand their Comfort Zone (get more conversational) as they go along over time. The idea is to break the habit (worse the further north you go) of keeping to yourself as you go about your (lonely?) day. The idea is to become more open to your fellows. In sales it prepares for selling. In life it prepares for selling yourself, for being connected.

No matter what we do in life, that's always our job—to be connected—to someone, somehow—connected. Mature humans want loving, supportive, non-judgmental companions. We want to be seen. That requires being connected—really connected. What's the worst that could come of such actions? Less loneliness? More fun? More maturity?

Recent scientific studies are showing that we actually increase our number of brain cells and our problem solving ability by talking to new people. This is apparently the case because we use more of our thinking and reasoning processes in such circumstances. Turns out, disComfort becomes us! Our brains on high alert get smarter! Who'd have thought it? Want to know more? Read *Dental Floss for the Mind* by neurologist, Bernard Croisile, M.D., Ph.D.

What do you think?
Do you have the will to be more friendly?
Do you need to "get over yourself!"?
What part of you is reading this?
What lies outside your Comfort Zone?
If you are operating out of your Inspired Self, chances are it's you!
Are you comfortable with any of this?

Worry

The worry habit is rampant in a world where those in charge are not dependable or predictable. That seems on the surface to make sense. If there is not a real adult in sight, it would seem to make sense to start worrying! Not so fast!

What is worry? It's been called the "What If?" disease. On close examination it turns out to be an irrational response to whatever it is a response to! It is wasted energy that gives the worrier the illusion that they are accomplishing something. It gives the duped worrier the impression that the thing worried about can be staved off or prevented with just the right amount of worry. It is that feeling of over responsibility that, if there is a chance in Hades that "I" could prevent "blah, blah, blah" from happening, then I am responsible (even if I have no idea how to proceed)! In IT terms worry is the DTL talking up a storm to the KID! (LL). Worry fills the worrier (KID) with painfully scary emotions and the brain is then stimulated to stimulate worry chemicals and send them sailing throughout the body. Lots of stress is worry based. It certainly can seem crazy to get all worked up, and even harm the body, over things undetermined that may *never* actually come to pass!

What's the antidote for worry? Live in the present. One day at a time. *The Power of Now*. There is only one part of you that *always* lives in the present. If you are worrying, by definition, it is about some future possibility. It has not happened! It does not exist in your present moment. If you are worrying, it is unnecessary and dysfunctional. If you live in the present, you can't worry. Once you let the KID off the impossible (and not even the KID's job) hook of some possible future something or other, you are instantly free. If you live in the present moment you are free. You are free to function and that may even actually serve to prevent some future horror. What part of you has the wisdom and power to do that?

If you are worrying, you are not operating out of your True Self. If you are worrying, you aren't really you.

Need a mantra to break the worry spell?

"God, give me something else to think about."

Repeat as necessary. (You can add "Please! and Thank You!" if you want.)

No one can think two thoughts at the same time. By saying the mantra you start the Shift. Only when the Inspired Self is on the Throne taking care of business, is the KID in you freed from the past (memory) and the future (worry) and able to live free as intended in the present! Only in the present is the KID fulfilling its promise.

In the words of Dr. Abraham Low and Recovery, Inc.,

"Keep your mind where your feet are."

Adults don't worry. (Does this worry you?)

Acceptance

Acceptance is truly an adult virtue. When you accept what is, you can then move beyond it and create what can be. Children (including the KID inside) can rail against the forces of evil. They focus on what is "right" in their opinion, rather than on what "works." To spend time and energy on what "ought" to be but won't ever be is a waste of time and energy. That's not to say we should not protect ourselves from real possible future problems or attacks. Rather, the point is to not spend a lot of energy crying over spilt milk. Better to accept that it is spilled and needs to be cleaned up. With that, perhaps something can be done to prevent future occurrences. Accept, plan future prevention strategies, and then move on. Accept what is.

Whenever confronted by a tyrant, tormentor, teacher, friend, or foe (they all mean the same thing) remind yourself, "This moment is as it should be." Whatever relationships you have attracted in your life at this moment are precisely the ones you need in your life at this moment. There is a hidden meaning behind all events, and this hidden meaning is serving your own evolution. --Chopra (1994, pp. 59-60)

There is a story on page 417 in the Big Book of Alcoholics Anonymous that has a paragraph that I'd like to quote here. I've never seen a better way of saying it.

And acceptance is the answer to all my problems today. When I am disturbed, it is because I find some person, place, thing, or situation—some fact of my life—unacceptable to me, and I can find no serenity until I accept that person, place, thing, or situation as being exactly the way it is supposed to be at this very moment. Nothing, absolutely nothing, happens in God's world by mistake. Until I could accept my alcoholism, I could not stay sober; unless I accept life completely on life's terms, I cannot be happy. I need to concentrate not so much on what needs to be changed in the world as on what needs to be changed in me and in my attitudes.

--Alcoholics Anonymous

The above paragraph is one of the most quoted paragraphs by A.A. members from the Big Book. It was written by a physician who came to find sobriety and serenity only after surrendering from a life of dissatisfaction with what is. He let go of the dissatisfaction.

As I was typing the wisdom of Deepak Chopra and the words from the A.A. Big Book into the manuscript before you, it struck me that I was in such an inner struggle myself. There was a person in my life that seemed in need of a tune up and I felt focused on that idea to my own misery. Just typing those two amazing quotes onto the page reminded me that I have the power to free myself from that which is not my business! I made a Shift, and decided to let it go. People who have done that very thing (myself included) will tell you that, "When I let go, things have a way of straightening themselves right out!"

When I was working in the Runaway Shelter for teens I worked with families in distress. With Reality Therapy as our model we helped many a distraught family member give up what they *thought should work* for what was *going to work.* It was a new concept for most. So many lives are made miserable by somebody's concept of what is "right." Looking instead for solutions that would "work" helped put an end to the wasted focus in those families on blaming, and helped move them along to what could be better.

There is a great old question floating about: "Would you rather be *right*, or would you rather be *happy*?" Apparently, sometimes the two don't go together. Just ask any happily married person.

Adults accept what is. Adults never stand on the beach with their arms and hands and fingers outstretched and try to hold back the incoming ocean. They just don't do it.

Can you accept that?

Connectedness vs. Competition

In our current common culture, competition reigns. We say we bond in teamwork as we battle the enemy. We say we bond in our stadiums and in our big screen TV living rooms as we root on our team to victory, or lament the bad luck of common loss. But does that really connect us at the levels that really count?

We cover our flaws and compete for jobs, for power, for respect from our peers. We value success in business over love and marriage.

David Brooks, a well-respected American journalist, has just released a new book that might challenge these ideas. In *The Social Animal,* he looks at the results we get when we follow the teachings of our culture today. According to the research he has pulled together from various fields of study, we are suffering.

But do not worry. There is a counter-culture that is silently growing in our very midst that challenges the old rules that isolate us—that challenge the old order that holds us captive to our false, public relations images. There is a quietly growing gathering of those who would seek integrity. It is a coming together, not in our established institutions, not necessarily in our churches, our schools; but rather it is appearing in circles of people who reach out to each other for a hand up to recovery from the traps so many of us find ourselves in—from the traps laid by our cultural beliefs in superiority and inferiority, in good and bad, in black and white. It is a coming together in holistic healing centers, in recovery centers, in spiritual circles of like-minded seekers.

Some are beginning to realize that we are each equal in value. Some are beginning to realize that we each have much to offer to the common good. Some are beginning to realize that we are each at our very core all connected—that what we do to others, we do to ourselves. Some are beginning to realize that there is room for all of us at the top, and that only by recognizing that, and only by working together will we get there.

A human being is a part of a whole, called by us a universe, a part limited in time and space. He experiences himself, his thoughts and feelings as something separated from the rest… a kind of optical delusion of his consciousness. This delusion is a kind of prison for us, restricting us to our personal desires and to affection for a few persons nearest to us. Our task must be to free ourselves from this prison by widening our circle of compassion to embrace all living creatures and the whole of nature in its beauty.

--Albert Einstein

Adults are humble.
Adults are inclusive.
Adults don't judge others.
Adults encourage and assist the temporarily fallen to rise.
Adults are magnets.
Adults inspire.

Lazy Is a Four-Letter Word

Are you ever lazy? Chronically? Do you know someone who is? Would you like to know what to do about it?

Funny thing is, *there is no such thing!* "Lazy" is a myth. There is no such thing as lazy. It is a myth that causes a lot of misery.

Well then, you might ask, just what is this thing we call lazy? Just what is this thing we accuse our teenagers of? Just what is this thing we call ourselves when we drag our feet on this or that? Just what is this thing that entire groups of people sometimes seem to be suffering from? Just what is this thing that makes us feel superior about ourselves when we see others dragging their feet? Just what is it?

Sometimes people just feel like taking a mental health break or an R&R Day. That's not what we're talking about here. What we're looking at here is a broad tendency to avoid something or everything. We're looking at the tendency to avoid doing this or that *consistently. The simple answer is that what we call lazy is frozen feelings or feelings that are so fraught with trouble that they actually cause a kind of paralysis.* Beyond that it can get complicated. But the bottom line is if a person's feelings are frozen it can take most of their energy to keep them frozen! So, what appears to be a lazy person is someone who is very busy working on a tremendously industrious project. If it is in fact the person's stored feelings that cause the paralysis, there is a lot of hard work going on. The point is there is nothing lazy going on.

How do you fix just being lazy? There is no way. By labeling yourself or others as lazy you are just adding the impossible to the existing misery. But, frozen feelings? Now you have something to work with. What frozen feelings? Where do they originate? And why are they frozen? Paralysis? What's causing it? What is the treatment for it?

Depression:

Depression is often said to be anger turned inward. Who are you really mad at? People are often unaware of their anger because it is not permitted in their family system or because the anger they've witnessed in others (or in themselves) is so destructive. So, they use their energy unconsciously to contain their anger. There is no energy left over to do the tasks in question. Or, they are consciously or unconsciously mad at the beneficiary of the task well done. Or, they can't take their concentrated focus off anger containment (even unconscious anger containment) to do the task because if they did, the unconscious fear is that the anger would explode on the scene.

Fear:

Fear of failure. Fear of inadequacy. Fear of success. People can feel overwhelmed by fear if they lack the skills to break the task or project down into manageable pieces. Or, if they outshine you or mom or dad, they may bring rejection or retaliation upon themselves. If competition reigns in the relationship, this can occur.

Shame:
They may feel that there is something wrong with them for not easily knowing exactly how to accomplish the task at hand.

The list goes on. The point is that people are *never* lazy. All behavior is purposeful, and unless and until they are living the Inspired Life from the Inspired Self, people are always just trying to survive. They are doing what they believe they need to do *to survive*. In IT terms, the DTL is convincing the KID that it would be unsafe in some way to attempt the task. Further, the DTL also gets to berate the KID for being lazy! The problem is that it is not the KID's task to do. The KID is on the Throne and abandoned by the True Adult part. The solution? Make the Shift, deal with the KID's fear, anger, or shame, and then "Get 'er done!"

Accomplishment is a key ingredient to happiness. People want to accomplish. People are curious and filled with exuberant energy for the better life. People are natural doers. If little is getting done it is a clue that the KID is in some way overwhelmed and abandoned and in need of rescue. If you or someone you know is being "lazy," they are giving clues to all watching that they are living the miserable Lower Life. They are suffering and in need of rescue.

Adults are never lazy.
Children are never lazy.
Lazy is a myth.

Boredom

Boredom is another one of those myths that confuse us. People don't really get bored. They may *feel* bored, but they're not bored. Boredom is a myth. People are naturally curious and creative. If they feel bored they do not have access to their enthusiasm and curiosity. Something is blocking their vitality. The universe is brimming with opportunities for pursuit and promise. The universe is brimming with wonder. The universe is ever calling us with secrets and mystery to be explored.

What would ever possess a person to make him feel bored?

Boredom is another disguise for depression. What is being depressed? IT would say it is the Self—the Inspired Self. The Inspired Self is ever renewed with Inspiration! IT would suggest the KID has been inhibited due to current abandonment. IT would suggest that the person is feeling powerless to know what interests him, or to do what interests him, or both. IT would point the bony finger at the DTL. When the DTL becomes the great inhibiter, the entity sighs with boredom and life loses its sizzle.

When you are living the Inspired Life you live life inspired. Inspiration abounds! The very word "Inspiration" comes from the Latin word for "infilling of spirit."

"In order to live free and happily, you must sacrifice boredom. It is not always an easy sacrifice." --Richard Bach
Illusions

Boredom is a Lower Life condition. If you feel bored ask yourself:

Who am I mad at?
What am I afraid of?
What do I find fascinating?
Who am I?
What do I need to do to unblock the inflow of Spirit and to find my SELF?

Curiosity

"You are led through your lifetime by the inner learning creature, the playful spiritual being that is your real self." --Richard Bach
Illusions

Curiosity is pure spiritual air—oxygen of the spirit. It is a huge ingredient at the core of our true nature. Curiosity is a driving force. It is what takes us, moves us, pushes us forward into the realms of the unknown licking our chops with anticipation and joy! We are naturally *driven* to "know." If you have little or no access to your Curiosity it has been buried. Curiosity is buried by terror or tragedy, by fear or abuse, or by a sense of hopelessness. If missing, your natural Curiosity has most probably been buried by your admitted or secret tragic experiences. If your life is not filled with passionate wondering you have to ask yourself why.

Our natural Curiosity is the true antidote to boredom, laziness, depression, and even anxiety. It *can* overcome all fears and shame, but hard work is usually necessary for that to happen.

There is a bit of the Cheshire Cat in all of us who, like poor little Alice, have been overly polite and living stifled lives. It can prod and prick our dormant Curiosity to new life and point us in the direction of real adventure!

Curiosity is the most obvious of our Four Foundational Links to the Divine. *

Curiosity is the very blood and pulse of life. It breeds excitement, enthusiasm, and zest. It is delicious! And it leads through wonder to creative endeavors.

Who are we?
Where are we going?
Why are we here?
Says Who?
What and where *is* here?
What is this "soup" made of?
What is around the corner?
What is the lifespan of:
A Gnat?
The Universe?
Our Consciousness?

Curiosity is central. If you want to know your life purpose just uncover your Curiosity and follow.

Curious?

*Our Four Foundational Links to the Divine:

1. Love. (Our spiritual flesh and bones—our connectedness.)

2. Wisdom. (Our spiritual brain—guidance.)
3. Curiosity. (Our spiritual blood and oxygen—spice.)
4. Creativity. (Our spiritual productions—outcomes, expressions, activity, purpose.)

Anger

Anger is not a primary emotion. In fact, in some systems of psychology, there are only two primary emotions. Some label them Love vs. Fear. Some would say Positive vs. Negative. Others would categorize them into Feel Good Feelings vs. Feelings that make you Feel Bad. It is probably obvious that anger would fall under the fear based, negative, feel bad category.

So what underlies anger?

Fear
Hurt
Loss
Fear, hurt, and loss
Fear of loss
Loss of self-esteem
Loss of life and limb
Loss of possibilities
Loss of being loved
Loss of being seen
Loss of others
Loss of food, shelter, and belongingness
Loss of existence—annihilation

That stuff really makes us mad, mad, mad! Mad feels safer than fear.

So, what part in us gets mad? Ah, yes, it is the unprotected, abandoned KID.

In our culture it is not uncommon to believe that anger is justified under certain circumstances. It is then deemed acceptable to act out the anger by yelling or worse. This is a left-over from the Survival Phase. Today, as we are becoming more civilized and more aware of boundaries, some, an enlightened few, are realizing that it is *never* justified to act out anger. It is OK to be angry, but not to express anger to others. Disagreement can be expressed, but expressing (acting-out) anger is actually quite uncivilized and immature. Getting angry, being angry, realizing you are angry, of course are each and all acceptable. Acting out on your feelings of anger is not. Anger needs to be dealt with internally (in your head). In cases of danger or life and death, taking action can be necessary. Anger can add energy to do what is called for to ensure safety. But if life and limb are not threatened there is no reason to act out anger.

On the other side of the coin, people early in treatment often make a simple but definitive error. Because they don't want to *get* angry at this or that, or at this person or that person (for lots of reasons already stated in Chapter 4), they think they can "decide" not to. They resist the idea that what happened *makes* the KID in them mad. They resist the truth. What they don't realize is that it is not about making a decision. They *are* angry. Uncovering the anger you are secretly (from yourself) harboring doesn't *make* you mad, it makes you admit that you *have been* and *are* mad. It is a major part of getting free. It is called integrity! It is called in some circles "self honesty." MAD, MAD, MAD! Anger in the KID is not right or wrong. It just is. Unless you give the KID in you *permission* to *have* all the feelings that are stored inside, the KID can't get over it. It is childish to get mad. It is foolish to avoid dealing with it once the error is uncovered. It is a boundary violation to act it out on any one out there. The abandoned KID in you is the angry part. The KID needs the anger to be contained and validated. The KID needs an Inspired and Inspirational Adult at home.

Both anger and rage can also be found located in the DTL, but there it is just a recording. It needs to be shut off. How do you tell the difference? Validate, validate, validate, and then tell the KID to go and play, that you will take care of it. If, after several applications of that medicine, you don't feel yourself calming down, and if the rage increases, those are good indicators that you are dealing with Dead Tapes. Sometimes it just feels over the top even to you, especially the more you get a sense of the observer (the IS) in you. Also, a good therapist could help.

Adults don't get angry.
Adults don't let the KID or the DTL out.
Adults just deal with what is internally and externally.
Deal with it!

Criticism

Don't Do It!
Just Don't Criticize.

Constructive Criticism?
There is no such thing!
Criticism is not constructive.

In human relationships (even parent to child) it is not constructive to criticize. To criticize means to find fault with. Feedback and setting reasonable limits is one thing, but it is never constructive to criticize. In the twelve-step programs people talk about "taking the other person's inventory." The practice is very highly discouraged and for good reasons.

A child that is raised with severe criticism does not get raised. Criticism stunts growth, kills confidence, shames, and makes the child self conscious and unable to function spontaneously. When such a child becomes a parent, it is not unusual for them to externalize the perceived "bad" part of themselves onto one of the children. Have you ever seen a parent in public attacking a child verbally? Did it feel like a gross overreaction to you? Did you feel upset for the child? Perhaps the attacking parent was regularly criticized as a child and has unconsciously chosen a scapegoat. If the "bad part" can be externalized onto someone else, the person has a momentary illusion that only the "good" part is left. For that brief moment the unconscious self-hate is lessened.

An adult that is dealing with severe criticism from significant other(s) can become withdrawn, self-conscious, and be less and less able to function well, and can loose spontaneity, or can lash out in self-defense.

It is always easy to find things to be critical about in anyone. We all do things differently. If you are busy noticing what is "wrong" with others it suggests you are looking "out there" for what may actually be upsetting you "in here."

The fact is that it seems to be time in the great evolutionary scheme of things to turn our attention inward in search of attitudinal healing rather than the old time honored practice of looking for blame "out there." As we begin to discover what it really means to be empowered, we are surprised by the realization that empowerment is our natural inheritance. We are surprised to understand that only we can disempower ourselves. The more that we begin to recognize that we do have real power over our own lives (powers of choice that seem to elude us) the less we are tempted to criticize others.

It is always easy to find things to be critical about in anyone. We all do things differently. If you are busy noticing what is "wrong" with others it suggests you are looking "out there" for what may be upsetting you "in here."

Criticism is related to control. If I feel out of control in my own life (disempowered), I will likely try to control those around me. If my inner world is in turmoil, I can gain a false sense of calm or false sense of control and safety by criticizing and exerting control over my outer world—namely you.

It is always easy to find things to be critical about in anyone. We all do things differently. If you are busy noticing what is "wrong" with someone else it suggests you are looking "out there" for what may be upsetting you "in here."

Remember the story of the African village in Chapter 3? Criticism and punishment seem to go hand in hand. Remember what Dr. Bob Smith always says: "Punishment teaches only one thing—avoidance of the punisher!" Criticism teaches that too, that and deep shame.

The truth is that I am giving you my power when I criticize, or I am giving you my power and criticism naturally follows. If I am pointing out your "flaws," I am avoiding my inner world. Maybe I need to believe I am perfect. If I need to believe I am perfect, then I must always look outward at the first sign of discomfort. I must find the reason for my discomfort in you. I am perfect—you must be at fault. Why do I carry such a heavy burden?

Boundaries are sacred. Our boundaries help define who we are. They define where I stop and you begin. Boundaries protect my rights. When I point out your "flaws," I am invading your boundaries. I am taking liberties with your psyche and your soul that you have not given me permission to take. And remember, I am doing this to avoid discovering my own humanness or to grab for myself a false sense of calm.

What if you are abusing me, you ask? In that case, again, criticism is not the answer. I need to set my boundaries. This does not mean I have a right to attack you. It may mean I need to be willing to lose you—to leave you. What is the difference between feedback and criticism? Feedback honors your boundaries. Feedback does not criticize. Feedback states a behavior (yours) and a feeling (mine) and leaves you with freedom of choice. Criticism (so-called constructive or otherwise) says you are:

a. obnoxious
b. drinking too much
c. out of control
d. unfair
e. hurting yourself
f. stupid
g. selfish
h. etc.

You will feel attacked and invaded if I say this to you and your defenses will naturally go up. You will most likely focus on the boundary invasion—on the fact of attack—and be unwilling or unable to make any constructive use of the content or the information. You most probably will be tempted to criticize me back! (Good guess, huh?) This is not a system that works.

Criticism has a high cost:

It leaves you reeling with indignation.

It helps me avoid looking at my inner world.
It invites attack.
It destroys good feelings and trust.
It is NOT relationship!

Who has given me the right to take your moral inventory anyway? Did you hand that over to me when you agreed to be my friend? I think not. When you married me? I think not. My criticism of you dishonors and disrespects your right to your own imperfections (if they are even that). And my criticism of you dishonors my right to be imperfect.

Society teaches us to develop judgment and yet in every openly expressed judgment of another is an intrinsic criticism and potential rejection. We are taught to point out each other's mistakes. That keeps me focused outward. It keeps me trying to manipulate the environment instead of adjusting to reality. It is safe to stop judging and trying to control others. I can begin to count on myself and walk away from abusive or unsafe people and situations. This does not mean that I stop working through my issues from childhood. On the contrary, childhood is a time when others did have real power over us. If that power was in any way abused (intentionally or not) we need to get into reality about it. If we were heavily criticized as children, this probably left its mark in the tendency to rebel, or act it out on others, and suppress our creative selves.

Adults give feedback and only when invited to do so, or when it is necessary for the safety or development of a child. The DTL is the critic. Immature people criticize. Criticism is what people who feel superior do to those they feel (or want to feel) superior to. Or criticism is a way to get rid of the "bad part" inside and dump it out (project it) onto someone else. Pure illusion. Self-hypnosis. A damaging lie.

If I am in the habit of criticizing children, if I am in the habit of criticizing peers (and most of us are), I may want to begin really examining what the benefits are: Feeling superior? Acting out anger? Avoiding my issues? If I am in the habit of criticizing others, I may want to STOP.

Criticism, labeled constructive or not, is a terrible part of the Lower Life.

You've no doubt figured out that people living the Inspired Life don't criticize.
Got something constructive to say?
Don't criticize!

Strength

We have it in abundance. For many of us, however, we have been trained to lose our access to it.

When people begin working with me, before very long they will hear me say, "That must make you feel good about yourself!" I may say it in response to a report of a time when they stood up for themselves. They always look shocked. And they hate it! It takes a lot of convincing on my part that it is going to be important to recognize what they are doing "right." At first most people really fight hearing, "That must make you feel good about yourself!" They feel conceited if they claim their goodness. This seems to scare them, as if they expect some form of retribution. So, they explain to me why they do not feel good about themselves. Like that proverbial dog with a bone, I persist! They get kind of mad at me. I accept that and persist. We then can begin to explore why that makes them feel so uncomfortable.

In fact, self-care, appreciation, and recognition, when based in accurate truth grows our strength. We need to begin to approve of ourselves. Just like in that African village, our behavior becomes less devious when we recognize our worthiness—our unfathomable *worth!*

In IT terms what is happening is that we are wrestling the poor little over-criticized KID from the mighty grip of the nasty Dead Tapes. Over time in therapy people's strength emerges more and more. They learn that they can count on themselves. They learn that they *do* feel good about themselves!

Which part contains our glorious strength?
How do we grow it?
We are strong.
We can count on it.

Safety

Survival—We have to come to understand that we have already survived. We know that our troubles are mainly of our own making. We have to come to a better understanding that we are Safe. Once we know we are Safe, there is nothing to fear. Once we know that we are really Safe, that there is nothing to fear, we can release the negative fear-based emotions and beliefs that bind us to our Lower Life. We can stop creating problems for ourselves. This seems to call for some kind of faith. As we each discover and draw the Inspired Self more and more into daily life we discover that fear fades.

Self Development—We are developing, moving more and more into our true nature. As we do this we are discovering we can count on ourselves for more and more of what we need and what we really want.

Creation—The key to feeling Safe is coming to understand, discover, develop, and operate from our higher, wiser nature. We have been referred to as the "…salt of the earth." We have been told that we have the capacity to achieve miracles. Only the Inspired part in us can take us there.

What are we waiting for?

"Nothing real can be threatened. Nothing unreal exists."

--*A Course In Miracles*
Introduction

Security

It all comes down to security.

We all want it.
We all seek it.
We sure do seem to need it.
On what do we base our feeling of security today?
What makes us secure?

What is our security?
--The stocks in our portfolio?
--The Euros or dollars under our mattress?
--The ice at the poles?
--The "solidity" of matter?

Who among us is really secure when it comes to earthly standards? When it comes to depending on outside forces? When it comes to depending on others "out there"?

What is true security?

In 2008, 2009, 2010, and even into 2011 we watched the global economy change dramatically.

Two of the "Big Three" American automakers seemed to think of the American Government as their security. But what about all those Chrysler and GM dealerships who after decades in business got their licenses yanked? And what about the autoworkers themselves that lined up at the unemployment office? Ask Michigan, "What is security?"

Is security a tent to keep out the rain? For some, it seems, it has come to that.

We've all come down a peg or two.

Does it make you think? About what?

How does the delicate balance of the world economy stay so stable much of the time?

What is our real security?

Is it what the quantum physicists call the Quantum Field of All Potential? (That one doesn't even sound secure!) But is it?

How does it (real security) all work?

In June 1, 2009 GM got nicknamed Government Motors. They have since recovered, but, where-in lies their ultimate security?

Even as I write these words, the global economic free-fall is slowing and seems to be heading toward an upswing.

People are buying again! Are they stupid? Or is something afoot?

Why do things always seem to work out?

And some would say we are prospered by an ever abundant, constant flow of ideas. Where do they come from?

And then there's this to think about.

For eons people did not want to believe (despite evidence from ancient Egypt, ancient Greece, the Mayan Empire, etc.) they didn't want to believe that this "solid" earth we stand on was nothing more than a pretty ball swirling in seemingly empty space!

"Yeah, that's it….the earth is flat! That's secure, right? Flat. Solid. We can stand on that! And we'll kill anyone who says different! (Killing the naysayers will keep us secure, right?)

Oh, wait a minute! What's "it" on?

OK. How about a strong guy—a

really strong guy—Yeah—Atlas—That's it!

Yeah. The earth is flat

And a strong guy is holding it up! Whew!

That was a close one!

But wait… what's holding the strong guy up?

Oh, yeah, how about this:

Two elephants!

Elephants are very strong!

That'll do it! Yeah…

But wait—what are the elephants standing on?

Um…

Um…

Um…

Eureka!!!!!! How about a giant turtle that swims through empty space!?! Now, that makes sense, right?

Oh, but wait, what's the deal with the sun?

What keeps it all the way up there?

What keeps it from falling on us?

Oops. Here we go again!"

So, just what *is* security for anyone or anything? What does all we see, all we touch, all we want, all we have stand upon?

Real answers can be hard to come by in the realm of the physical. (Just ask those quantum physics guys. Turns out not even an atom or the nucleus thereof is solid!)

Even our beloved Einstein began to ponder the galactic glue that creates all things, is all things, and can't be touched or seen, yet holds all things together.

Adults seem to "know" how to ride out the storms.
Adults somehow mysteriously find real security.
Adults "know" things.
How do they do that?
Become one and find out!
(Adults sure are something!)

So, here's the deal. It seems that our only security is to become adult.
"Nothing real can be threatened. Nothing unreal exists."
- -A Course In Miracles
(Where have we heard that before?)

Maybe, just maybe, Love thinks.
LOVE THINKS.
Secure that thought.

Getting Your Correct Change

Personality Integration Therapy's 5 Steps Toward Self Mastery

How to Change from the Inside Out

1 Admit/Recognize there is a part of you that never grew up that gets your life into hot water.
2. Understand there is another part that can change your life for the better.
3. Decide to do the work necessary to make the Shift in consciousness. (Who's in charge?)
4. Do the work. Develop and exercise the mental determination and mental discipline to become self-honest, self-protective, self-nurturing, and self-developed.
5. Share the wealth—pass it on.

Q and A

Ask Yourself

1. Q: Am I beginning to realize how much of my life is spent in Lower Life pursuits? How much is it?
   A:

2. Q: What are my major Lower Life indulgences?
   A:

3. Q: How committed am I to working to operate more and more as an adult?
   A:

4. Q: What kinds of things do I need to do to further my growth to adult living?
   A:

5. Q: What can I do to help others?
   A:

6. Q: What will it take to get myself to do it?
   A:

7. Q: Am I curious? About what?
   A:

8. Q: Am I creating? What, and in what ways?
   A:

9. Q: Am I getting a glimpse of my phenomenal true self worth?
   A:

10. Q: Who M I?????
    A:

Summary

1. Perfection #1 in this Perfect Universe is a paradox. Perfection #1 is: *Change Is the Only Constant.*
2. We are in the process of changing our race mind (our collective mind set) to a more positive view of our potential as individuals and as a species.
3. We are safe if we believe it and stop using our creative powers to make messes for ourselves!
4. We can create a world of real adults if we each quit monkeying around and do our part to grow up.

Commentary

Creativity

We are all creators.
We all create.

We are in fact continually creating. We talk, we write (tweets, e-mails, memos, etc.), we dream, we daydream, we joke, we plan, we imagine, we make, we do. At our essence we are creators. If we were each equal in confidence, if we had each been equally focused on, nurtured, protected, disciplined, and encouraged by our caregivers during our childhood years, we would, I believe, be happily on with the business of expressing each our unique brand of creativity. We would be free to be and to do. When we are born or adopted into dysfunctional families, however, we are not really *seen*. We are not really nurtured. We are not really disciplined. The caregivers are too caught up in crisis, chronic difficulty, or trauma, or their own unmet needs to be able to focus on the child. They cannot therefore ask of the child, "Who are *you*?" They cannot draw out the individuality of that child to grow, to come forth, to play, to experiment, to be developed. The Inspired Self of that child is not encouraged to unfold. Life is too difficult, or too serious, or too demanding, or too important for such "luxury." But is it really luxury to become who you really are? And what price is our world paying for the lack of it?

"But I was given piano lessons," you say. Ah yes, but did you really want to play the piano?

Remember that sometimes children are shaped rather than observed, and nurtured, and allowed to unfold. Formed rather than discovered. Controlled rather than supported. Forced rather than encouraged. Punished rather than disciplined. Selected for "greatness" in a given area such as music or sport rather than provided a variety of experiences to choose from. Pushed rather than appreciated.

What if, like the snowflake and our own fingertips, we each were born with something truly YOUnique, a one of a kind creative urge? What if that fountain of creative energy did not meet the Lower Life needs of our caregivers? The survival instinct would wisely take over and the child would set about to please the hands that feed it. Even if you believe you wanted to play the piano, did you ever ask yourself why? Was it to fulfill an inner urge to discover and express? Or was it to gain approval from mom and dad? And if the latter was true, what does that say about mom and dad? Certainly not that they were *intentionally* harsh or cruel or abusive. But we now know full well that their *intent* is not what you are left to deal with. You are, remember, left to deal with the *impact*. What does it say about mom and dad?

At the very least, it would seem that they did not trust in your YOUniqueness to unfold, or even that it existed at all. And what message did that give you about yourself? What did you "learn to be true" (true or not) about you? And then what impact did that "learning" have on your creative self? Many of us, I believe, learned to deny who and what we really are in order to survive. But who and what we really are will not go away. It takes tremendous energy to hold back our creative urges, to hide them from ourselves. As we begin to be more honest with ourselves, to move more into reality about dysfunction in the family of origin, as we find the courage to face the pain of an imperfect childhood, we release the energy used to keep us in the dark. Our Inspired Creative Self pours forth. We surprise ourselves with the power of our ideas, our talents, our curiosity, and our new-found energy to create!

Epilogue

The Vision: Living IT

"The original sin is to limit the Is. Don't." --Bach
Illusions

Real Life in the Image and Likeness of Our Creator

A deep strand of genius and creativity has threaded its way throughout human history and moved humankind out of the jungle and into the penthouse. It has served the god of practical purpose (with good reason) for thousands upon thousands of years. It is that same strand that begins ever more to blossom for the pure joy of expression in the third stage of our evolution.

We are creators. We are creative at our very core, artists all. Creative thought, word and deed emanate from our true deep nature. Once we have discovered the "artist within," once we have unearthed the strand of creativity inside each and every one of us, and watered and nurtured it with belief; once we have discovered our unique orientation to it, and use of it; we find encouragement in the companionship of others on the artistic trail.

With all of this we begin to get a glimpse of our true and glorious life purpose. In the destination phase of our evolution (which is actually the beginning for our species as fully developed beings), a fourth need will emerge in our list of requirements for happiness. The fourth need is, "full and consistent creative expression." This will set us each and all free. And we must be free in order to achieve it. A paradox.

The leftovers and hangovers of our Survival Phase (Phase I) intrude everywhere in the Self Development phase (Phase II), and on into the beginnings of the Third Phase, the Creativity Phase. In our pre-Phase III families we are encouraged to be practical. When our artistic nature does dare raise its head we are admonished with comments such as, "That's fine, *but* how will you support yourself?" or "That's just pie in the sky!!!" Julia Cameron, author of the bestseller *The Artist's Way,* claims that, "We live in an anti-art culture with an anti-creativity conscious." (Cameron, CD). All of that is just a remnant of the Phase I mind set. But even back in the deep recesses of the darkest caves of our ancestors we made art. Art then made us. It made us brighter and stronger and took us out of the dark. Art played a part in the very survival of our species.

The Vision

About Phase III and Creativity

"Minds of the strongest and most active powers fall below mediocrity and labor without effect if confined to uncongenial pursuits."

~~ Alexander Hamilton

It is only when the KID (the Key Individual Dynamic) is integrated into the divine nature (the Inspired Self) that the KID is empowered to create wonders.

In Phase I we were concerned with preserving the species. We were focused on survival. Our Phase I Life Purpose was to survive and to aid in the survival of the species. In Phase II the great Shift to awakening is occurring. As a function of Phase II life, we are in the process of awakening to our true nature and we are concerned with serving others toward the same end. As people discover their Phase II Life Purpose they find it is always about serving humanity, or the animals, or the planet in some way as a part of the Great Awakening. Once our awakening to True Adulthood is well under way, and we have served or are serving that purpose, our third (and *real*) Life Purpose emerges. It is *always* to create.

The evolutionary push is to awaken self and others. Phase III will be about what we concern ourselves with as high-minded enlightened beings "…in the image and likeness of The Creator…"

Phase III Focus

Just as we do in a marriage, as a culture we need to stop focusing on the "flaws" of the other. We need to process our own inner issues and to be free to focus on *seeing* ourselves, our children, and each other. We need to really properly raise our children to develop their creative natures. We need to focus on our own true creative promise. And we need to focus on our journey together. The same holds true for our great society as it does for our smaller groups, communities, and families. We need to start focusing on this great adventure we find ourselves in. We can be companions and witnesses all to one another. We can have one another to "tell it to."

It is in this Third Phase of living that our unique personalities emerge. By getting the KID off the control panel of our lives, s/he is freed of an impossible burden, and thusly able to concentrate on play, which can often result in art. When our lives are run by a competent adult (IS), s/he (KID) can play and bring individuality into our everyday lives. We are fun. We have fun. We create. With the Key Individual Dynamic (KID) properly integrated our creative uniqueness emerges, and does so with energy.

As we work out our differences with each other, and any inequities we discover during the current Self Development Phase, we have moved beyond mere Survival and on toward wholeness—the True Self. We are clearing the way for real freedom to create—for each of us to create. As we achieve a realization of safety, life for each and all will be focused on contributing our unique creations to humanity and for the joy of it!

The Four Needs for Happiness

In this "destination phase" of human existence (our true beginning), people will have a fourth need that must be fulfilled in order to achieve happiness.

1. Belonging.
2. Accomplishment.
3. Authenticity.
4. Full and Consistent Creative Expression.

The Phase III need, the fourth condition for happiness introduced here—abundance of expression, will become the new focus. Our job as human beings is to:

1. Get all physical needs met. (Survive)
2. Get Self Control. (Self Develop)
3. Help all others achieve #s 1&2 above. (The Great Awakening)
4. All play, create, and express joyously! (Create)

People will create, enjoy the process, and enjoy each other's creations. It seems that we are to use the clay of the three dimensional world together with our fourth dimension access to create. What a life! To get to that point in our human journey we've certainly got our work cut out for us.

The Case for Laughter

"Laughter is the best form of unity." --Michelle Obama

Laughter triggers the creative side of the brain. It stimulates creativity. It creates a sense of connectedness. Laugh more. Laugh often. Laughter is a "now" experience that can't happen without at least a moment of faith. Laughter is empowering. How do you feel when you are laughing? Heavenly? Safe? Laughter deserves a high priority in our lives. Laugh not at the expense of others, nor in hedonistic, irresponsible moments or situations, but in release and joy. Laugh first at yourself. Be humble. Life is not some contest. No *one* is best at life.

The KID is the container of our feeling life. When we are on track, on purpose in our lives, the KID feels safe. The more the KID is integrated in our psyche, the more often the KID shows up to sprinkle laughter, spice, curiosity, and fun in our lives. You can speed things up by lightening up, and as you lighten, up the KID feels freer to play the appropriate role in your life.

A word of caution is called for here. Sometimes, as a coping mechanism, the KID part will develop a habit of smiling or laughing as they tell of terrible things that happened to them. They do this as a survival technique to avoid letting painful feelings overtake them. A smile or laugh can keep painful feelings at bay. This is a survival skill. It is not congruent laughter and it needs to be dealt with as a therapeutic issue. When a client does this in a session I gently ask them if they realize they are laughing as they make their report. Usually they don't. I then ask them to repeat the telling without the smile or the laugh. They have trouble doing so, but as they accomplish the task, tears well up and we can process the pain. That is not what we are talking about here.

What we are talking about here is dropping the judgment of the DTL that tells you that you are silly, or will look foolish, or you will not be taken seriously if you appear to be having fun. What we are talking about here is not letting the DTL stop you from having fun any longer. What we are talking about here is using discernment to quash the Tapes and give that KID in you permission to belly laugh!

William Glasser points out in Reality Therapy that we *learn* by having fun. When we are having fun we are more relaxed. When we are relaxed we are able to take in what is going on around us. When we are relaxed our curiosity and our creative juices are not restricted with anxiety. Phase III life will be peppered with laughter and joy. Laughter can speed its arrival.

It seems that this life is *not* meant to be a "…vale of tears" after all! The actor, Michael J. Fox recently completed a documentary that he made as a part of his journey through life with Parkinson's disease. The documentary is titled: *Adventures of an Incurable Optimist.* It ran on ABC TV in May, 2009. In it he traveled to Butan, a country high in the Himalayan Mountains. Butan is a country where they believe in and focus on "Happiness For All!" Instead of a Gross National Product (GNP), they monitor the GNH: The Gross National Happiness. They value relationships, family, friends, and community. They prioritize family, community, country. They focus on happiness for every person. They laugh a lot. The colors are vivid and gorgeous. The smiles are contagious.

It is the Dead Tape Library in us that tells us life is hard and we should be serious. *Being serious pushes people away.* Laughter is magnetic. It brings down walls. It brings down defenses. Laughter bonds the laughers. Laughter is contagious. The more the KID in you is off the Throne and protected from the DTL the more that laughter naturally comes into your life.

As it turns out, laughter is one of the most serious and important emotions given to us by our Creator. It is good medicine. And by the way, guess what they do at Mensa (the high IQ society) meetings. They play! The Mensa slogan: "Mensa—where we get your joke." (Do you get it?!?)

Hey! Are they saying that laughter makes us smarter? Or, that the smarter we are, the more we laugh? Hmmmm…This is serious!!!!!!

Are we having fun yet?????????????

The Three Faces of Adam

We now know that on the "species" level the three faces of Adam are:

1. The Face of Survival.
2. The Face of Self Discovery and Self Development.
3. The Face of Creation.

On the level of the individual we see Adam as:

1. The Key Individual Dynamic (KID).
2. The Dead Tape Library (DTL).
3. The Inspired Self (IS).

Further, #1 and #2 can and are intended to be properly integrated into #3 (on both levels) and thereby form a beautifully functioning whole. IT defines health not as Freud might say, "a balancing act," but rather as an issue of proper integration and Self Mastery. Health is a living, breathing, flowing, growing, unfolding, organic wholeness.

Our True Life Purpose

When you get to the bottom of the concept of life purpose, it seems there are three stages or categories of life purpose for each of us, one for each Phase of our evolution.

1. Preserve. To preserve creation. (Survival).
2. Serve. To awaken and to help others awaken. (Self Development).
3. Create. To create that which only ***"I"*** can create. (Creativity).

The artist in each of us actually performs all three life purpose functions at once. As we find our creative thrust and produce our creations, we do preserve the species, awaken each other to ever widening aspects of consciousness and life, and we create.

Ahhh, the Vision

"Greater works than these...."

We have come indoors. The only saber-toothed tigers we now need fear are the ones we create ourselves. This is misuse of the creative energy. And misuse it, we do. It can seem to many of us that the world is in an impossible state of chaos and devastation. Our economies are struggling; our world citizens are suffering from starvation, disease, exposure, ignorance, and violence. Yet, in the very midst of such impossible conditions, and against all seeming odds, there can be found shining examples of a greater humanity rising; and the audacity of hope. What are the optimists among us hoping for? I think that matters.

It has been said that, "Without vision, the people will parish." So, what is our vision? Why not a world in which we each become adults? Why not a world where in each of us is sharing our genius and our creations? Can we get there? Is such a world possible? Go back in time even one hundred years and ask yourself, could any world citizen ever have envisioned the world, as we know it today? So much of what we have today would have been dismissed as impossible. Haven't almost all meaningful breakthroughs in human history come from believing in the possibilities of the impossible? I think John Lennon said it best in one of his last gifts to the world—in his song, *Imagine*.

It may be even simpler than all of that. What if *you* begin to open to *your* inner artist? What if you really begin to take yourself and your artistic ideas and urges and curiosities seriously? What if everyone does just that?

My Story

Finding My Purpose

Years ago, in the late 1980s, I attended a little church in Fairfax, Virginia. The minister, Rev. Helice Greene, would speak to the congregation from time to time on the idea of life purpose. She maintained that the clues for each of us were there for us to follow, and that a person's own specific life purpose was with them from early childhood. It reminded me of a book I had once come across that suggested that if you ask any child why they are here, they will say something like "I'm here to help the trees, or the animals, or the people, etc." After reading that I admit that I tried it out on an occasional child, and I never got a noteworthy result. But the idea that we have a passion, and that it is connected to our journey from early on did make sense to me. So, when the minister suggested the same idea, I began to search my own history for clues. I found some dots, and I began to connect them.

From a young age I was fascinated by what motives people have. My older sister and I shared a room, and when our parents would entertain in the evening, we were tucked away upstairs. Of course, instead of sleeping, we'd listen to the sounds of tinkling glassware, silver on dishes, and bursts of laughter sprinkled throughout the rollercoaster rise and fall of chatter. An occasional clear and intact sentence or two would slip through and stir my interest. Ignoring the nasty rise of cigar and Lucky Strike smoke in our little nostrils, it would be then that I would talk with my sister, Judy, about what made Vinnie Dodd, or Mary Boyle, or Jack Fenton tick. Figuring these adult personalities out was just plain fun!

People have always fascinated me with their ways. The motives underlying their behaviors have seemed "clearly" obvious. I guess you could say, "I see people." Though I dreamed of becoming an airline stewardess like Vickie Barr, or a nurse like Cherry Ames, depending on which series I was reading at the moment, it was really why people did what they did that was so interesting to me. My amateur analysis continued throughout all my school years, but it never occurred to me to choose psychology as a career. In fact, it didn't really occur to me to think about that at all. My mom had always wanted to be a teacher, but her plans were sadly cut short by the great depression and family tragedy. I did love my English classes and writing (Shakespeare in particular—a master blend of psychology and poetry). So, I decided to become an English teacher. The clues: I was curious about people and had a penchant for analyzing them, I wrote poetry off and on my whole life, and I loved to draw. English teacher it isn't. But here's the thing, the minister I spoke of suggested that we had most probably dismissed the idea that there was any importance to the fact that we had "that particular passion" and we probably used some other criteria to determine our life plans. What is our problem? (Read Chapters 1-5 to get *that* answer.)

So, like so many of us, I took a circuitous path to find my real life work. I know that I am in the minority, and one of the lucky ones to have found it and to be achieving it, but in truth, many others can be, too. I never really liked teaching in the school setting, but what I did like were the kids and their issues and ideas. I naturally began working closely with Brenda Cavenaugh, the guidance counselor at the high school where I taught English, and she suggested that I should get my masters in counseling. That's all it took—one person to encourage me. I took that ball and ran with it. A few years later I awoke one morning with the thought, "I've come to help the children." With it a powerful feeling came attached. But since working directly with children as a counselor has never been my field of interest, it just seemed strange to me. Strange, but moving. It was a few years later when I began to formulate my personality theory and really put stock in the concept of the inner child. It was then that I again thought of that phrase, "I've come to help the children," that had resonated so powerfully within my bones. I realized finally that what I was doing in my work was helping the stuck and suffering children inside the adults I was working with.

Today I know that that is my Phase II Life Purpose. And even as I realize it my Phase III creative purpose emerges. In the mid 1990s I began working with *The Artist's Way* (Cameron) and I began doing what Julia calls "the morning pages," which is a way of journaling. It turns out that I had a number of children's books inside me waiting to be expressed. The little stories just began showing up on my journal pages almost as soon as I began consistently putting pen to paper! Once they began flowing out onto the pages, it was as if a dam had burst!

My Phase III Life Purpose? I believe it is to help, encourage, entertain, and enjoy the children inside you and me as well as the little ones out there. Life has become a fun and wonderful adventure.

"Of all that heaven has produced and earth nourishes, the greatest is man. Heaven's purpose is contained in our nature." --Confucius 500BC

Q and A

Ask Yourself

1. Q: Do I have a vision for my life? For humankind?
   A:

2. Q: Do I laugh often?
   A:

3. Q: What is my Phase II Life Purpose?
   A:

4. Q: What is my creative genius?
   A:

5. Q: Am I taking my artistic urges seriously?
   A:

6. Q: Am I creating?
   A:

7. Q: What is my Phase III Life Purpose?
   A:

8. Q: Who the heck am I?
   A:

Summary

1. Congruent laughter will help to hurry in the next phase of evolution. Do your part. Laugh like an innocent often. This will help you to, "Live long and prosper." --Gene Roddenberry
   Star Trek
2. The fourth need for human happiness is to create abundantly.
3. When we are whole (fully integrated as individuals and fully developed and on track as a species) our genuine, fully integrated personalities will emerge and because the safe and nurtured and properly disciplined KID will be free to perform its proper and intended function, life will be filled with curiosity, fun, laughter, and joy.
4. The third and highest Life Purpose is to use the clay of this material world to create that which no one else can. It seems that we are here

to each put our unique creative mark on this glorious creation we are living!

5. If we are created in the image and likeness of our Creator we must also be creators. Then what could be more natural than to live abundantly as genius-artists all?
6. We are fundamentally good. We are powerful. We are purposeful.
7. We are free!

Appendix

This Perfect Universe

We live in a perfect universe. Things can seem imperfect to the untrained eye, but things are not imperfect. Fractals are a perfect example of the order that underlies what can seem to the naked eye to be random, even chaotic. All is in perfect order. Ask the mathematicians. Ask the fractal artist. Ask the technicians who create computer generated special effects and movie sets. Chaos and what seems random are illusions. They just reflect a perception. In truth, we live in a perfect universe.

The following Perfections in this Perfect Universe are listed in random order:

Perfection #1:

Change Is Constant.
Change is therefore the only constant. Therefore challenge and mystery and adventure are eternally promised.

Perfection #2:

You Have Full Power To Heal (Whole) Yourself.
You have within you the power to become fully integrated. You have the power to be whole.

Perfection #3:

In Every Situation You Have Power.
You are never powerless.

"The point of power is always in the present moment." --Louise Hay

Perfection #4:

Using (asserting) Your Power Can Never Cause Harm.
What is really best for you cannot harm me. What is for your highest good can never clash with my highest good. This is because we are all divinely connected. This is a perfection that sets us free.

Perfection #5:

No One Can Take Your Power.
Only you can give it away. It is *never* wise to do so.

Perfection #6:

It Is *Never* Too Late.
You can *always* take your power back.
You can always find your power and use it.
You can *now* create your real life.

Perfection #7:

Who You Really Are Can Never Be Destroyed.
You are safe.
"Nothing real can be threatened." --*A Course In Miracles*

Perfection #8:

Time Is Temporary/Now Is Eternal.
Time Is Temporal/Eternity Is Now.
Time Passes/Eternity Is.
We Play In Time/We Live In Eternity.

Perfection #7 + Perfection #8:

Time Is The Playground For Your Eternal Soul.
Time is a schoolhouse;
Eternity is your inheritance.

Perfection #9:

Nothing Ever Happens By Accident.
There are no accidents.
There are no coincidences.

Perfection #10:

Everything Can Be Turned To Good.
"The only thing to fear is fear itself." -- F. D. Roosevelt

Perfection #11:

No One Is Ever Alone.
We are all connected
-to each other
-to "The All There Is"
Always.

Perfection #12:

There Is Only Love.
"...Nothing unreal exists." --*A Course In Miracles*

Perfection #13:

This Perfect Universe Never Gives Up On You.

Perfection #14:

LOVE.

Perfection # 15:

YOU.

Let's Begin...

About the Author

Diane Light, MA, has worked in the fields of education and mental health since the mid-seventies, first as a teacher, then as a counselor, psychotherapist, and professional life coach. Her focus as a mental health professional has always been on wellness with a keen awareness of the client's innate potential for growth and wholeness.

A former AirAmerica Washington radio show host for *Life Coaching Live/The Diane Light Show*, today she maintains a private practice in the Washington, DC area. She is the author of many upcoming children's books that encourage creativity and help build self-esteem.

Diane is available to provide private sessions, workshops and seminars to promote the understanding and application of *Personality Integration Theory and Therapy.*

She can be contacted through her website at www.dianelight.com and by email: dianelight@aol.com.

Bibliography

and

Recommended Reading List

Abrams, Jeremiah, ed. *Reclaiming the Inner Child.* Jeremy P. Tarcher, Inc., Los Angeles, 1990.

Alcoholics Anonymous. 4th edition. A.A. World Service, New York, 2001.

Amen, Daniel. *Magnificent Mind at Any Age: Natural ways to unleash your brain's maximum potential.* Harmony, New York, 2008.

Bach, Richard. *Illusions: The adventures of a reluctant messiah.* Delta Publishing, New York, 1977.

______. *Running From Safety: An adventure of the spirit.* Delta Publishing, 1994.

Bell, Rob. *Love Wins: A book about heaven, hell, and the fate of every person who ever lived.* Harper Collins, New York, 2011.

Bem, Daryl J. *Feeling the Future: Expiramental evidence for anomalous retrospective influences on cognition and affect.* American Psychological Association Journal of Personality and Social Psychology, 100, 407-425, 2011.

Braden, Gregg. *The God Code: The secret of our past, the promise of our future.* Hay House, Inc., 2004.

Brooks, David. *The Social Animal: The hidden sources of love, character, and achievement.* Random House Group, 2011.

Brown, Dan. *The Lost Symbol.* Doubleday, 2009.

Brown, Nina W. *Children of the Self-Absorbed: A grownup's guide to getting over narcissistic parents.* New Harbinger Publications, 2001.

Burstein, Julie, and Andersen, Kurt. *Spark: How creativity works.* Harper Collins Publishers, 2011.

Buss, A. R. *The Structure of Psychological Revolutions.* Journal of the History of the Behavioral Sciences, 14, 57-64, 1978.

Butterworth, Eric. *In the Flow of Life.* Unity House, 1995.

Cameron, Julia. *The Artist's Way: A spiritual path to higher creativity.* Putnam Group, New York, 1992.

_______. *The Artist's Way: A spiritual path to higher creativity* CD. Penguin Audio, 2006.

Capaccione, Lucia. *The Power of Your Other Hand: A course in channeling the inner wisdom of the right brain.* Newcastle Publishing, North Hollywood, CA., 1988.

Carrol, Louis G. *Alice in Wonderland.* Macmillan, 1865.

Chopra, Deepak. *The Seven Spiritual Laws of Success: A practical guide to the fulfillment of your dreams.* Amber-Allen Publishing, Inc., San Rafael, CA, 1994.

______. *Reinventing the Body, Resurrecting the Soul: How to create a new you.* Harmony Books, New York, 2009.

Coue', Emile. *My Method.* The Leidecker Institute, Shaumburg, IL, 1999.

Cousins, Norman. *Anatomy of an Illness as Perceived by the Patient: Reflections on healing and regeneration.* Norton, New York, 1979.

Donaldson-Pressman, Stephanie, and Pressman, Robert M. *The Narcissistic Family: Diagnosis and treatment.* John Wiley and Sons, 1997.

Dreikurs, Rudolf, and Stoltz, Vickie. *Children: The challenge.* Penguin Books, New York. 1964.

Dyer, Wayne. *The Power of Intention: Change the way you look at things and the things you look at will change.* Hay House, Carlsbad, CA, 2004.

Eastwood, Clint. *Every Which Way But Loose.* (movie) Warner Bros. Pictures, 1978.

Eagleman, David. *Incognito: The secret lives of the brain.* Canongate Books, Ltd., Edinburgh and London, 2010.

Fast, Julie A., and Preston, John D. *Loving Someone With Bipolar Disorder: Understanding and helping your partner.* New Harbinger Publications, Inc., 2004.

Fieve, Ronald R. *Bipolar Breakthrough: The essential guide to going beyond mood swings to harness your highs, escape cycles of recurrent depression, and thrive with Bipolar II.* Rodale Books, 2009.

Fossum, Merle A., and Mason, Marilyn J. *Facing Shame: Families in recovery.* WW Norton & Co., New York and London, 1986.

Foundation For Inner Peace. *A Course In Miracles.* Mill Valley, CA, 1976.

Fox, Emmet. *Find and Use Your Inner Power.* Harper Collins Publishers, New York, 1937.

Fox, Michael J. *Adventures of an Incurable Optimist.* Aired on ABC TV, May, 2009.

_______. *Always Looking: The Adventures of an Incurable Optimist.* Hyperion, New York, 2009.

Frankl, Viktor. *Man's Search for Ultimate Meaning.* Harper Collins Publishers Basic Books, New York, 2000.

Gilman, Charlotte Perkins. *The Yellow Wallpaper.* The Feminist Press, Old Westbury, NY, 1973.

Glasser, William. *Reality Therapy: A new approach to psychiatry.* Harper & Row, New York, 1965.

_____. *Control Theory: A new explanation of how we control our lives.* Harper Collins Publishers, New York, 1985.

Goldberg, Natalie. *Writing Down the Bones: Freeing the writer within.* Shambhala Publications, Boston, 1986.

Gottman, John M. *Why Marriages Succeed or Fail: And how you can make yours last.* Simon and Shuster, 1995.

Greenbaum, Judith, and Markel, Geraldine. *Finding Your Focus: Practical strategies for the everyday challenges facing adults with ADD.* McGraw-Hill, 2005.

Greene, Brian. *The Hidden Reality: Parallel universes and the deep laws of the cosmos.* Random House, 2011.

Greven, Philip. *Spare the Child: The religious roots of punishment and the psychological impact of physical abuse.* First Vintage Books, New York, 1992.

Grof, Stanislav. *Dimensions of Consciousness and New Perspectives in Psychotherapy and Inner Exploration.* SUNY Press, Albany, NY, 1988.

Haanel, Charles F. *The Master Key System: Your step-by-step guide to using the law of attraction.* Jeremy P. Tarcher/Penguin, New York, 2007.

Hamilton, Alexander. *Report on Manufacturers.* 1791.

Hay, Louise. *You Can Heal Your Life.* Hay House, Carlsbad, CA, 1984.

Helmstetter, Shad. *The Self-Talk Solution.* William Morrow & Co., 1987.

Hendrix, Harville. *Getting the Love You Want: A guide for couples.* Henry Holt and Company, New York, 1988.

Howard, Ron (Director). *A Beautiful Mind* (movie), starring Russell Crowe. Universal Studios, 2001.

Hughes, Judith M. *From Freud's Consulting Room: The unconscious in a scientific age.* Harvard University Press, 1994.

International Profile. *Sigmund Freud: Analysis of a Mind.* A Production of History International, HI Channel (TV), Aired on September 18, 2010.

James, John W., and Friedman, Russell. *The Grief Recovery Handbook: The action program for moving beyond death, divorce, and other losses including health, career, and faith.* Harper Collins Publishers, 2009.

James, William. *A Pleuralistic Universe: The continuity of experience.* University of Nebraska Press, 1996. Originally Published in 1909.

_______. *Essays In Radical Empiricism.* Longman's, Green and Co., 1912.

_______. *Varieties of Religious Experience: A study in human nature.* Longman's, Green and Co., 1902.

Kaku, Michio. *Physics of the Impossible: A scientific exploration into the world of phasers, force fields, teleportation, and time travel.* Doubleday, 2008.

Kaufman, Gershen. *The Psychology of Shame: Theory and treatment of shame-based syndromes.* Springer Publishing, New York, 1989.

Kornfield, Jack. *The Wise Heart: A guide to the universal teachings of Buddhist psychology.* Bantam Books, New York, 2008.

Kreisman, Jerold J., and Straus, Hal. *I Hate You, Don't Leave Me: Understanding the borderline personality.* Avon, 1991.

Laing, R. D. *The Politics of the Family and Other Essays.* Travistock Publishers, 1971.

Landsman, Karen J., Rupertus, Kathleen M., and Pedrick, Cherry. *Loving Someone With OCD: Help for you and your family.* New Harbinger Publications, 2005.

Lanza, Robert, and Berman, Bob. *Biocentrism: How life and consciousness are keys to understanding the universe.* BenBella Books, 2009.

Lennon, John. *Imagine* (song). Label: Apple, EMI. Producer: John Lennon, Yoko Ono, Phil Spector, 1971.

Lipton, Bruce. *The Biology of Belief: Unleashing the power of consciousness, matter, and miracles.* Hay House Inc., 2008.

Low, Abraham. *Mental Health Through Will-Training: A system of self-help in psychotherapy as practiced by Recovery, Inc.* Willet Publishing, 1973.

Lucas, George. *Star Wars Episode I: The Phantom Menace.* (movie) 20th Century Fox, 1999.

Melody, Pia. *Facing Codependence: What it is, where it comes from, how it sabotages our lives.* Harper Collins Publishers, New York, 1989.

Middelton-Moz, Jane. *Children of Trauma: Rediscovering your discarded self.* Health Communications, Inc., Deerfield Beach, FL, 1989.

Miller, Alice. *For Your Own Good: Hidden cruelty in child-rearing and the roots of violence.* Farrar, Straus and Giroux, New York, 1983.

______. *Thou Shalt Not be Aware: Society's betrayal of the child.* Farrar, Straus and Giroux, New York, 1984.

Monte, Christopher, and Sollod, Robert. *Beneath the Mask: An introduction to theories of personality.* Seventh Edition. John Wiley & Sons, Hoboken, NJ, 2003.

Nasar, Sylvia. *A Beautiful Mind: A biography of John Forbes Nash, Jr.* Simon and Schuster, 1998.

Newberg, Andrew, D'Aquill, Eugene, and Rause, Vince. *Why God Won't Go Away: Brain science and the biology of belief.* Ballentine Books, New York, 2001.

Noir, Michael and Croisile, Bernard. *Dental Floss for the Mind: A complete program for boosting your brain power.* McGraw-Hill, New York, 2005.

Nuckols, Cardwell C. *The Ego-Less Self: Achieving peace and tranquility beyond all understanding.* Health Communications, Inc., 2010.

Orlov, Melissa. *The ADHD Effect on Marriage: Understand and rebuild your relationship in six steps.* Specialty Press, 2010.

Osteen, Joel. *Become a Better You: 7 keys to improving your life every day.* Free Press, New York, 2007.

Pera, Gina. *Is It You, Me, or Adult A.D.D.?: Stopping the roller coaster when someone you love has attention deficit disorder.* 1201 Alarm Press, 2009.

Pressfield, Steven. *The War of Art: Break through the blocks and win your inner creative battles.* Warner Books Edition, New York & Boston, 2002.

Rapoport, Judith. *The Boy Who Couldn't Stop Washing: Experience and treatment of obsessive-compulsive disorder.* Harper Collins, 1990.

Roddenberry, Gene. *Star Trek.* Bantam Books, 1964.

_______. *Star Trek.* Desilu Productions, NBC TV, 1966.

Rowe, Stephen C. *The Vision of James.* Element Books Ltd. Rockport, MA, 1996.

Satir, Virginia. *Conjoint Family Therapy.* Science and Behavior Books, Inc., Palo Alto, CA, 1964.

Schreiber, Flora R. *Sybil: The true and extraordinary story of a woman possessed by sixteen personalities.* Warner Books, New York, 1973.

Schwartz, Gary E., and Simon, William L. *The Afterlife Experiments: Breakthrough scientific evidence of life after death.* Atria Books, 2002.

Storr, Anthony. *Solitude: A return to the self.* Ballantine Books, New York, 1988.

Talbot, Michael. *The Holographic Universe.* Harper Collins Publishers, 1991.

Thigpen, Corbett, and Cleckley, Henry. *The Three Faces of Eve*. Arcata Graphics, Kingsport, TN, 1957, Rev. 1992.

Tolkien, JRR. *The Lord of the Rings Trilogy.* Allen & Unwin, 1954-1955.

Tolle, Eckhart. *The Power of Now: A guide to spiritual enlightenment.* New World Library, Novato, CA, 1999.

Vitale, Joe and Hew Len, Ihaleakala. *Zero Limits: The secret Hawaiian system for wealth, health, peace, and more.* John Wiley & Sons, Hoboken, NJ, 2007.

Walker, Richmond. *Twenty-Four Hours A Day*. Hazelden, Center City, MN, 1954, Rev. 1975.

Warner, Rex, ed. *The Confessions of St. Augustine*. Penguin Books, New York, 1963.

Walt Disney Studios. *The Kid.* (movie), starring Bruce Willis. 2000.

Wilson, Bill. *As Bill Sees It.* A.A. World Service, New York, 1967.

Williamson, Marianne. *A Course In Weight Loss: 21 spiritual lessons for surrendering your weight forever.* Hay House, Inc., 2010.

Yogananda, Paramhansa. *Autobiography of a Yogi*. The Philosophical Library, New York, 1946. Reprinted, Crystal Clarity Publishers, 2005.

The greatest use of life is to spend it for something that will outlast it.

--William James

20575120R00167

Made in the USA
Middletown, DE
01 June 2015